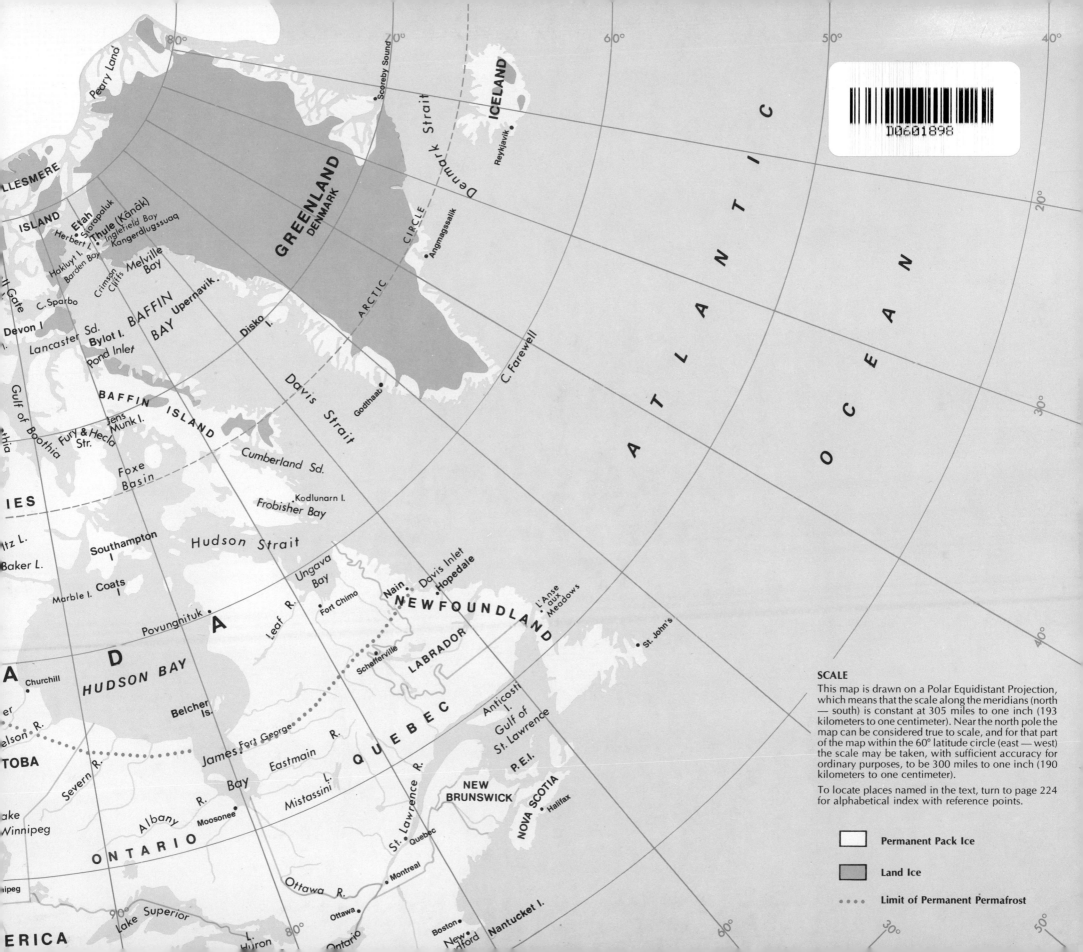

Peary Land

80°

70°

Scoreby Sound

ICELAND

60°

50°

40°

20°

30°

GREENLAND
DENMARK

Reykjavik •

ELLESMERE

ISLAND

Etah
Siorapaluk
Herbert I. **Thule (Kânâk)**
Inglefield Bay
Kangerdlugssuaq

Hakluyt I.
Barden Bay

Crimson
Cliffs

Melville
Bay

t Gate

C. Sparbo

BAFFIN

Upernavik.

ARCTIC

CIRCLE

Denmark Strait

Angmagssalik •

ATLANTIC

Devon I.

Lancaster Sd.

BAY

Disko I.

Gulf of Boothia

Bylot I.
Pond Inlet

BAFFIN ISLAND

Davis Strait

Godthaab •

C. Farewell

thia

Fury & Hecla
Str.

Jens
Munk I.

OCEAN

Cumberland Sd.

Foxe
Basin

IES

Kodlunarn I.
Frobisher Bay

tz L.

Baker L.

Southampton
I.

Hudson Strait

Marble I. Coats
I.

Ungava
Bay

Davis Inlet
Nain • Hopedale

L'Anse
aux
Meadows

Povunghituk

Leaf R.

Fort Chimo

NEWFOUNDLAND

St. John's •

Churchill

HUDSON BAY

Schefferville

LABRADOR

SCALE

This map is drawn on a Polar Equidistant Projection, which means that the scale along the meridians (north — south) is constant at 305 miles to one inch (193 kilometers to one centimeter). Near the north pole the map can be considered true to scale, and for that part of the map within the 60° latitude circle (east — west) the scale may be taken, with sufficient accuracy for ordinary purposes, to be 300 miles to one inch (190 kilometers to one centimeter).

Belcher
Is.

A

D

Anticosti
I.
Gulf of
St. Lawrence

er

Nelson R.

TOBA

Fort George

James

Bay

Eastmain

R.

QUEBEC

P.E.I.

Severn R.

R.

L.
Mistassini

St. Lawrence R.

**NEW
BRUNSWICK**

**NOVA
SCOTIA**

Halifax •

To locate places named in the text, turn to page 224 for alphabetical index with reference points.

ake

Albany

Moosonee

ONTARIO

R.

St. • Quebec

Lake

Winnipeg

St. Lawrence

Montreal •

nipeg

Ottawa R.

Ottawa •

Boston •
New
dford

Nantucket I.

☐ Permanent Pack Ice

■ Land Ice

•••• Limit of Permanent Permafrost

90°

80°

60°

50°

Lake Superior

L.
Huron

L.
Ontario

ERICA

30°

THE ARCTIC

THE ARCTIC

hotography and text by fred bruemmer

or Limited, Information Services Division, Montreal

torial and Graphic Contributors:
sign: **Gilles Daigneault** *Editing and Research:* **Hugh Shaw and Anna Ozvoldik** *Cartography:* **Michel Lanctôt** *Production assistant:* **Pierre Legault**
duced under the direction of Infocor Limited, Information Services Division

To Maud with love

Preceding pages: At Baker Lake, Eskimos bury their dead
under piles of stones as no graves can be dug in the frozen ground.
Inukshuks, man-like stone pillars, were built
by Eskimos to scare caribou towards a hunting place or served as markers.

Evening along the northwest coast of Greenland near Kangerdlugssuaq.
The weirdly eroded north shore of Inglefield Bay.

Great icebergs drift past the lichen-painted cliffs of an island
in Inglefield Bay, northwestern Greenland.
Icebergs from the great icecap of Greenland drift down a fiord.

The silken bolls of arctic cottongrass glisten in the midnight sun in northern Greenland.
Golden poppies on the Pribilof Islands in the Bering Sea.

The white phase of the gyrfalcon, largest of all falcons, is most common in the high Arctic.
A polar bear mother and her yearling cub. Cubs remain with their mother for about two years.

A Polar Eskimo girl in Kânâk, northwest Greenland.
An Eskimo hunter from Jens Munk Island, rimed after a long dog team trip.

Introduction

Vast, varied, millions of square miles, thousands of years — an immense world of extremes, contrasts, enlightenment, wonder, humanity—come to rest in your hands and come alive in your mind. The Arctic, Nunassiaq, Sib-ir. This book is one man's thoughts and photographs of those immense stretches of land and sea, their nature, history and inhabitants. It is the most comprehensive single book on its subject matter ever presented.

If that sounds much, be encouraged for this book ranges from Deshnev, the Cossack Yermak Timofeyvich and the misted Aleutians, past Naskapi camps, a Lapp wedding, and caterpillars producing glycerol anti-freeze to survive the arctic winter, through botany, zoology, glaciology, archaeology and history into the drab, spongy summer Barrens and the rolling Scandinavian taiga to the poetic Saltatha, Ottar the Norse explorer and to Odâq who took Peary as his navigator to the North Pole.

Fred Bruemmer has travelled widely in the North and lived close to it in several places. He has been sentient, perceptive and learning. The results of his tundra and taiga experience, distilled over thirteen years, coalesce in *The Arctic*, an unusually balanced and ranging blend of thoughts, facts, feelings and images.

Contemporary man is now beginning to understand these bare, beautiful regions, now, in part, because he senses how fundamentally important they are to him. The store and stories of arctic natural resources fuel the belief that our voracious, dependent economy can be sustained by their exploitation. The future may well validate this rather simple and widespread belief and surely the continuing development of technological expertise gives it credibility. Believing in those resources and the development of the remarkable technology and other means necessary to extract, transport and use them is one matter. There remains, by contrast, a large and sinister danger — the myth of technological competence. While there is some reason to believe in the growth of technological expertise over the past century, there exists also some, perhaps substantial, reason to doubt a parallel growth in wisdom to handle this powerful expertise competently. The clever, elaborate harvesting of arctic resources will not be the wise application of technology unless it derives also from an understanding of the Arctic. This book adds to that needed general understanding.

Those insights, of course, come in part from a second basic importance of the Arctic for all of us, as an area of scientific study. For example, the practical value of research on arctic ecosystems appears clear in attempts to build on permafrost, to assess long-term viability of Greenland fish as an economic base or to plan arctic marine transport relative to sea ice. Also, we are beginning to appreciate the world significance of the arctic basin through oceanography and of its weather through meteorology. Such obvious examples underline the urgency, if the Arctic is to be used sensibly, of better comprehending the subtle and surprising interdependence of natural forces in the northern world. Further, such research has general value, for in learning more of the Arctic we know more of the world: through the study of man and nature in distinctive or unique arctic settings there occur increases in data and theories to the general growth of knowledge. And the increase of knowledge continues vital and among the few enduring monuments shared by mankind.

And after all the talk of ecosystems, resources and knowledge there, in that often terrible, sometimes loving, land, stands man — where he has stood for millennia. That circumpolar quest, that awesome human achievement shared by Indians, Europeans, Eskimos, Asians, tells us much of our own earlier ancestors and of the tenacity and wit of this northern-most species. Ultimately the men and women reading this book are the same as those whose arctic lives seem so different. And thus the third aspect of the fundamental importance of the Arctic for southern man is the new perspective it gives to our own lives. Self-knowledge has been a persisting goal for some 2,000 years in the development of western man. By seeing how arctic cultures proceed you can see your own tribe in a fresh perspective. In the cares of a Lapp mother and the work of an Eskimo hunter we can find our own concerns re-stated. While learning from these people we must become aware that the wise use of the Arctic requires a full appreciation of their place in the cultural ecology of the North.

Thus, for many varied reasons, some noble, others sadly selfish, the direct importance and value of the Arctic to all of us increases. Even if you are familiar with it, the words and photographs that follow will provide the pleasures of exploring and the joy of discovery.

William E. Taylor, Jr.
Director
National Museum of Man
Ottawa

CONTENTS

ADDENDA

reface

Somewhere in this book I used the expression "long ago." When asked to be more precise, I re-read the passage and realized with a shock that the event I was describing had taken place 53 years ago. Yet in the Arctic change has been so abrupt, so drastic, that time has taken on a different meaning, and half a century is indeed a very long time ago.

In 1893, when the explorer J. W. Tyrrell crossed Canada's Barren Grounds, "of almost this entire territory (more than two hundred thousand square miles in extent) less was known than of the remotest districts of 'Darkest Africa' . . ." In 1973, near Kazan River Falls, discovered by Tyrrell, I saw the stakes of a mining company. If the ore body is large enough, a uranium mine may soon flourish there. In 1917 and 1918, Vilhjalmur Stefansson discovered Meighen, Borden and Brock Islands. Now companies are drilling for oil on these islands.

Ekalun, a 65-year-old Eskimo hunter, with whom I lived for six months at Bathurst Inlet had been ten years old when he had been "discovered." His early youth had been spent in conditions probably similar to those of our own ice age ancestors of the Magdalenian period, some 15,000 years ago. Now he used a snowmobile, took his automatic Swiss watch apart and repaired it, and listened to the news from the world at large on his transistor radio. Into his lifetime had been compressed, to some extent, 150 centuries of our own technological evolution.

That this technological revolution which we have brought to the circumpolar regions has made the physical existence of its natives easier, is certain. Whether it has made them happier, is quite a different question, and I, for one, doubt it. Above all, the changes we have brought to the north, the decimation of wildlife, the threat of widespread ecological upheaval, the introduction of a complex technology, a burgeoning bureaucracy, and an intensely materialistic ideology, have doomed the ancient, simpler, nature-linked cultures of the north.

This book, then, deals largely with an Arctic of the past. If a certain pessimism and sadness pervade its text, it is something I cannot help, because to me it has been sad to witness the decline of the native cultures, which, over millennia, had existed in harmony with this harsh land.

I have wandered in the north now for thirteen years: a summer on Spitsbergen with a Scottish expedition; a year with the Lapps in northernmost Norway and Finland; and eleven years in North America, from Alaska, through the Canadian Arctic to Greenland. To all those who have assisted me go my sincere thanks, particularly to the scientists and technicians of the Canadian Wildlife Service and the Arctic Biological Station of the Fisheries Research Board of Canada whom I have accompanied on many field trips. I am grateful to the librarian and staff of the Arctic Institute of North America library in Montreal who have helped me with my research.

Above all, I owe thanks to the native peoples of the north; Aleuts, Eskimos, Indians, and Lapps. I usually came unannounced and uninvited, yet they put me up, and put up with me for weeks and often for months, and they took me along on hundreds of trips, where I was rarely an asset and often, no doubt, a nuisance. To all of them my thanks for their kindness, their hospitality, their forbearance, and their understanding for what I have been trying to accomplish during all these years — to preserve a record of a way of life and a land, before both are irrevocably altered.

Fred Bruemmer

The History

"Men wanted for hazardous journey.
Small wages, bitter cold, long months of complete darkness.
Constant danger, safe return doubtful.
Honour and recognition in case of success."

**Advertisement placed in London newspaper by Ernest Shackleton.
It attracted hundreds of volunteers.**

Overleaf: Graves of members
of the Sir John Franklin expedition
on Beechey Island,
under a pale midnight sun, flanked by
even paler mock suns.

surrounded by bones,
remnants of long-ago feasts,
this great boulder,
a glacier-carried erratic, figures
prominently in the legends
of the Polar Eskimos of northwestern Greenland.
Here, they say,
their ancestors fought with the Tunit,
the Dorset culture people.

preceding page: Kodlunarn Island
in Frobisher Bay,
Baffin Island, the goal of a fleet
of 15 ships led by
Martin Frobisher in 1578.

It has taken explorers more than twenty centuries to complete the discovery of the Arctic. Only a few generations ago less was known about vast regions of Arctic tundra, sea and ice than is known today about the surface of the moon. Yet the search has gone on almost without letup since the ancient Greek philosophers and astronomers in the fourth century B.C. predicted the existence of a frozen region far to the north where the summer solstice would be a time without night and winter a season of perpetual darkness.

They called it Arktikos, for the constellation Arktos, the Great Bear.

About 325 B.C., the explorer Pytheas, a mathematician and navigator of the Greek colony of Massilia (Marseille) set out in a bireme to explore the north.

He travelled along the coasts of Portugal and France to England and Scotland. From there, he sailed six days north, to a land where the sun barely tipped below the horizon in summer, and he gave it an immortal name — Thule, Ultima Thule, the uttermost land, the end of the known world.

Scholars still argue about the location of Pytheas' Thule. Some think it was Iceland, and say his last day's travel took him half-way to Greenland; others, more modestly, opt for central Norway.

By the first century, A.D., the northern horizon had widened.

Tacitus, the Roman historian, knew enough about the distant, primitive peoples of the north to be aware of the remarkable serenity of their lives.

"The Fenni" (meaning probably the Lapps), he wrote "are extraordinarily wild and horribly poor . . . yet it is this people's belief that in some manner they are happier than those who sweat out their lives in the field . . . they have achieved the most difficult thing of all: they have ceased to feel the harrying of men's desires."

In the early middle ages Irish anchorite monks in search of islands of solitude in the wilderness of the northern sea, discovered and settled the Faeroes. By the end of the seventh century they had reached Iceland, inspired, no doubt, by the legends of Ireland's saintly navigator, Brendan. St. Brendan was a learned abbot, founder of several monasteries, whose fame survives in the fanciful saga of his expedition launched to search for the "Land of the Saints."

In 530, accompanied by eighteen monks he set out on his travels in a large curragh.

St. Brendan's sea-going curragh (some of these boats at that time were large enough for sixty people) was a craft of willow-basket framing "covered with oak-tanned ox-hide and caulked with ox-tallow."

Sailing north, "against the summer solstice," St. Brendan and his monks presumably visited Iceland and may have reached Greenland, for one of the marvels they met on their travels was "a floating crystal castle," the color of a "silver veil" yet hard as marble, and the sea around it was "smooth as glass and white as milk."

This is a beautiful (and history's first) description of an iceberg.

The peace of the monks under the midnight sun was shattered when sea wolves came prowling out of the north, swift raiders in high-prowed dragon ships — the Norsemen who went "i viking," by which they meant voyages of piracy and plunder.

The Norse in their sleek ships ranged the Atlantic and the Mediterranean, conquered, pillaged, settled and founded powerful states in Normandy and Sicily.

They also ventured north. Ottar, a Norse chieftain who lived "farthest north of all Norwegians" (probably in the Kvalöy — Tromsö region) visited King Alfred the Great of England and told him of his travels. Ottar was a wealthy man, who owned six hundred tame reindeer, a mighty lord to whom the Lapps paid tribute in furs, bird's down and seal and walrus skins. About 870, he set out on a trip to see "how far the land extended due north." He followed the coast, past the farthest region to which Norse whale hunters ventured, until the land "veered due east." He had passed North Cape, Scandinavia's northernmost point, and sailed east along the land for four days and then south for five. Seven centuries before Richard Chancellor and Willem Barents, he had discovered the Barents Sea and the White Sea.

Though Ottar went, in part, to explore, "chiefly he went there . . . for the walruses, for they have very fine ivory in their tusks, and their hide is very good for ship's cables." So reported King Alfred.

By 870 A.D. having already occupied the Faeroes, the Orkneys and Shetlands as well as parts of Scotland and Ireland, the Vikings began to settle Iceland, hitherto uninhabited except for the few hundred Irish monks who had lived there in ascetic solitude.

Iceland was empty, rugged and inhospitable. Volcanic debris covered immense regions, swamps and lakes alternated with tundra, heath and mountains, and ice fields covered one-sixth of the island. Yet the Norsemen colonized it quickly.

The narrow valleys of their native Norway were crowded, and young men hungered for new land.

In less than 50 years, 25,000 Norsemen had settled on the island, and by 930, all suitable land had been occupied.

A late-comer, who had to flee Norway, as the sagas laconically report, "because of some killings," was Thorvald with his teenage son Eric, red-headed, hot-tempered and later known as Eric the Red. In what one might be tempted to call "good Norse tradition" (for tales of multiple murder and mayhem the sagas are hard to beat), Eric in due course committed his share of killings and was banished from Iceland for three years.

Following up reports of land to the west, he discovered Greenland and spent his three-year exile exploring the great fiords of its southwest coast. Like a shrewd real

estate promoter, he called it "Greenland," for he argued that men would be drawn to go there if the land had an attractive name.

Land shortage in Iceland, and the allure of green pastures across the sea, gave Eric a sizable following and in 986 he set out to colonize Greenland, leading a flotilla of 25 ships. Some perished, some turned back, but 14 safely arrived, with about 400 people, as well as livestock, house timbers and provisions.

For a while the Norse prospered. They had about 300 farms, 16 churches, a cathedral at Gardar, seat of the bishop of Greenland, an Augustine monastery and a Benedictine nunnery. At least 3,000 people inhabited the two main settlement areas, both on the southwest coast of Greenland.

While most settlers looked after their sheep (the same regions now support in excess of 20,000 sheep), and their meagre cattle herds (the bishop had 75 cows), fished, or hunted caribou in the neighboring valleys, the more venturesome undertook extensive voyages far to the north. They may have reached or even passed Melville Bay, with its glittering parade of glaciers and it is certain that they reached the Upernavik region, where a runic inscription left by them was discovered in a cairn. That these voyages were both frequent, and frequently fatal, we can surmise from the fact that one of the sagas mentions a man who was a sort of free-lance corpse collector. Lika-Lodinn (Corpse-Lodinn) made it his profession to search the northern shores for drowned mariners, and to bring them south for burial in hallowed ground, presumably for a fat fee.

These far-north hunting expeditions were vital to Greenland's economy.

They provided the colony with high-priced export goods: live polar bears and polar bear skins, walrus tusks and walrus hide, white gyrfalcons, and narwhal tusks. Most of these goods were luxury items and brought fabulous prices. A live polar bear had the equivalent value of a ship plus cargo or a bishopric. Narwhal tusks, shrewdly sold as "unicorn horn" which reputedly could detect and

neutralize poison were worth several times their weig[ht] in gold, and the superb gyrs, the "falcones alba," we[re] worth a royal ransom. In 1396, the Duke of Burgun[dy] offered 200,000 gold ducats in ransom for his son, ca[p]tured by Sultan Bayazid. The sultan instead demande[d] and got, 12 white gyrfalcons.

In 1002, Eric's son, Leif, called "the Lucky" set o[ut] with 35 companions to explore land to the west of Gree[n]land that had been sighted by another Norseman. Th[ey] reached a barren rugged coast with great glaciers "a[nd] the intermediate land from the sea to the glaciers was li[ke] one flat rock," and Leif called it "Helluland" — Flatsto[ne] Land. This was Baffin Island.

They sailed south and "discovered a second land . [. .] low-lying and wooded" and Leif named it "Markland" [—] Woodland. He had arrived in Labrador. The journe[y] ended in a land he called Vinland, where they "ma[de] large houses," and spent the winter. In 1960, the N[or]wegian scholar Helge Ingstad discovered the remains o[f a] Norse settlement near the tiny village [of] L'Anse-aux-Meadows at the northern tip of Newfoun[d]land. In all probability, this was Leif's Vinland, called [in] the sagas "Vinland the Good."

The Norsemen had overextended. They made a fe[w] more recorded voyages to Vinland, and presumab[ly] many unrecorded trips to Markland to get the timber th[at] Greenland lacked, but distance and hostile natives (D[or]set culture Eskimos and, in Newfoundland, the now e[x]tinct Beothuk Indians) simply made it impossible to sett[le] the new land.

After flourishing for two centuries, the Norse sett[le]ments in Greenland went into a gradual decline.

The reasons for this were many, but the crucial on[e] perhaps, was that they insisted on living as Europea[n] style husbandmen in a region which by its very natu[re] made this form of existence marginal. Nor were the[y] self-sufficient. To maintain the traditional aspects of the[ir] culture, they depended on a trade life-line to Europe f[or] metal and metal implements, for clothes, and grains.

From the latter part of the 13th century on everythi[ng] went against them. After the "climatic optimum" that ha[d] prevailed at the time they settled Greenland, when a[n]nual mean temperatures were about 5.4°F warmer th[an] they are now, it became much colder. Immense ice fiel[ds] swept down out of the north, blocked the east coast [of] Greenland, and currents carried part of the ice up t[he] southwest coast. This made trips to Greenland mo[re] dangerous and difficult. Political problems in Sca[n]

avia and later the ravages of the Black Death militated
inst voyages to far-away, hard-to-reach Greenland,
I finally, in the coldly dispassionate view of com-
rce, it simply wasn't worth it.

Norse hunters no longer brought back wealth from
rthern hunting trips and, in any case, the bottom had
en out of the ivory market. Africa now supplied Europe
h vast quantities of relatively cheap elephant ivory.
The very conditions that brought decline and doom to
European-culture Norsemen, favored the Arctic-
ture Eskimos. Increasing ice cover lured seals south
d with them the Eskimos, the Skraelings as the Norse
led them. The Icelandic Annals for the year 1379
ord that "The Skraelings attacked the Greenlanders,
ed eighteen of them, and carried off two boys." Some
he Norse may have merged with the Eskimos, but there
ittle evidence to support this pet theory of several arctic
nolars. Their sad but true fate is probably one of isola-
n and abandonment, of the gradual sapping and with-
ng away of a once-vital people, of quiet despair and
imate lonely death. In 1492, the year Columbus disco-
ed America, Pope Alexander VI, in a letter to his
hops in Iceland evinced a laudable worry about his
t flock in Greenland "situated at the end of the world."
His concern came too late. About this time, it is
ought, the last Norseman on Greenland died.

The Elizabethan explorers of the 16th century sailed to
Arctic with a purpose quite different from that of the
mesteading Norse. They saw the lands and polar seas
t as a region to settle and raise sheep, but as a mighty
d annoying, but surely not insuperable obstacle barring
road to Cathay, and the vast wealth of the East. The
rtuguese and Spanish had pioneered and more or less
e-empted the southern routes to India and China. This
t the English and the Dutch, both just emerging as
jor sea and trading powers, literally out in the cold. If
y could not reach the fabled wealth of the East by the
uthern routes, they were going to find a northern one.
d thus began the centuries-long quest for that Holy
ail of the Arctic: the Northwest Passage and its equally
sive twin, the Northeast Passage.

To the discoverer of a feasable northern route to the Far
East, and to his financial supporters, it would have meant
immediate and immense wealth. The delusion was that it
would be easy to find such a route.

"The voyage to Cathaio by the [north] East is doubt-
lesse very easy and short . . ." wrote the Flemish geographer Gerhardus Mercator, inventor of the Mercator's
projection that revolutionized map making.

In a long "Discourse of a Discoverie for a new Passage
to Cataia," Sir Humphrey Gilbert, (who had claimed
Newfoundland for England), argued that; 1) it would be
easy; 2) it could be done "without danger and annoyance
of any prince living, Christian or Heathen, it being out of
their trades"; 3) it would relieve unemployment, since in
new lands discovered, England might settle some of her
poor "which now trouble the common wealth."

Playing shrewdly on English national phobias, Sir
Humphrey hints darkly that the crafty Portuguese had
boycotted the search for a Northwest Passage by giving
the Emperor Charles V a bribe of 350,000 crowns "to
leave the matter unattempted," and clinches this argu-
ment by saying the emperor would not have received
"such summes of money for egges in mooneshine."

Martin Frobisher, one of the most accomplished English sea adventurers and explorers of his time, approached the Northwest Passage in a mood that reflected
the general optimism. On his first voyage to the north, in
1576, he discovered what he took to be a strait and with
superb assurance he named it "Frobishers Streytes, lyke
as Magellanus at the Southwest ende of the world

*" . . . we seven miserable persons
who were still lying there alive,
looked mournfully at each other,
hoping every day that the snow would thaw
and the ice drift away."*

**Jens Munk, 1620, a Danish explorer searching for
the Northwest Passage. Of his crew of 64, 61 died of scurvy
near the present town of Churchill on Hudson Bay.**

hauing discouered the passage to the South Sea . . . called the same straites Magellanes streightes." Unfortunately, this was not a strait, but Frobisher Bay on Baffin Island, a long way from China. Ten years later, John Davis, returning from his first voyage with those two lovely-named ships, the "Sunneshine" and the "Mooneshine," wrote confidently to Sir Francis Walsingham: "The northwest passage is a matter of nothing doubtful, but at any time almost to be passed, the sea navigable, void of yce the ayre tolerable and the waters very depe." His "northwest passage" was Cumberland Sound, just north of Frobisher Bay.

Frobisher, like others seeking sea routes to the East, was motivated in part by an expectation that the north might yield gold, silver and jewels, riches such as the Spanish were reaping in their conquests far to the south.

From his first voyage to Baffin Island, Frobisher took back a chunk of rock which he gave to Michael Lok, a prominent London merchant and one of his principal backers. Lok took it to several government assayers who, quite accurately, pronounced it worthless. Unwilling to take no for an answer, Lok, who apart from being a wealthy businessman also seems to have been a first-rate sucker, kept making the rounds of free-lance assayers until he found one, an Italian, who declared the rock to be rich in gold.

After a second expedition returned to England with "a good store of ore," Frobisher's third expedition was organized and sailed in 1578 — a company of 15 ships, the largest assault on the Arctic until quite recent times. So many men, sailors, soldiers and miners, crowded onto the little Countess of Warwick Island, that Frobisher saw himself forced to issue the north's first anti-pollution regulations: 1) no person shall wash his hands "or anye other things" in the spring on the island (actually a small pond); 2) no person shall "doe his easemente but under the cliffes where the Sea maye washe the same awaye . . ."; 3) no person "of what nature or condition soever" may cast any "ballast or rubbish" into the sea.

Frobisher was a superb seaman, and a likeable, if at times rather gruff and hot-tempered, person. He looked after his sailors. His men, on the last voyage, had several changes of clothes, an unheard of luxury for sailors of the time.

To wash down the monotonous ship's diet of salt pork, salt beef, and salt fish, he carried enough beer to provide each man with a gallon a day for six months, plus barrels of "aquavite" to relieve the chills, and butts of sack and malmsey for the officers.

Although Frobisher tried to be friendly, his relations with the natives were bad. On the very first voyage they kidnapped five of his sailors, and he, in turn, captured one Eskimo, and three more (a man, and a woman with a baby) on his second voyage. They fought frequently and once the Eskimos "chased them back to their boats, and hurte the Generall in the Buttocke with an arrow, who the rather speedily fled back . . ."

On his third voyage Frobisher again referred to the "savagenesse of the people" which he gave as a reason, along with the appearance of "many straunge Meteors" (the aurora borealis) for his decision not to attempt to winter in the Arctic.

He intended to return. Before leaving, the party built on the island a house of "lyme and stone," and in it an oven with "breade lefte baked therein, for them [the Eskimos] to see and taste." They also sowed "pease, corne, and other graine to proue the fruitfulnesse of the soyle against the next yeare."

But there was to be no next year. The 1,350 tons of ore they carried back to England yielded no treasure. It was pyrite, "fool's gold," and was finally and ignominiously used for road repairs. Frobisher was in disgrace, and Lok in debtor's prison. The proverb "All is not golde that glistereth" acquired new currency.

The financial fiasco of the Frobisher voyages (they had cost over £20,000 in an age when an ocean-going ship "all equipped" sold for £120) put a damper on any further searches for arctic gold. With a few exceptions, such as the ill-fated Knight expedition of 1719, all of whose members died, the search for arctic treasure "couched within the bowels of the earth" was not resumed until our era, when technology first made it possible, and then by its own demands, necessary.

Wooden slabs on a lonely coast ma
the graves of the first m
of the Sir John Franklin expediti
to die in the Arct

On left: Only a stone circle remains of a semi-subterranean house in northwestern Greenland, once the home of a Polar Eskimo family.

Battered by ice, wind and age, the figurehead of a 17th century whaling ship lies on a northern Spitsbergen beach.

The weather-scarred grave marker on Beechey Island of "John Torrington who departed this life January 1846 on board H.M. Ship Terror . . . aged 20 years."

On right: The remains of an ancient, semi-subterranean Eskimo house on Coats Island in Hudson Bay. Around it lie the bleached bones of walruses, seals and caribou, remnants of successful hunts.

Gravestone for a member of the 1849-1850 ''North Star'' expedition in search of Sir John Franklin. Forced to winter at Wolstenholme Sound, northwest Greenland, four members died, including ''Wm. Sharp . . . aged 26 years.''

Only the mast remains of the yacht ''Mary'' which Sir John Ross brought to Beechey Island in 1850 on a search for the Franklin expedition.

Mountains of ice,
at stop the imagined way
eyond Petsora
stward to the rich Cathaian coast.''
ton, "Paradise Lost".

But the quest for a passage to the glittering treasures of Cathay continued. There were dozens of expeditions, both east and west, poking, ever hopeful, into every bay and bight, finding straits where there were none, ramming their frail ships against the monstrous ice barriers of the north, and leaving their share of dead, victims of scurvy, to rot on remote arctic beaches. Although they failed to achieve their objective, their determined efforts yielded some dividends: they opened the way to arctic whaling; to the establishment of the Muscovy Company and extensive trade with Russia; and to the formation of the Hudson's Bay Company.

Furs, in the Middle Ages as now, were partly prized for their warmth and beauty, but primarily as visible symbols of status and affluence.

In Germany, in France and to a lesser extent in England, the laws of rigorously hierarchical societies made furs into badges of class: marten, sable, and ermine were reserved for royalty and great nobles; beaver, otter and lynx were worn by the lesser nobility; and the poor, if they wore furs at all, had to be content with those of cats and dogs.

The advent of a wealthy merchant class disrupted many conventions of this established order. Badges of eminence no longer were for the ennobled few, and rich furs, among the most coveted symbols of privilege, soon were in short supply all over Europe.

In the 17th century the search for furs became a worldwide commercial quest that was to take white men across the most distant northern reaches of North America and Asia, precipitate a century of bitter competition and conflict and forever alter the ecology and the lives of the native peoples in the vast territories where the fur trade flourished.

Mercantile and political empires were founded on furs: on the silky-soft sable of Siberia; on the glossy-brown beaver of North America whose barbed hairs were uniquely suited for felting and for the making of hats; and on the lustrous, dark-brown, silvery-frosted fur of the sea otter, the prize of Alaska and the northwest coast of America.

The French started it. The wealth of New France, especially in its early days, was furs. During three years, 1693, 1694 and 1695 (at the time Frontenac was governor), 500,000 beaver pelts per year were shipped to France, worth a total of about 500,000 pounds sterling, an immense sum at the time.

The furs were brought to the French settlements by Indians, or obtained from the Indians by far-roving coureurs de bois.

Among the more daring of New France's explorer-traders, best remembered because his renegade appeal to the British sparked the founding of the Hudson's Bay Company, was Pierre Esprit Radisson.

Radisson and his brother-in-law, Médart Chouart Sieur des Groseilliers, were men whose knowledge of the wilderness and the fur routes was valuable to the French but whose taste for travelling and trading outside their circumscribed limits frequently caused them to run afoul of the fur trade bureaucracy in Quebec. By the 1660s Quebec had developed a complex system of regulations and prohibitions that frequently were invoked to justify severe fines and confiscation of the furs brought in by independent traders. Offended at such treatment after a lengthy journey to Hudson Bay, and discouraged by the lack of French interest in the Hudson Bay region, the pair decided to offer their services to the English.

In London in 1666 they dangled in front of money-hungry nobles the prospect of great wealth to be had by tapping the fur resources of Canada from the north, via Hudson Bay and James Bay, both already well-known through the exploratory voyages of all those hapless Northwest Passage seekers.

On May 2, 1670, Charles II, with that gracious largesse of kings giving away what does not belong to them, signed the charter of the "Governor and Company of Adventurers of England trading into Hudson's Bay," better known as the Hudson's Bay Company, or, today, simply as "The Bay." It was a generous document.

By the time the scriveners had finished listing "all those seas, streights and bays, rivers, lakes, creeks and sounds . . . (&) all the lands, countries and territories . . ." they had made the Adventurers of England "true and absolute Lordes and Proprietors" of roughly 1,400,000 square miles, more than a third of the total territory of the future Canada.

bandoned buildings
the west coast of Hudson Bay
ar Cape Fullerton,
ce housed RCMP officers
ho kept check
American whaling in the bay.

One clause in the charter enjoined the company to explore its lands in general and, in particular, to seek a Northwest Passage. This it preferred to ignore. For many years it was busy establishing forts in James Bay and Hudson Bay, and wrangling for their possession with the French who did their utmost to kick them out. And after these problems had been more or less settled, the company concentrated on trading and making a pleasant profit. In 1739, a fairly average year, the posts "on the Bay" shipped to London the skins of 69,911 beavers, 15,196 marten, 355 otters, 1,011 wildcats (lynx), 853 wolverines, 266 bears, 454 wolves, 76 elk (moose), and 14 deer.

In return for these furs, the Indians received kettles, guns, ammunition, clothing, brandy, ivory combs, vermilion paint, hatchets, needles, and many other goods they soon came to regard as essential.

In 1769 the company asked Samuel Hearne, one of its most devoted servants and best explorers, to find and examine the copper deposits near the mouth of the Coppermine River.

After two abortive starts Hearne set out on his third attempt to reach the arctic sea overland, a trek that would last 18 months. For the Indians, a major enticement to make such an arduous journey, was the joyous hope of finding and killing some Eskimos. In this they were successful, butchering every man, woman and child of a small camp at a place known to this day as "Bloody Falls." It was a few miles from Hearne's goal, the mouth of the Coppermine River, and the Arctic Sea, "full of islands and shoals . . . (&) ice." On July 18, 1771, he "took possession of the coast, on behalf of the Hudson's Bay Company."

On July 14, 1789, Alexander Mackenzie of the North West Company, arch rival of the Hudson's Bay Company, threading his way through the maze of channels and islands of the just discovered Mackenzie Delta arrived at the Arctic Ocean. Four years later, after a gruelling journey across the Rocky Mountains, he reached the Pacific.

By the middle of the 19th century, the Hudson's Bay Company (it had merged with the rival North West Company in 1821) reached its apogee of power and extent. It owned, or administered, more than half of Canada, as well as parts of Oregon. It had trading posts and forts from Labrador on the Atlantic, to Vancouver Island on the Pacific, from Hudson Bay to California, and Sir George Simpson, for 34 years the governor-in-chief of this vast domain, was justly nicknamed "the little Emperor." In 1869, the company, in its "Deed of Surrender" sold this realm, some thirty times the size of England, for £300,000 to the newly created Dominion of Canada.

The Hudson's Bay Company's expansionary drive had been westward, across the fur-rich landmass of Canada. When the whalers left the Arctic, having despoiled it of its sea mammal wealth, the company moved north to fill the trading vacuum created by their departure. The Russian drive was from west to east, across an even vaster continent.

In the late 12th century, the fast-riding Mongol armies of Ghengis Khan, having conquered the major portion of central and eastern Asia, swept into Europe. His successors occupied most of Russia, and reduced the northern Slav princes to tribute-paying vassals. Inevitably, the decentralized and overextended Mongol empire eventually disintegrated into a multitude of quarrelling khanates.

As Mongol power diminished, Moscow's conquest of the Asian Arctic began and the penetration from Northern Russia across Siberia, north to the arctic coast and east to the Pacific, was accomplished with unruly, often violent, haste.

The wealthiest city of northern Russia in the 15th century was Novgorod, near Lake Ilmen, at the centre of a network of river routes used since ancient times: west to the Baltic Sea, north, via the Dvina, to the White Sea, and to the east and south via the Volga.

The Stroganovs of Novgorod were a merchant family who enriched themselves with the land, furs and minerals in the regions to the north. They were wise enough recognize very early the ascending star of Moscow and grand princes, and to shift their allegiance, and t taxes, to them.

Throughout the 15th century, and with increas speed in the 16th century Moscow's might increase conquered Novgorod and became ruler of the no Under Ivan III, better known as Ivan the Terrible, Russ troops swung south and east, defeated the Mongols occupied their strongholds of Kazan and Astrakhan, m ing Moscow master of the Volga, and opening the roa Persia. In the northeast, the Stroganovs, under char granted by the tsar, extended their domain to the U Mountains, the "Iron Gate" as it was called. Beyond it Siberia, "Sib-ir," "the sleeping land" of the Mongol

Ivan assumed the title "Commander of all Siberia of the North Parts." However, he owned, as yet, no pa Siberia. A Tartar prince called Kuchum styled him "Tsar of Siberia," and occupied a good portion of i

But Ivan was not only terrible, he was also very shre In 1574, he rented Siberia, for a period of 20 years, to Stroganovs. How to take possession of it would be t problem.

Since among their retainers the Stroganovs could m ter only 300 armed men of somewhat dubious mili prowess, they engaged, in addition, an "army" of Cossacks. This force was led by the Cossack hetr Yermak Timofeyvich, a man of questionable antecede but unquestioned courage.

For an undertaking such as the conquest of Sibe these Cossacks of the border regions were, milita speaking, ideally suited. They were hardy, resource and immensely courageous. They had to be. Kuchu forces outnumbered them by fifty to one.

In 1581, Yermak led his army across the Ural Mo tains. The "iron gate" barring the way to the east been broached.

In a series of battles he defeated Kuchum's forces then he himself was killed. His death was only a temp ary setback. More Cossacks arrived and the fighting renewed. Kuchum suffered his final defeat in 1587 died in 1598. Siberia lay wide open.

A few of the vast number of Siberian tribes fought invaders. The very last to be discovered, the Koryaks, Chukchi, and the Kamchadales of the Kamchatka Pe sula resisted most stubbornly. But generally the invad met little opposition from man; only the very vastnes

eria was a giant obstacle. By 1630, they reached the
na; in 1632 the Cossack captain Peter Beketov built the
strog" (fortified town) of Yakutsk, and by 1639 they
d reached the Sea of Okhotsk. In the 58 years since
rmak led his little army across the Urals, the Cossacks
d spanned and conquered a continent.

In 1648, Semyon Ivanovich Deshnev, a government
assak" (tribute) collector, sailed a fleet of six frail,
-bottomed "kochas," Cossack boats of the "let's-
pe-to-God-they-hold-together" variety, down the
lyma River to the Arctic Sea.

There he turned east, rounded the eastern tip of Asia
ow called Cape Deshnev), was driven by a storm
ough Bering Strait, 80 years before Bering "discov-
d" it, and ended up near the mouth of the Anadyr
ver. It is indicative of the somewhat chaotic conditions
Siberia at the time that this amazing voyage did not
come known until 88 years later. The historian of
eria, G. F. Müller discovered Deshnev's report in 1736
ried in the archives of Yakutsk.

Siberia's wealth at the time was measured primarily by
magnificent treasure of furs it yielded. The Russian
vernment, amazed but delighted by the speed with
ich it was acquiring an empire, immediately de-
anded a lion's share of Siberia's "soft gold," as furs
re called. As early as 1590, Moscow asked for, but did
t necessarily get, an annual tribute of 200,000 sable
ns, 500,000 squirrel skins, and 10,000 black fox skins.
the middle of the 17th century, Russia obtained annu-
y from Siberia, furs worth a total of more than 600,000
ables, representing a third of the empire's entire
come.

Even in the latter part of the 19th century, Siberia still
roduced" each year the skins of 20,000 sables, 20,000
nines, 20,000 red foxes, 2,000 blue foxes, plus tens of
ousands of skins of bears, wolves, marten, mink, lynx
d squirrels, and even tiger and leopard skins from the
gions of the Ussuri and the Amur.

The headlong rush across Siberia was followed by a
riod in which the Russian presence imposed itself more
wly beyond the few scattered ostrogs established by
erchants and trades.

The logistics of transport were staggering. There were,
yet, no industries in Siberia. Everything had to be
transported from European Russia with pack horses and
barges in summer, with horse-drawn sled caravans in
winter. There were no roads. Summer trails often turned
into quagmires. Locally built barges and rafts were held
together, in the absence of hard-to-obtain nails and ropes,
by osier withes and fervent prayers. In winter, snow in the
forest lay deep and soft. Any sled that strayed off the
beaten path, was engulfed by powdery snow, and sometimes it took hours to get the sled and the frantically
struggling horses back onto the packed trail. It was cold.
Temperatures could drop to -40ºF and -50ºF, and stay
there for weeks. In the Yakutsk region it could be -70ºF.
Then human breath freezes instantly with a crackling
noise which Siberians rather poetically call "the whisper-
ing of the stars."

The distances that had to be traversed under these
conditions were enormous. Moscow goods, destined for
Okhotsk had to be transported more than 5,000 miles,
further than from Halifax to Vancouver.

The Okhotsk merchant who ordered such goods might
have to wait four years for them to arrive — if they arrived
at all. In Okhotsk a pound of fresh salmon sold for two
cents, a pound of iron for forty cents.

Despite these difficulties, the drive to the east continued. The fact that Siberia's easternmost tribes were also
its most war-like, and resolutely opposed Russian occupation and the exaction of fur tributes, seems to have
served as an incentive rather than a deterrent. The Cossacks invaded the land of the Chukchi, a region larger
than France. They subdued the fierce Koryaks. They discovered Kamchatka, a peninsula twice the size of England, and established several posts despite almost constant attacks by the Kamchadales. They heard of land to
the south and set off across the open sea in boats whose
planks were sewn together with thong and caulked with
moss. On the Kuriles they found and promptly despoiled
the islands' mysterious inhabitants, the Ainu, the "hairy
Ainu" as both Russians and Japanese called them, of a
new type of fur, that of the sea otter, exceeding in beauty
and value even the sable.

"The whole of the country
. . . has so hard and severe a winter,
that there prevails
there for eight months an altogether
unsupportable cold."
Herodotus c. 430 B.C.

Most of his life, Peter the Great fought valiantly and often brutally to turn his nation west. Shortly before his death in 1725, he looked east. What lay beyond Siberia? To provide the answer, he sent out an expedition under Vitus Bering, a Dane who had served for many years with distinction in the Russian navy. It took three years to move men and matériel the 7,000 miles overland from St. Petersburg to Nishne-Kamchatsk on the west coast of the Kamchatka Peninsula. In comparison, the real expedition was brief. Bering left on July 13, 1728, discovered St. Lawrence Island (the Chukchi had already informed him of its existence), sailed farther north and passed through the strait dividing Asia and America which Captain James Cook named fifty years later in his honor.

A new expedition was organized this time on a truly grandiose scale. Its aims were broad and based to a large extent on urgent geopolitical considerations.

Russia simply had to know more about its eastern realm, and the lands that lay beyond. The expedition task forces were expected to explore, scientifically, a major portion of eastern Siberia, to map and explore Kamchatka, to chart the Kuriles and establish contact with Japan. Bering and his second-in-command, Chirikov, were to find and map the land beyond the sea. Scientists from diverse fields were assigned to the expedition. Many would remain in Siberia for ten and more years. Some, like the brilliant young biologist Georg Wilhelm Steller and Bering himself, would die there. More than 900 people took part in the expedition, scientists, sailors, and servants. They and the thousands of tons of equipment (including everything needed to build the expedition ships on the Pacific) had to be transported by horse and boat across the breadth of Siberia. Bering was fifty-one at the inception of this expedition. He was sixty by the time he sailed east from Kamchatka.

On July 16, 1741, feast day of Saint Elias, they saw in the distance the glittering peaks of snow-covered mountains, now called the St. Elias range.

After 16 years of incredible difficulties and hardships Bering had reached his goal, the land beyond the sea, "Al-ey-as-ka," the "great land" (or mainland) as the Aleuts called it. But the burden had been too great, the elan was gone. Like some of his men, Bering was already suffering from scurvy. He looked at the land, shrugged, and quietly turned away. On July 20, they landed on Kayak Island to replenish their water supply prior to returning. Steller was bitter. "We had only come in order to take American water to Asia," he wrote.

The return voyage was dismal. They skirted the Aleutians, that 1,000 mile chain of islands hidden in near-perpetual fog and ominously and aptly known as the "Cradle of Storms." In November, their ship broke up on land which they hoped was Kamchatka. But it was an island, and they named it Bering, after their dying commander. Bering died during the severe winter and so did many of his men. Only Steller, the biologist, found the ordeal rewarding. On this bleak, barren island, he found animals no westerner had ever seen before. There was a strange flightless cormorant soon to be exterminated. Colossal, dim-witted sea cows, their skin like the bark of ancient oaks, munched seaweeds in the shallows. Discovered in 1741, they were extinct by 1768. In spring, the fur seals came in tens of thousands to breed on the island. Most important, sea otters were numerous near Bering Island. They had never met man, and were tame and gentle. And each of their skins was worth at least 100 roubles, more than the annual salary of a Russian worker.

When the survivors of Bering's crew returned (in a boat built from pieces of their wrecked ship) with 900 sea otter pelts, the eyes of Siberia's "promyshlenniki" (fur traders) glittered with greed. Within five years, 15 "companies" were active to exploit this new-found realm of furs. There was one problem. They had no ships, nor was there iron available for ship construction. So they built "shitiks," a type of vessel whose name is derived from the Russian word "shi-itj" — to sew. Made of green lumber, they were literally sewn together, with thong when available, otherwise with thin tree roots or osier withes. In such ships during the mid-to-late 18th century the promyshlenniki crisscrossed one of the world's stormiest, foggiest seas. Bancroft in his monumental *History of Alaska* lists some 90 of these voyages, and the words "wrecked in a storm" and "the men died of scurvy" recur like a sinister refrain. This was a breed of northern conquistadors, courageous and hardy, cruel and greedy, and here the gold was fur.

On the south coa
of Ellesmere Island, the remai
of a Thule culture hous
built with the bones of their main pre
the giant bowhead wha

Overleaf: Whaler's grave at Cape Fullerto

On the north coast
f Spitsbergen,
long-abandoned
apper's cabin.

Sailing from island to island, they enslaved and ravaged the Aleuts with such ferocity that within decades these proud people were reduced from about 20,000 to a cowed, subservient remnant of 2,000.

Imperial policy opposed such barbarities but returning promyshlenniki brought with them such a wealth of furs, local officials were glad to forgive any trespasses committed beyond the sea in a land as yet only vaguely known. Several ships returned with cargoes of sea otter and fox pelts worth more than 100,000 roubles.

Gerassim Pribylov discovered the Pribilof Islands, their beaches covered with more than two million fur seals, in 1786, and came home from a single voyage with furs and walrus ivory worth a total of 258,018 roubles, the equivalent of at least a million dollars today.

In 1784, Grigory Shelikov, a wealthy and venturesome Irkutsk merchant, sailed to Kodiak Island and subdued the fierce and hostile Koniags. He built a fort, traded, and after some years, returned to Siberia, leaving behind a minuscule but permanent Russian settlement.

The man to whom Shelikov entrusted his colony was Alexander Baranov, a trader, who arrived on Kodiak Island in 1791, when the settlement consisted of a few mud huts, a granary, and two log houses inhabited by Russian hunters.

In 1797 Tsar Paul signed the charter forming the crown-protected Russian-American Company with a twenty-year renewable trading monopoly. Baranov was the company's first administrator.

Baranov was a builder and a brilliant administrator. He constructed houses and ships. He built new settlements, pacified the Indians, and organized large-scale Aleut sea otter hunting expeditions. Between 1802 and 1804, furs valued at 2.5 million roubles were shipped out of Russian-America.

By the time Baranov retired in 1818, after 27 years of service as governor, Russian-America was a going and lucrative concern, and the Russian-American Company (increasingly state-controlled) was one of the greatest commercial enterprises in the world.

Although Russian-America grew into a reasonably prosperous extension of the Russian realm, the government in St. Petersburg, more than 8,000 miles away, was acutely aware of its vulnerability. It simply lacked the manpower and, above all, the naval strength needed for its defense. The California gold rush was seen as a grim omen. A similar gold find in Alaska would have started a stampede to the north, which the Russian authorities would have been incapable to repel or even regulate. (The Russians did, in fact, find gold in Alaska but kept it secret.) During the Crimean war, disaster had only been averted by an agreement between the warring parties to exclude the territories of the Hudson's Bay Company and the Russian-American Company from hostile action, since, after all, business is business.

Furthermore, in the middle years of the 19th century, the Russians were busy in southeast Siberia, occupying vast territories of the lower Amur and Ussuri regions, and there was the distinct possibility of war with a decaying, but nevertheless still powerful imperial China.

Under these circumstances, the government in St. Petersburg began to look upon Russian-America as a liability. In its decision to sell Alaska to America, the powers in St. Petersburg were in part motivated by an honest desire to please the United States government and its people. At $7,200,000, two cents an acre, Alaska was a bargain, and the Americans, who had been so obligingly pro-Russian during the Crimean war, deserved this good deed. That, unfortunately, was not the way the American people and Congress looked upon Alaska, after Secretary of State Seward had negotiated the sale in 1867. "Walrussia," they called it, and "Seward's Ice Box," and Russia had to await payment for one-and-a-half years, while Congress dragged its feet. Yet in twenty years, net revenues to the U.S. Treasury from the sale of Alaskan fur seal pelts alone, paid for this vast land, eleven times the size of England.

The northern explorations of the 16th, 17th, and 18th centuries were prompted occasionally by political but primarily by mercantile aspirations and goals. In the 19th century this changed. Expeditions were no longer sponsored by "merchant adventurers" but by governments and, especially towards the end of the 19th, and at the beginning of the 20th century, by wealthy publishers, shipping magnates or beer barons, all of whom received their share of immortality by having islands, capes and glaciers named after them.

People of the 19th century romanticized arctic exploration, endowed the arctic regions with a largely misplaced aura of glamor, and created an arctic mystique which lingers on to this day. The Arctic was a challenge to western man. Polar explorers were "heroes," who fought "battles," and they "conquered" everything from the now useless Northwest Passage to the equally useless North Pole. The fact that they, or more often the men they led, died in droves, hardly mattered.

Sir John Franklin, whose early expeditions were near-disasters, and whose last expedition was a total disaster, ending with the death of 129 men, was a popular hero. Dr. John Rae, who explored about as much territory as Franklin did, and who never lost a man, was little known, and was in his time regarded as a bit of a heel for having made public the fact that some of Franklin's crew, in their final agony, had resorted to cannibalism. The public did not want to learn such dismal facts about its romantic heroes.

The explorers of the 19th century were a product of their time. They considered themselves superior men, and usually referred to the natives as "savages." Given this gulf, it was unthinkable for them to concede that the "savages," who obviously seemed to prosper in these inhospitable regions, might possibly know best how to live in this land, and to emulate them. To do so, in the view of 19th century western man, would have been a denial of his own inherent superiority. They paid for this illusion with incredible suffering and endured it, as a rule, with magnificent fortitude. The marvel is that they achieved so much with so little understanding of the regions they assaulted.

The last of the great explorers, Nansen, Stefansson, Cook and Peary combined native knowledge with western technology to achieve their results. In 1913, Russian explorers discovered the Severnaya Zemlya Islands north of Siberia. In 1915 and 1916, Stefansson found and mapped the hitherto unknown Brock, Borden and Meighen Islands in the northwestern Canadian Arctic. The last blank spaces on the arctic map were being filled in.

With that, interest in the Arctic faded. Denmark ruled Greenland with gentle paternalism, educating the people, but keeping them "on the land" and shielding them as much as possible from corruptive outside influences.

Canada showed little interest in her vast arctic domain. She established a few Royal Canadian Mounted Police posts in the north, mainly as symbols of her sovereignty, and for the rest was content to leave the north and its natives to traders and missionaries, both devoted to maintaining the status quo. Alaska lay in quiet isolation, a romantic hinterland of little consequence. Only in Siberia, the winds of change began to blow. Russia, racked by war and civil war, impoverished but ambitious, needed Siberia's treasures. There had been many mines in tsarist times. But the exploitation of Siberia's mineral wealth on a vast scale, began after the revolution.

The Arctic of the western nations was abruptly yanked out of its isolation, first by the realization of its strategic importance, and more recently by understanding that it, too, is a treasure trove of mineral wealth, particularly desperately needed oil and natural gas. Technological progress made it possible to find and extract minerals in the remotest regions of the Arctic.

Fifty years ago, or even less, a resource industry could move into a region and start operating on as large a scale as the situation warranted with little consideration for the permanent damage its activities might be causing to the Arctic's incredibly fragile natural environment.

Now it is different. The Arctic, no doubt, will be exploited but, it is hoped, with care. For in our crowded and polluted world, it is a land apart; the last immense wilderness region on earth. It is a land of beauty and diversity, a land of infinite space. It can be rugged and harsh and hostile, primeval and powerful, and as delicate as the filigree of red lichen on a tundra boulder. It is a new land, in the sense that much of it has only recently emerged from beneath the mile-thick glaciers of the Pleistocene.

And it is an ancient land, where shaggy muskoxen still wander over the vast tundra, as they did, millennia ago, together with lions and mammoths.

Samuel Hearne engraved his nar
on a sloping ro
on the west coast of the Churchill Riv
in 1767. Three years la
he travelled from here to the Arctic Ocea

War

From their legends and latter-day experience the Eskimos understood the violence of raids and murder but war was an alien concept. When Diamond Jenness in 1915 explained the World War to Eskimos who had only recently been "discovered," they were horrified and felt that "white men who deliberately used their extraordinary knowledge and powers for the wholesale massacre of each other were strangely unnatural and inhuman." And John Ross, with the memory of the protracted Napoleonic wars fresh in his mind was startled that the Polar Eskimos whom he discovered in 1818 "could not be made to understand what was meant by war." The Eskimo language, which has more than one hundred words for different kinds of snow, lacks a specific word for war. The best they can do is to add a plural suffix to the noun "killing" or "murder," thus turning it into "mass killing" or "mass murder."

Recall

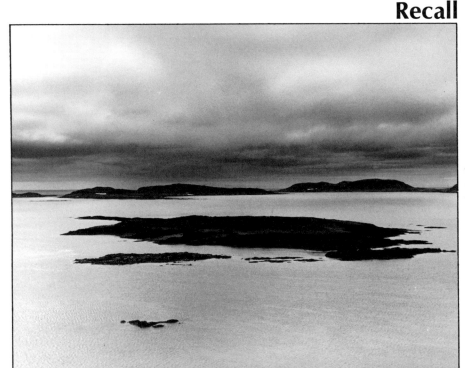

The Eskimos of Baffin Island still vividly remember Frobisher's visits. In 1862, the explorer Charles Francis Hall lived amongst them, and an old woman told him that "long, long ago" white men had come to Frobisher Bay, with one ship the first year, two the second, and with a great many the third. Hall visited the Countess of Warwick Island, called Kodlunarn (White Man's) Island by the Eskimos and found many relics of Frobisher's stay. More than a century later, and nearly four centuries after Frobisher, I visited Kodlunarn Island, with some Eskimos, and the story was still vividly alive. We saw the great trench where the "gold ore" had been mined, the remnants of his house of "lyme and stone," and the sloping ditch where, the Eskimos recalled (accu-rately!) the "white men repaired the ships." From a high cape on the neighboring mainland we looked down on the little twenty-five acre island. It was an ideal vantage point. In all likelihood four centuries ago, Eskimos had stared down from here in wonder, watching Elizabethan sailors and miners inexplicably load their ships with rock and, their last day, march around the island, flags flying, trumpets blaring, and ship cannons firing a farewell salute.

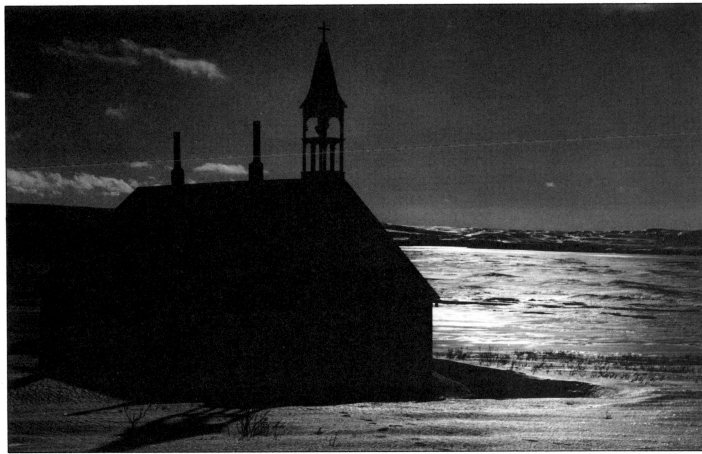

Impact of Whites

Four groups of white men have responded to the lure of the north. The explorer and scientist sought knowledge, adventure and fame; the whaler, sea mammals; the trader, furs; and the missionary, souls. The explorers' direct impact upon the land and its people was, as a rule, minimal. But they opened up the north and made it accessible and desirable to other men from the south. The whalers, sealers and walrus hunters killed, in some instances almost to the point of extinction, those sea mammals upon which the native peoples relied for food. They equipped the natives with guns to provide crews with fresh meat, and thus contributed to the massive slaughter of arctic land mammals.

They brought diseases which decimated many groups and destroyed some completely. The traders destroyed the natives' ancient self-sufficiency. Before the advent of the traders, the native peoples of the north had been poor but independent. Now they were dependent and still poor. The missionaries replaced the culture of the northern people, which saw man essentially as an integral part of nature, with a new one that proclaimed man was nature's master. Inevitably, the cultural conflict produced an emotional dichotomy that continues to this day.

One animal, above all others, inspired ice age man with reverential awe. This was the mighty cave bear, a huge beast, (similar in appearance to Alaska's Kodiak bear), eight feet tall when it reared up on its hind legs. It weighed as much as 1,500 pounds. The cave bear was probably a placid enough plant eater, until cornered when it became a fierce and formidable foe. Yet Neanderthal man pursued it with puny stone-tipped spears, killed it, and probably worshipped it. Bear skulls and bones, carefully cached perhaps fifty centuries ago, have been discovered in European caves. The cult of the cave bear may have been man's first, and certainly has been his most enduring form of animal worship. Like an echo from the dawn of man, the cultic killing and veneration of the bear by most circumpolar peoples has persisted nearly to our day.

To the Lapps, the bear was the king of animals and ancestor of man. They killed and ate it with elaborate ritual, carefully buried all its bones and reverentially assured it: "With the coming of next spring, you will rise again and roam the hills . . . Pardon us now, forget that we have killed you . . ."

The Ket (Ostyaks) a tribe of central Siberia, similarly regarded the bear as both animal king and ancestor. Even now they call it "gyp" — grandfather, or "qoi" — stepfather. The bear was killed with many apologies for the "inconvenience" and eaten with great ceremony and reverence. The skull was set up in a forked tree (a practice still observed by a few Cree Indians on James Bay), and the bones were buried to ensure the bear's resurrection.

Dorset culture Eskimos, who held sway over much of the North American Arctic for nearly 2,000 years, from about 800 B.C. until 1300 A.D., may have had some worshipful feeling for the great white bears that roamed the north. Next to man, the bear was the most common subject of their art, and this art, it is believed, was basically religio-magic. The subsequent Thule culture Eskimos, the recent ancestors of today's Eskimos, did not worship the bear, but since, in their belief, the bear, as well as all other animals, had a soul, utmost care had to be taken not to offend it. A killed bear was treated with great respect.

It was customary to thank the animal for letting itself be killed, thus providing the hunter and his family with food and fur. Such polite treatment, and the observation of a multitude of appropriate taboos, it was thought, would please the bear's soul. When it returned to the realm of bears, it would spread a good report about the hunter, and its fellow bears would be pleased to let themselves be killed by such a pleasant and polite man who observed the proper spiritual punctilio.

Fighting the great bear, so powerful it can kill an 800-pound seal with one stroke of its massive paw, was the Eskimos' test of manhood. Yet nearly all the Eskimos did it routinely, and usually alone. Typical was an incident witnessed when Charles Francis Hall's expedition wintered near Etah in 1873. A polar bear passed the camp and the aging Polar Eskimo Awatok immediately set out in pursuit with his sled, a team of dogs and a four-foot spear as his weapon. He remained out all night in a northeast gale with the temperature in the vicinity of -30°F. Late the next day he returned with the bear's carcass on his sled.

Hall adds a footnote to the record of this episode: "When the old man took off his jacket to dry it, his back, marked with the scars of what appeared to be frightful wounds, showed that he had previously had fights with the same enemy."

In a poem, translated by Knud Rasmussen, Orpingalik, an old Netsilik Eskimo, recalls his fight with a bear.

"It threw me down
  Again and again,
  Then breathless departed
  And lay down to rest,
  Hid by a mound on a floe.
  Heedless it was, and unknowing
  That I was to be its fate.
  Deluding itself
  That he alone was a male,
  And unthinking
  That I too was a man!"

Bears

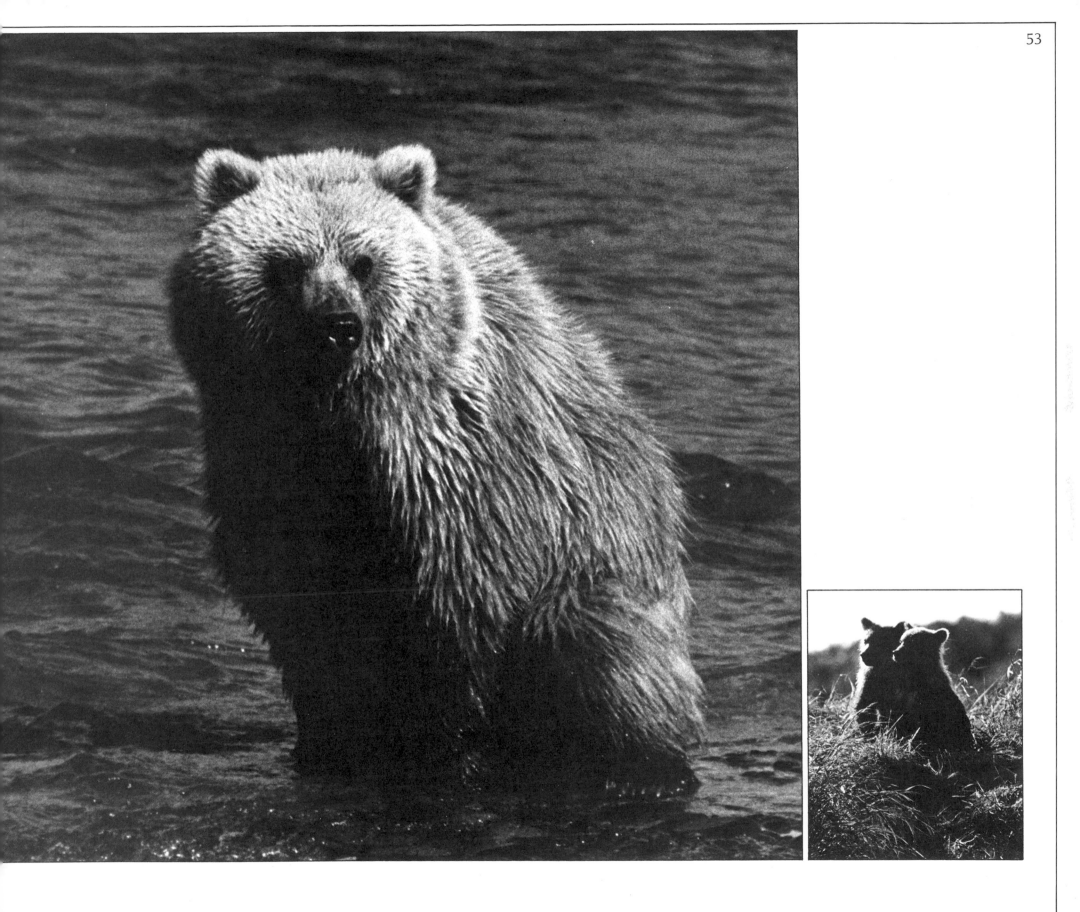

The Land

"No vines are there to provide men with drink,
. . . one night in this region may last no less than two months . . .
for eight months of the year snow and ice cover all land and all water . . . (in) summer,
the air is noxious with mosquitoes and midges which come in such hosts
that the sun is obscured. All this being so, one would surely hold that
the country cannot be inhabited by so much as wild beasts . . .
Yet inhabited it is."

Description of Lappland
by the 17th century Italian priest Francesco Negri
in his book "Viaggio Settentrionale".

Spitsbergen . . . an arctic island

Driftwood from the great rivers of Siberia lies strewn over a beach
on this glacier-covered, treeless island.

A muskox herd in Adventdalen, a great river valley.

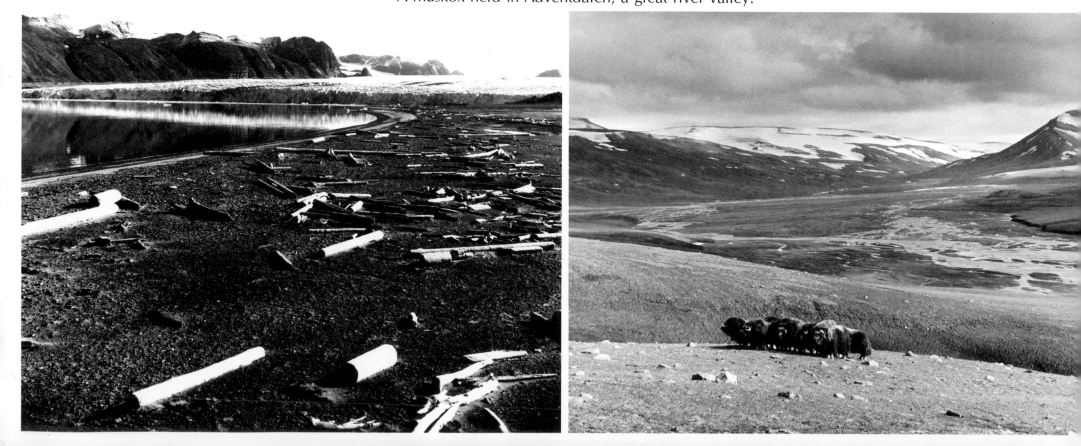

The mountains and a fiord between them covered by clouds.
Flowing slowly over uneven ground,
a glacier responds to stresses by breaking into a maze of crevasses.

zan River Falls
the Canadian Barrens.

Most of the physical geography of the Arctic is of recent post-glacial origin, its barren landscapes appearing today much as they did when they were uncovered by the retreating ice 10,000 years ago.

In the far north the ice age persists and the people share an ice-age culture with a heritage that by-passes the entire recorded history of modern man.

This bridge to pre-history is found today, amazingly preserved, in the lore of the Polar Eskimos.

My neighbor at Kangerdlugssuaq, the narwhal hunting camp on the south shore of Inglefield Bay in northwestern Greenland, was Kutsikitsoq, son of the famous Odâq who had accompanied Peary to the North Pole.

Until a few years ago Kutsikitsoq had been one of the best and most daring hunters among the Polar Eskimos, that tiny isolated fragment of humanity living farther north than any other people on earth. Now a widower, nearing seventy and still a good hunter, but lonely, he often sat in front of this tent for hours and stared silently at the land, the broad iceberg-studded bay and the mountains and glaciers beyond.

The snow-streaked mountains, and the glittering glaciers and icebergs gave the scene a certain chill grandeur.

But it looked empty, unfinished as if God had abandoned its creation before giving it life, leaving this narrow strip of barren rock surrounded by an infinite expanse of ice — the icecap of Greenland.

Sometimes, when Kutsikitsoq and I drank tea together, and the mood was right, he would tell me about this land, and to him it was not drear and dead, but superb and alive, "Nunassiaq," the beautiful land.

In pragmatic Eskimo fashion, he saw its beauty primarily in terms of food, and his stories were mostly about a lifetime of hunting experience and hunting travel.

In this land ninety-five percent covered by ice, at the edge of a sea frozen nine to ten months each year, Kutsikitsoq and his people, for uncounted generations, had survived by ceaselessly pursuing the region's game animals, moving with them as the seasons changed, knowing their habits as intimately as they knew their own. Kutsikitsoq, in his prime as a hunter, had travelled at least 2,000 miles each year.

Now, in summer, sleek single-tusked narwhal and milky-white beluga whales surged through the dark waters of the bay. Hunting with kayaks, the men had killed many of them, and their meat and fat formed the bulk of our food. Seals were numerous and farther west, we had hunted walrus in spring on the ice. Caribou had once been common. Eighty years ago, Peary had obtained his winter supply of caribou meat in the valley just behind our camp. Unfavorable climatic fluctuations, and over-hunting by the now gun-equipped Eskimos, had exterminated caribou locally. Some hunters made the long trip to Inglefield Land in the north to get caribou, crossing a spur of the mighty Greenland icecap. The people no longer feared "sermerssuaq," the giant glacier, as the Polar Eskimos call the icecap. But their ancestors, Kutsikitsoq said, had avoided it. It was, they believed, the abode of evil demons. Now many white men had crossed the icecap, and Eskimos with them, Kutsikitsoq said, but there really was nothing there, only ice and hunger, just as there had been nothing at the Pole when his father had finally reached it with Peary. "Kingmersoriartorfikssuaq," the place where one only eats dogs, he called the North Pole.

When I spread a map in front of Kutsikitsoq, it immediately came to life. "This place is called 'Ulugssat,'" he said, pointing to the southwest coast of Herbert Island. "People used to go there, long ago, to get a special stone to make 'ulus,' [the crescentic women's knives]. This island, [Hakluyt Island], is called 'Agparssuit,' because the 'agpa' [murres] nest there. Here," he pointed to Barden Bay, "people hunt seals at their breathing holes in spring. There once was a camp, here, at 'Natsilivik,' at the great stone. Long ago the Tunit lived there. Our people attacked them. One Tunit fled onto the great stone. But one of the Eskimos shot an arrow into him, it pierced his body and he died." His folk memory was spanning the ages. Since Tunit are Dorset culture people, who gave way to Thule culture Eskimos about 800 years ago, the fight Kutsikitsoq was describing so vividly and in such detail, must have occurred some eight or nine centuries ago.

I had been to Natsilivik in spring. The Eskimos with whom I travelled had been hunting seal at the floe edge, the limit of landfast ice. A storm sprang up at night, it looked as if the ice might be driven out to sea, and we sought refuge on firm land at Natsilivik. The "great stone" was a giant erratic, a house-high rounded boulder brought thither, eons ago, by a glacier and deposited on a flat rock shelf at the very edge of the sea. It was encrusted and blackened by a thick layer of congealed and hardened fat, because on top of this boulder Eskimos had stored, perhaps during centuries, meat and fat beyond reach of their voracious sled dogs.

Near the boulder were remnants of old houses. Once these homes had been ingeniously roofed with great, flat, cantilevered slabs of rock and then covered with turf. Now the roofs had collapsed, the semi-subterranean house depressions were filled with rocks, rubble, ice and snow and looked singularly dreary and uninviting.

Some weeks later, I lived in Siorapaluk, the northernmost village in the world, with an old couple, Inuterssuaq and his wife Naduq, and found, to my surprise, that Naduq had been born in one of those stone houses at Natsilivik and remembered her home and childhood there with warm nostalgia.

Near Siorapaluk are many-mile-long scree slopes, some rising to a height of more than 1,000 feet. Under this mass of rocks and boulders, with its myriad clefts and fissures, nest the dovekies, black and white sea birds about the size of starlings but chubbier. Their colonies number millions. With an estimated population of eighty million they may be the most numerous sea birds on

earth. To the Eskimos they have always been an important source of food. Inuterssuaq and Naduq spent their days on the slopes, scooping low-flying dovekies out of the air with long-handled nets. On good days, they caught between 400 and 500 birds. Some we ate, others, marinated in blubber, were cached for the coming winter.

At night, after supper, Inuterssuaq liked to tell me about his people's past. "Aglani, aglani . . ." long, long ago, he invariably began, and unfolded for me the tale of his people, who had lived, since time immemorial, in the shadow of sermerssuaq, the giant glacier. Once I asked him: "The Eskimos of the western Arctic make the cat's-cradle figure of an animal they call 'kilivaiciaq.' Do you know it?" He thought a moment, his dark, handsome face a mask of concentration. "Maybe it is the same we call 'kiligfagssuk,' " he said, and made a figure with a piece of netting twine. Not only was the name similar, but the figure was identical to the one Eskimos in the west had made for me, thousands of miles away, people with whom the Polar Eskimos must have lost contact at least seven centuries ago. "What is a 'kiligfagssuk'?" I asked. "It is an animal," he said. "A very large animal. It has four legs, like a muskox, but it is much bigger. It existed a long time ago. No one here has ever seen it. Even the oldest people have never seen it."

Nor have their parents, or grandparents, nor any people for 300 generations because in this string figure, handed on from generation to generation, the Eskimos have preserved, for more than 10,000 years, the memory of the mammoth, the great shaggy elephant of the north. This figure was first created, perhaps by a paleolithic hunter in Siberia, at a time when the ice age was not just here, at Siorapaluk, at the very edge of the world, but in much of North America and Europe, at a time when Stockholm, Oslo and Ottawa lay under mile-thick sheets of ice, and Stone Age man hunted mastodon and muskox in New York State.

Ice ages are not common. There have been about 1(
the last 600 million years of our earth's history, the las
the Permo-Carboniferous Period some 150 million ye
ago. Nor was the North Pole always where it is now. It
quite a peripatetic history. At one time it was in
neighborhood of Hawaii. For millions upon millions
years, the earth's climate was nearly uniformly ben
and the north was warm and wooded.

A gift from that era, are the vast oil and coal deposit:
the far north. On Spitsbergen, near a glacier where I li
for one summer, we used to find shale-type rocks, bear
fossilized imprints of the lovely, tropical-looking pla
that once had grown there in ages of warmth.

But during the Pliocene (which lasted about 13 mill
years) the climate gradually deteriorated; no one re:
knows why. Very slowly it became colder. The No
Pole by this time had moved to its present position, and
the beginning of the period called the Pleistocene, ab
two million years ago, the first glaciers began to form
the mountains of the far north.

Glaciers are born when annual snow fall exceeds
nual melt for a long period of time. To flourish t
require cold and sufficient precipitation to permit
accumulation of snow that gradually turns into ice.

There are great glaciers on some of the high mounta
of New Guinea, just three degrees south of the equa
and less than 70 miles in a direct line from
sweltering-hot jungles of the coastal plain. By contr
Peary Land, the size of Maine, at the north tip of Gre
land, only 500 miles from the North Pole, is ice free. It
frigid land, but drier than most deserts. Its annual prec
tation of about an inch is insufficient for glac
formation.

The snows of winter, only partially melted in summ
are re-frozen, compacted, and covered by new layer
snow. These snows of yesteryear change their crysta
graphic structure, become coarse and rounded, and
called firn, or névé. As more snow is piled on them
weight turns the porous, granular firn into solid glassy
But individual ice crystals in this mass are separated fr
each other by exceedingly thin films of water contain
dissolved impurities, such as salts, and the crystals
glide along these planes of separation. Thus the ice m
of a glacier behaves like a very viscous fluid.

A glacier on the move is a thing of awesome we
and power. If it flows through a valley, it gouges rocks
of the mountain sides and piles them into vast, irregul
strung-out heaps, as lateral moraines. It rips out g

cks of rock and transports them along, often for hun-
ds of miles.

s the glacier creeps on, rocks and even boulders
ome embedded in its sole so that it grinds over the
d like a billion-ton rasp. Stones are ground to dust. It is
"rock flour," finely suspended in water, that gives
cier streams in the mountains their peculiar milky
oring. Ice and stones cut and groove the underlying
k, and from the glacier front meltwater streams, laden
n sediment, fan out in a braided maze, forever branch-
and rejoining, over the outwash plains beyond.

Cold, drying winds sweep down from the ice sheets,
iccate the periglacial regions, pick up dried fragments
oil and carry them, often for hundreds of miles, into
land beyond. Slowly these aeolian sediments settle,
caught by plants, enrich the earth, and form the loess
dra-steppes with a rich vegetation for enormous herds
ce-age herbivores, who in turn are food for predators
n fox to sabre-toothed tiger, and for that ultimate
dator of the late Pleistocene, man.

Once the conditions favoring the formation of the ice
ets are reversed, when the climate becomes warmer,
cipitation decreases, and annual melt exceeds
nulative annual snow fall, the glaciers begin their
eat. Although their advance is usually slow, their re-
at can be, geologically speaking, quite rapid. Ten
usand years ago, most of Canada was covered by
e-thick ice. Today only mountain glaciers are left, in
Rockies and on the eastern arctic islands.

Upon the land, the passing of this icy juggernaut has
a lasting imprint. The étapes of its retreat are marked
terminal moraines, the dumped mass of rock debris at
glacier's face. The great eskers that wind like mis-
ced railroad embankments over hundreds of miles of
tic tundra are the sediment deposited by ancient sub-
cial streams. Because they are high and dry and consist
narily of sand and gravel, they are one of the preferred
ning areas of arctic foxes, wolves, and ground squir-
s. To the detriment of these original claimants, eskers
now also a favorite source of fill for the builders of
tic roads and pipelines.

Drumlins, low ovoid hillocks, consisting of glacial till,
accumulated and dumped by the ice around cores of
rock, all neatly aligned to show the path of the retreating
glaciers, cover vast areas of the north.

On the hills, where glaciers ground over hard rocks,
they left them rounded and abraded, looking from afar
like flocks of resting sheep, and because of this geologists
call them roches moutonées.

In the south, where the climate was relatively mild,
plant invasion and plant succession after the ice's retreat
was fairly rapid, and soon the jumbled, chaotic mess of
boulders, gravel beds, moraines, kames and drumlins,
was covered by a hiding and protective mantle of forest.
When George Vancouver in 1794 sailed along the coast
of what is now southeastern Alaska, he found the present
Glacier Bay barred by "an immense body of compact,
perpendicular ice, extending from shore to shore, and
connected with a range of lofty mountains on each side."
Today, Glacier Bay, for a distance of more than 50 miles
is free of ice, though glaciers tower on the mountains and
in the valleys above. Where Vancouver saw nothing but
ice, giant hemlock forests now cover much of the land.

In the north beyond the treeline, this concealing forest
cloak is missing. The vegetation is low and scant, a mere
veil over the rasped and riven body of the land. The
glaciers, advancing and retreating, have stamped and
moulded this land, and when explorers first saw it, its
rawness and solitude frightened them. "Vast and dreary
plains," said J. W. Tyrrell, of the Canadian Geological
Survey, and Warburton Pike, the English explorer, who
saw the land in winter, wrote 70 years ago: "A monotonous snow-covered waste. A deathly stillness hangs over
all, and the oppressive loneliness weighs upon the spec-
tator until he is glad to shout aloud to break the awful spell
of solitude." The people of the land saw it differently.

"My father, you have spoken well;
you have told me
that Heaven is very beautiful;
tell me now one more thing.
Is it more beautiful
than the country
of the muskox in summer,
where sometimes
the mist blows over the lakes,
and sometimes
the water is blue
and the loons cry very often?"
**Saltatha,
Warburton Pike's Indian guide,
talking to a priest.**

Warburton Pike's guide, Saltatha, asked a priest who had extolled the marvels of heaven: "My father, . . . you have told me that Heaven is very beautiful; tell me now one more thing. Is it more beautiful than the country of the muskox in summer, where sometimes the mist blows over the lakes, and sometimes the water is blue and the loons cry very often?"

Four times during the Pleistocene the ice sheets advanced to cover much of Europe and North America, and four times, during the interglacial periods, the longest lasting about 200,000 years, they receded.

The interglacials, though generally mild, had some nasty and prolonged cold spells, and the ice ages were interrupted, from time to time, by so-called interstadials, brief periods of relative warmth. We are pleased to call our present period the post-glacial. Whether, in fact, it is that, or merely another interglacial, or perhaps even a short-lived but exceptionally warm interstadial, we don't know.

The water needed to form glaciers and ice sheets comes, ultimately, from the oceans, and to the oceans it returns when ice sheets and glaciers melt. At the height of the last ice age, (it started about 80,000 years ago, and reached its maximum extent roughly 20,000 years ago), ice sheets covered 4,300,000 square miles of North America and 1,200,000 square miles of Europe. More than 10,000,000 cubic miles of water were locked within this monstrous mass of ice, and the level of the world's oceans was 300 feet lower than it is now. Millions of square miles of continental shelves were exposed, and land bridges linked countries and continents. In the Arctic the shallow sea north of Siberia receded for hundreds of miles, leaving behind a vast land where mammoth and muskox roamed, and Asia and America were connected by the thousand-mile-wide Bering Land Bridge. Across it cold-adapted animals, and man, invaded the New World from Eurasia. Animals and man could roam freely, in search of pasture and of prey, because while large parts of Europe and North America were covered by ice sheets, most of Siberia and much of Alaska were free of ice.

It was an age of giants, a last spectacular proliferation of mighty mammals in the north, often in great herds. The imperial mammoth of the American plain stood fourteen feet high at the withers, and carried tusks of up to sixteen feet in length. The woolly mammoth of the far north was only nine to ten feet high but it was so numerous, half the world's ivory comes from its fossil tusks. In Russia alone, the remains of some 175,000 mammoths have been found. A. E. Nordenskjöld, the Swedish scientist-explorer who made the first voyage through the Northeast Passage, wrote: "The nearer we come to the coast of the Polar Sea, the more common are the remains of the mammoth . . . Nowhere, however, are they found in such numbers as on the New Siberian Islands. Here Hedenström in the space of a verst [three quarters of a mile] saw ten tusks sticking out of the ground, and from a single sandbank . . . ivory collectors had . . . for eighty years made their best tusk harvest."

Castoroides, the Pleistocene beaver, was the size of a small bear. The woolly rhinoceros was common in Europe and Siberia, but did not cross to North America. Muskoxen roamed the tundras from France to Siberia and the North American periglacial lands which included New York State; they are still around in the far north of Canada, and Greenland, and died out in Alaska only in the last century (they have since been re-introduced), but their mighty cousin, the woodland muskox did not survive the Pleistocene. Bison were bigger than now; one species, Bison crassicornis, carried a six foot sweep of horns. Saiga antelopes, puffy-nosed cold-steppe animals, now living only in Russia, were then at home in southern England as well as northern Alaska. Camelops, an immense, knob-kneed camel paced over the Alaskan plains, while in the valleys nearby the dimwitted, twelve-foot-high ground sloth Megalonyx munched placidly the leaves of dwarf willow and birch.

Patterns of the tund
polygons
the Mackenzie River del

t is more dream-like
nd supernatural
an a combination of earthly features . . .
is a landscape
ch as Milton or Dante
ight imagine,
- inorganic, desolate, mysterious.''

**sha Kent Kane, 1855,
herican arctic explorer.**

These mighty herbivorous mammals were prey to an equally impressive array of Pleistocene predators. Lions roamed over Alaska and Siberia, and the sabre-toothed tiger, larger than any tiger today, whom scientists, with a slightly sinister sense of humor have named Smilodon, probably stabbed his prey to death with dagger-like six-inch fangs.

Man, during much of the Pleistocene, avoided the chilly northern regions. He had originated in Africa, a product of warmer climes, and was as yet neither physiologically nor culturally prepared to cope with a cold climate. But when the last ice age began, Neanderthal man was well established in Europe and parts of Asia. He survived for some 75,000 years and was displaced about 35,000 B. C. by the Cro-Magnon people who with their successors, such as the men of the Magdalenian period, were skilful hunters.

By employing methods such as the fire drive, or the stampeding of herds over cliffs and into bogs, men could kill large numbers of animals. But in the late Pleistocene they were not as yet numerous, certainly not in Siberia and North America. In the waning years of the Pleistocene, as the ice sheets receded and it became warmer, forests moved northward. An animal like Ireland's giant elk with his bizarre spread of antlers was obviously a beast of the wide open spaces. Once forest covered the land, he got himself all tangled up and died out. The woolly mammoth seems to have been an animal of arctic tundra and brush land. As it grew warmer, Siberia's great forest moved northward, while the rising Polar Sea, reclaiming more than a million square miles of continental shelf, moved south.

The mammoth, caught between the rising sea and the advancing forest, found its pasturage area considerably shrunken, and to an animal which consumed about 300 pounds of forage per day, this undoubtedly was serious. To get more food, the mammoths may have increasingly frequented the flood plains of Siberia's great rivers, with the obvious hazard of being caught in a flood or getting stuck in mud with their pillar-like legs. Hunters, no doubt, took advantage of such situations and chased the great animals into dangerous bogs where, once they were well mired, they could easily be killed. Thus probably between cunning man and hostile nature, the mammoth was destroyed and, in a similar manner, perhaps, the other megafauna of the Pleistocene became extinct.

The ice sheets of the Pleistocene have vanished. Only Greenland and Antarctica remain almost totally covered by ice. About two million cubic kilometers of ice press down upon Greenland with such a stupendous weight, parts of the island, overlain by more than a mile of ice, have been squeezed so deeply into the earth's viscous mantle, they are actually below sea level.

Greenland's glistening carapace of ice covers an area as big as all of the United States east of the Mississippi. The Antarctic ice sheets are about eight times larger in extent, and contain ten times the amount of ice.

As year upon year new snow is added to the Greenland icecap, it flows outward and its glaciers ''calve'' some 10,000 to 15,000 icebergs annually into the sea, some of them 300 feet high. At that, they are mere dwarfs compared to Antarctic icebergs which can be two hundred and more miles long, with a surface area similar to that of some European countries. Greenlanders are now turning their icecap into an asset. They cut its pollution-free ice and ship it south to supply a marketable pure taste for chilled drinks.

Should the world's climate become warmer, the icecaps of Greenland and Antarctica will melt. The ocean levels will then rise by about 320 feet, drowning a large portion of the earth, and most of its great cities.

During the past two centuries it has been getting warmer. There was another warm period, a ''climatic optimum,'' about 1,000 years ago. Then, in the 14th century, it became much colder. It was the beginning of the "Little Ice Age," which lasted until the latter part of the 18th century. Eskimos left the farthest north of Greenland and the Canadian arctic islands. Only the Polar Eskimos remained, hemmed in by ice on all sides, but living in an area rich in game. As they passed centuries in total, frigid isolation, they came to regard themselves as the only people on earth, and the existence of other people was only vaguely remembered in legends. Farther south, the adverse climate hastened the decline of Greenland's once-flourishing Norse colony. As it became colder, the permafrost level rose in the ground, and Norse graves showed this climatic deterioration by becoming increasingly shallow.

Since about 1800, particularly in the present century, there have been visible effects of the warming trend. In northern Scandinavia, the annual growth rings of spruce, pine, and birch have increased in width. Animals, too, have responded. A quarter of all North European bird species have expanded their range northward. In Canada, moose were newcomers to the shores of the western Arctic Ocean about seventy years ago, and in the northeast, black bears are invading the realm of their white cousins. The shipping season to Spitsbergen has lengthened from three to six months because there is less ice. Cod, particularly sensitive to even small variations in water temperature, moved north. In 1915, twenty tons of cod were caught off southwestern Greenland; by the 1950s, the cod fishery, with an annual catch of 25,000 tons, had become Greenland's most important industry. But in the late 1960s, water temperatures seemed to have dropped slightly, the cod moved south again, and Greenland's fishing industry faced a decline.

As the glaciers of the last ice age receded, the land, freed of its burden of ice, began to rise. It rose rapidly at first, as much as five inches per year in some areas. Now the uplift is slower, about one to two inches annually in much of northern Scandinavia and Canada. Terrace-like raised beaches along many arctic sea coasts mark the upward movement of the land. The Eskimos like them. They make excellent camping areas.

Some regions of the Canadian Arctic have already risen more than 600 feet in the post-glacial era. In southern Baffin Island, cod were landlocked when the land surrounding a sea arm rose and turned it into a lake. Harbour seal have been trapped by rising land in lakes far in the interior of Labrador, and there are thousands of lakes with landlocked char throughout the Arctic.

While the grinding glaciers and the subsequent uplift have shaped and moulded much of the Arctic, it is essentially a land ruled by cold. The common assumption that it gets increasingly colder the farther north one goes, is wrong. The lowest temperatures registered at the North Pole are similar to those of cold winter days in Ontario or Manitoba. The areas of the northern hemisphere with the doubtful distinction of having the lowest winter temperatures are well within the forest belt: the Yukon with -81°F and Verkhoyansk in Siberia with -90°F, still cozy compared to the record -126.9°F measured by Russian scientists at Vostok, their antarctic research station.

The far north is not extremely cold, but the duration of cold weather is extremely long. In the land of the Polar Eskimos on northwestern Greenland, the average temperature of only one month of the year, July, is above the freezing point. With a Polar Eskimo party I travelled by dogsled on July 8 over sea ice which though rotten and dangerous was nonetheless strong enough to support us. Less than five weeks later, on August 10, the first snow storm of the season hit us. Summer for us was but a fleeting pleasant phase interrupting the ten-month winter.

This intense and prolonged cold of the north is responsible for permafrost, the vast layer of permanently frozen soil and rock, varying in thickness from a few feet at its

southern edge, to 1,620 feet at Winter Harbour on M ville Island in the Canadian Arctic and 4,265 feet in Sit ria's northern Yakutia. It extends over nearly one-fifth the earth's land surface: most of Alaska, half of Canac and about forty percent of the Soviet Union. Its southe limit coincides, to some extent, with the mean annu 25°F isotherm. But prolonged cold can start permafrost any locality. It was found, for example, in the grou beneath a long-used ice-storage house in Edmonto Alberta.

In more southern regions, permafrost may lie de within the earth, covered by a dozen or more feet unfrozen ground and here the northern forests can s flourish. Its trees may not be able to allow themselves t luxury of running taproots deep into the earth, but have be content with a lateral but extensive network of roo As one advances north, into regions with colder me annual air temperatures, the permafrost layer rises clos to the surface, and the trees become small and stunte Water seeping along the impermeable permafrost si face, is pushed up into icy ridges and domes, the s called naled or aufeis, and the trees above it lean crazi "The drunken forest," scientists call it. Farther nor beyond the tree line, the forest peters out and gives way the treeless tundra.

Finland proudly calls itself "The Land Of O Hundred Thousand Lakes"; Alaska claims to have thr million lakes; and Canada may have ten times th number. No one, I think, has ever counted them. Nea half of Canada's tundra region is covered by water, infinite maze of brooks and rills and rivers, of ponds a tarns and lakes, pieces of a watery jigsaw puzzle strew apparently, at random over the land. Yet much of t north has an arid climate; some regions receive less p cipitation than the Sahara. But the summer season short, evaporation minimal, and the impermeable lay of permafrost just below the land's surface, preve water from draining away into the ground. Without p mafrost, much of the Arctic would be a desert, one of t largest on earth.

In summer the surface of the land, the so-called acti layer, thaws to a depth of several feet in the more sou erly regions of the Arctic, and only a few inches in the north. This enables plants to grow by obtaining moistu and nutrients from the thawed soil. But theirs is a haza ous existence. The very stratum that gives them life strangely mobile, and can slide on its icy permafrost ba

on slopes having a gradient of only four or five per-
. This solifluction scars the land, it tears the roots of
ts, and on steeper hill sides, massive soil slips of
er-saturated earth in spring and early summer, bury
re plant communities with a mass of clay and rubble.
he alternating actions of thaw and frost squeeze and
ve stones within the soil, press them upward and
ward, and arrange them into circles, squares, or
gonal patterns. The ground itself is cleft by ice
ges within, formed in seepage zones filled by water
freezes and expands, cutting the soil into squares,
gles or polygons, so that from the air great areas of the
tic appear like the work of a creator obsessed with
metry. On a more down to earth level, the sharp-
ed ridges of stone polygons and circles, alternating
intermediate areas of soft, clinging, clayey soil,
e for miserable walking. They were also, in former
s, the despair of every Eskimo wife, because during
mer migrations the sharp stones wore out sealskin
ts as fast as she could sew them.
he folding of the earth's crust, eons ago, created
ntains. Water and wind, frost and thaw, level them
n. Their forces are slow and patient and powerful.
st arctic cliffs are banked by immense scree slopes,
ks broken off the mountains above by alternating frost
thaw. Water seeping into a fissure expands in volume
bout ten percent when it freezes and can shatter the
fining rock. The talus slopes look barren from a dis-
ce, and usually they are, except in the high Arctic
re some of the mightiest scree slopes are home to the
e colonies of dovekies. The auklets and murrelets of
ng Sea and Chukchee Sea regions also have chosen
e slopes for their homes.
he high Arctic is at its best in spring. It is often sunny,
sky is a pale robin-egg blue, merging into a cool-

greenish aquamarine near the horizon, or it is gayly streaked with cirrus clouds. In summer, along the coast, when it is cloudy, the cover is likely to be those uniformly dismal low stratus clouds that cast a pall over land and mind. In the interior, cumulus clouds are frequent, but everywhere in the Arctic thunderstorms are extremely rare. I was caught in one spectacular storm on Coats Island in Hudson Bay, together with a nineteen-year-old Eskimo. As the thunder crashed, the boy, Enoapik exclaimed: "Jet planes flying real low today!" With jets he was familiar, but this was the first thunderstorm he had ever experienced.

The Arctic has a not entirely deserved reputation for being stormy. It is so, no doubt, in the memory of all arctic travellers, because winter storms and even moderate winds are extremely unpleasant and to the unprepared they can be fatal. But meteorologists, compiling statistics with impartial accuracy in warm offices, say wind turbulence in much of the Arctic is less than in southern regions. When it does blow, an already cold climate becomes, due to wind chill, harshly colder, and ground drift cuts visibility. A moderate wind of 10 mph is sufficient to move granules of dry arctic snow across the land; at 20 mph the drift is high and dense; at 30 mph the hard snow

"The thawe began this yeare (1613)
about the 10th of June,
at which time there began to spring up
. . . a certaine stragling grasse,
with a blewish flower
. . . And this is that wher with all the deare
. . . become exceeding fatt;
but how they live in the time of extreame winter,
when all is couered with snowe,
I cannot imagine."
**Robert Fotherby, 1613,
English traveller in Spitsbergen.**

spicules sting your face like a thousand needles; and at 40 mph you can barely see the dogs pulling your sled.

Wind compacts and shapes the snow, it sweeps it off the ridges and packs it into hollows. The snow, so soft in the sheltered areas of the boreal forests that travel is possible only on snowshoes, is packed and hard in the wind-swept, treeless regions further north, and a five-ton tractor leaves only a two-inch deep track. Using hard, abrasive snow particles as its "tool," the wind sculptures the snow into long fluted ridges. Knowing his region's prevailing winds, an Eskimo uses these sastrugi as his compass when he is travelling blind in the swirling madness of a heavy ground drift, or in a white-out.

When land or sea are covered by snow, and the overcast is even, low and luminous, you usually have a white-out. The light is diffuse but may be so intense that it can snap the needle of a light meter. Sky and land merge into infinite even whiteness. All is without contour and relief, and depth perception is totally destroyed. A nearby rock looks like a distant boulder; an explorer mistook a tiny lemming for a mighty muskox in the distance; and once, while walking in a white-out across an area of the Barren Grounds I knew to be uninhabited, I was considerably startled to see two persons standing on a far ridge.

I waved to them, and with a shrill cry of anger and alarm they disappeared into the earth. My distant people had been two ground squirrels sitting bolt upright, as is their custom, near the entrances to their burrows just a few yards away. Pilots, understandably, hate white-outs. It is, they say, like flying in a milk bottle.

One can divide the circumpolar northern regions into four general zones: the sub-arctic boreal forest or taiga; the tundra; the land covered by permanent ice; and the islands of the Bering and Barents Seas.

Of these four zones, the boreal forest is by far the largest in extent. It covers more than half of Alaska, Scandinavia and the Soviet Union, and about half of Canada. From a plane, the deciduous forests of the south appear soft, light, rounded, and baroque. The primarily coniferous forests of the north look austere, dark, spired and gothic.

Spruce predominates the northern forests of Canada and Alaska, mixed or replaced in some regions with firs, tamarack, and jack pines. Larch, lighter, loftier and less severe than the North American spruces, is the most important tree of the eastern Siberian forests, and in the boreal forests of Scandinavia, sombre pines and firs alternate with silvery birches. In North America, the forest regions were inhabited by Indians; the tundra and the Arctic coasts were the Eskimos' realm. Some Indian groups, such as the Barren Ground Naskapi and the Chipewyans, pursued their main prey, the caribou, far out into the open tundra, and some Eskimos in Canada and Alaska live on sea coasts at the edge of the boreal forest. But essentially, the northern Indians are a people of the forests, and Eskimos prefer the treeless land beyond.

The treeless tundra covers about a fourth of Canada, nearly one million square miles. Roughly half of it extends over the northern mainland, the Barren Grounds or Barren Lands.

Barren Grounds seems an appropriate name when you fly over the Canadian mainland tundra. In winter its white monotonous infinity is only infrequently broken by the stark black lines of a rock ridge, a snow-free river bank, or low bluff. In summer, it is a low, rolling plain ten times the size of England, in black and brown and dun and olive, broken by a maze of lakes and rivers, many hemmed by bright green vegetation. It looks vast and empty and barren. It is a land without people.

Great icebergs glea
in Inglefield Ba
as a procession of Eskim
in kayaks ha
a dead narwhal hom

Overlea
Northumberland Islar

en and dogs
velling over the infinity
the frozen sea
ar Bathurst Inlet.

Once the Barrens had been bountiful. More than three million caribou migrated north each spring from their winter haunts in the northern forests, across the tundra, like a living and life-giving tide. J. W. Tyrrell of the Canadian Geological Survey saw them near the upper Dubawnt River in 1893: "The valleys and hillsides for miles seemed to be moving masses of reindeer (caribou). To estimate their number would be impossible. They could only be reckoned in acres or square miles."

Muskoxen were numerous. Samuel Hearne, travelling in 1771 from Churchill on Hudson Bay to the Arctic Ocean frequently saw "many herds of them in the course of a day's walk, and some of those herds did not contain less than eighty or an hundred head . . ." Seeing the immense number of caribou killed by the northern Indians, Hearne had marvelled: ". . . it is wonderful they do not become scarce, but so far is this from being the case, that the oldest Northern Indian in all their tribe will affirm that the deer are as plentiful now as they ever have been."

The tundra awes and humbles you with its immensity. It is a land both harsh and beautiful. In summer it is vividly and vibrantly alive. An icecap, by contrast is dead and desolate. I once flew over a part of the Greenland icecap in a helicopter, and it was white and void, from horizon to horizon, an icy dome more than a mile thick.

Despite its grim appearance, Greenland's icecap has attracted many men. The Norwegian explorer Fridtjof Nansen crossed it from east to west in 1888 and Peary traversed a major portion of the northern section. To glaciologists it is a fount of knowledge. They bore it and core it, and read in the icy samples extracted from its depth much of the history of our earth's climate.

In comparison with the giant icecap of Greenland, that of Vest-Spitsbergen, largest island of the Spitsbergen archipelago north of Norway, is of modest size and height.

The Greenland icecap has an apparently limitless, even, monotonous surface. The Spitsbergen icecap has a much more varied topography. Too thin to mantle the island completely, it is broken by mountains and even mountain chains that rise out of it and soar upward above its white expanse. Its surface is broken by many crevasses.

Crevasses, deep, wedge-shaped clefts in the ice, varying in width from a foot and less to 60 feet and more, form where a glacier flows over uneven ground, and its surface is bent and broken. A crevasse is a thing of beauty, provided you don't fall in. Its rim of recently compacted snow is a dull egg-shell white. Farther down, snow turns to ice, light green at first, then deep bottle-green, falling away into the cold blue and inky black of the abyss.

Spitsbergen and Bear Island, along with other islands of the Norwegian archipelago, form the western boundary of the Barents Sea.

Bear Island, wrapped in near-perpetual mists, looks bleak and dismal but once this island and the sea surrounding it, were home to a great wealth of wildlife. The walrus were exterminated, the great Greenland whales hunted to near-extinction, white whales and seals were reduced by incessant hunting to remnants of their former numbers, and polar bears now only rarely visit the island (for the latter's disappearance from Bear Island and its vicinity the warming climate is as much responsible as overhunting by man). Only the bird colonies remain, cliffs and crags crowded with hundreds of thousands of sea birds that find an abundance of food in the surrounding sea.

Similar to conditions in the Barents Sea are those of the Bering Sea, and the thousand-mile long Aleutian Islands chain is, on a much vaster scale, similar to Bear Island. The warm Japan Current, or North Pacific Drift, skirts the coast of Southern Alaska. Its warm, humid air rises against the coastal mountains, and drenches the land in torrential rains, or smothers it in snow. Some areas receive 180 inches of rain a year, almost twice as much as falls upon the Amazon rain forest, and at Thomson Pass, twenty-six miles from the Alaskan town of Valdez, the average snow fall is fifty feet, and during the winter of 1952-1953, the pass lay buried under a snow fall of eighty-one feet. In the Gulf of Alaska, the warm current is deflected in a southwesterly direction by the Alaska Peninsula and flows along the Aleutian Islands, where its waters mix with the icy currents rushing south through Bering Strait, causing near-permanent fog, a dismal land and a sea abounding in life.

These islands frequently and for long periods are hidden in fog and the entire region is so windy, it is often referred to as "The Cradle of Storms."

Here the warm humid air currents forming the semi-permanent Aleutian Low collide in titanic conflict with the dry air of the Siberian Polar High. The result, the U.S. Coast Pilot notes, is "the most unpredictable (weather) in the world. Winds of up to 90 mph are commonplace, and bad weather and howling storms may be expected at any time during the year." In addition, the mountainous Aleutian Islands are subject to local williwaws, freak gales that scream down mountain sides and whip through narrow valleys with gusts that have reached 140 miles per hour. Fierce rip tides churn through many of the channels dividing the islands and even on a rare calm day, heavy swells shatter against the jagged rocky coasts. Attu, the most westerly island of the chain, was described by U.S. soldiers in the Second World War as "the lonesomest spot this side of hell."

Yet when Vitus Bering and his second-in-command, Chirikov, discovered the Aleutians in 1741, these bleak, mountainous, fog-shrouded and storm-lashed islands were the most densely populated region of the entire Arctic and sub-Arctic, home to a people with a rich and varied culture, superbly adapted to life in this only apparently inhospitable region.

Despoiled and abandoned by the Russians, the Aleutian and Pribilof Islands, became a battleground in World War II which left most of the islands uninhabited, the Aleuts having been evacuated to mainland Alaska.

Arctic and sub-Arctic are neither the eternally frozen wastelands of popular fancy, nor are they the genial paradise painted nowadays by some romantic conservationists, who obviously haven't been bitten by enough mosquitoes, or spent a winter there.

It is a land as other lands where, as the Bible says "To every thing there is a season, and a time to every purpose under the heaven: A time to be born and a time to die." The Eskimo knew this, and the Indian, and perhaps we the invaders, knew this once. But now we are no longer content. We want to rebuild the Arctic land; we came to it as strangers, we reside in it as strangers and we dream of the day, when we can dome over its villages and cities with plastic, so that we can isolate ourselves from its reality and dwell in it as strangers forever. We covet its wealth, and we inquire little into the consequences of our actions and some day, when we are finished, we may have destroyed, beyond recall, its harsh and ancient harmony.

The native peoples of the north were an integral part of the land and its life, and subject to its laws. They could not dominate the land, they had to mould their lives to its demands. They developed a culture in harmony with the land, since the land was the only reality they knew. They lived at peace with nature and the land, and usually with each other.

The white man's attitude to the Arctic was diametrically opposed to that of the natives. He came to conquer and to subdue. At first, he came primarily to exploit the north's enormous animal wealth. Having accomplished this with great efficiency and ruthlessness, he temporarily lost interest. Now he returns, because the north promises new treasures. And now he comes armed with a technology that enables him to brush aside the ancient law of the land. He is, indisputably, the master, an alien master in an alien land.

Balanced against this triumphant northward march of technological man, spurred by the south's increasing need of the north's mineral wealth, is a new and, for white men, totally different awareness of the north. It is born of the realization that the vast lands of the north are our last great wilderness and that in our increasingly artificial world, we need a place of wildness and loneliness; a place where wolves run free; a place where the water is pure and the air is clear; a place where one can be alone; a place where nature is still master and where we can feel awe of her might.

Marmot Isla
off Alaska's west co

The natives of the north did not alter their environment, they were a dynamic part of it, skilled predators at the apex of the arctic food-energy pyramid. They formed part of nature's immutable cycle of life and death; what they took from the north, they had to return to it. They were not nature's masters, but lived subservient to its laws. Scattered over the vastness of the Arctic, they lacked the technological knowledge and capability to change in any way the delicate and tenuous balance of nature in the north.

Most arctic soils are oligotrophic, nutrient-deficient, often acid, usually poorly aerated, and lacking in those vital though invisible micro-organisms that hasten decay and regenerate the soil. There are millions (as many as 50 million) bacteria in a gram of southern soil, yet only thousands in an equal amount of arctic earth (and when scientists examined a pint of snow near the South Pole, they found in it one solitary bacterium!).

The soil is first formed by the mechanical and chemical weathering of rocks. This yields a fine, silt-type soil, acid and inimical to life. Lichens settle on the rocks. Their acids leach the stone and slowly crumble it. Centuries pass and millennia, the lichen dies and its fragments are added to the thin layer of soil.

Mosses settle on this earth and micro-organisms convert decaying plants into new, richer soil. Organic buffers develop and neutralize excess acidity or alkalinity. Little cushions of plants capture and hold wind-driven earth particles. Progressively, the more hardy pioneers, the lichen and mosses, make possible the existence of more complex and demanding life forms.

The vegetation mat offers shelter to minute insects, and to nematodes, mites, tartigrades and rotifers. They transform plant matter into energy which they return, in death, to the earth, or pass on to the predators that feed upon them and who in turn, will become earth. And thus the eternal cycle continues, from death to simple life, to more complex life forms and all eventually return the gift of energy that gave them life to the earth.

Arctic plants are opportunistic. Existing on soil generally deficient in nutrients, particularly nitrates and phosphates, they respond with exuberant growth wherever nutrients are plentiful. Multicolored lichens encrust, jewel-like, a caribou antler on the tundra.

Poppies and other plants form a dense mat of vegetation around a whale bone high on an arctic beach, obtaining nutrients from the slowly disintegrating bone. Wherever Eskimos and their dogs lived for any length of time, they fertilized the soil and even centuries after their passing, the spot is marked by luxuriant plant growth.

Botanical Environment

he Thule region of northwestern
enland is high Arctic, its soil thin
niggardly, its vegetation generally
se. But where the dovekies nest in
ons on the high scree slopes, the
en landscape changes dramatically.
rocks are aglow with the vermilion,
ophilous lichen *Caloplaca elegans*.
t growth beneath the colonies is
and varied, the earth black and
; even adjacent hillsides and val
where the birds pass on their flights
nd from the sea are carpeted with
, lumpy layers of bright-green mos-
In some places, the earth is 20 feet
. Yet even here it has taken thou-
ds of years to form this earth. The
ch scientist Jean Malaurie took peat
ples to a depth of 52 cm near Etah.
lowest level was dated at about
0 years. Thus, even under optimum
ditions, it had taken nature a time
al to that from the birth of Christ to
present day to create 1½ feet of
h.

Optimum conditions are rare in the
tic. As a rule growth and its con-
itant, decay, are both exceedingly
. The wooden slabs marking the
es of members of the Franklin ex-
ition on Beechey Island are as
nd now as when they were erected
846. The log cabins built by Russian
pers on Spitsbergen 200 and more
rs ago remain untouched by rot. The
ch clock, the bathtub made of wine
s, a manuscript written by Willem
ents in 1576 and placed in a powder
n, all were found in good condition
years later when Norwegian sealers
overed the spot where the Barents
edition had wintered on Novaya
lya. Cart tracks left by Sir Edward
y's expedition on Melville Island in
0 are now, a century-and-a-half
r, still clearly visible. And only
cks of lichen and moss grow in the
ches excavated by Sir Martin

Frobisher's men in 1578 on Kodlunarn
Island in their search for gold.

For men from the south, the main allure of the Arctic was an immense wildlife wealth which could be turned into
profit. To the traditional theme of ruthless, exterminative hunting as practiced
in the past, our age has added a sombre
coda: chemical poisoning and habitat
destruction.

First its strategic importance and then
the discovery of vast mineral deposits,
have spurred the south's interest in the
north. In a land where motorized vehi-
cles were rare only a decade ago, giant
tractors now carve out some 10,000
miles of seismic trails annually. Giant
equipment was moved in summer from
site to site on the Alaskan North Slope
by the simple method of "up-blading"
the thawed surface soil, and skidding
the machinery on the permafrost base
on tractor-drawn sledges.

The Arctic's thin, slow-growing plant
cover protects and insulates the underlying soil. When this blanket is ripped
and removed by tractor lugs during
seismic surveys, or in the course of
installing a pipeline, the ground thaws
deeply during summer, becomes unsta-
ble and, as the permafrost level is low-
ered, begins to slump.

A bulldozed line on a three percent
slope near Fort McPherson in the Mackenzie River valley became, in four
years, a gully 23 feet wide and eight
feet deep. Subsequent thermal and
water erosion can alter the drainage
pattern and topography of an entire
area. Already in parts of the Arctic, the
gracefully sinuous lines of nature are
crisscrossed by the starkly functional
rectilinear lines of industrial man.

In the south, given opportunity and
time, nature can heal the scars inflicted
upon it by man: a river can cleanse itself, grasses, bushes and trees can
cover, within decades, a devastated
area of land. In the north, time assumes
a different dimension: soil formation
and plant growth are reckoned not in
decades but in centuries and millennia.
The annual plant productivity of a given
arctic area in terms of weight is only
one percent of an area of similar size in
the south. A dwarf birch, creeping along
the ground, its stem needle-thin, can be
15 years old; a thumb-thick dwarf willow trunk may have 300 or more annual rings; and a patch of lichen no
bigger than the palm of your hand may
have begun its growth at the time King
Solomon built the temple of Jerusalem.
Yet it takes a tractor only seconds to
destroy them.

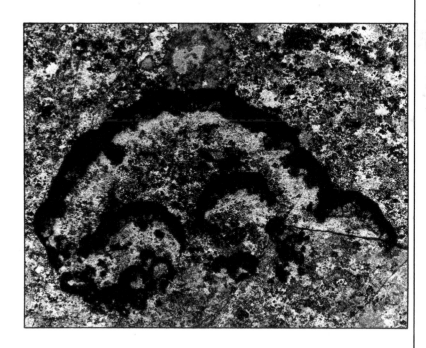

Away from such obvious sources of smell as sea bird colonies and human encampments, the Arctic is a nearly odorless land. Its air is free of dust, and the industrial haze covering so much of the south is totally absent. The air is cool and glassy clear. In spring, I took pictures with a long telephoto lens of glaciers on the other side of Inglefield Bay, 35 kilometers away, and they are clear and sharp.

In summer, though, the Arctic can be full of weird mirages, some of them due to temperature inversions. While land or sea are still cold, the sun-warmed air above is relatively hot. This produces horizontal distortion in distant scenes.

Low coasts become bizarrely elongated. A little iceberg, shimmering and twisting, seems to rise out of the sea to incredible heights. The far land soars up into the flickering air in strange and vibrant fluidity.

Intense refraction raises objects above the observer's natural horizon. The Labrador coast is famous for its "vanishing islands." Once, travelling on a little Eskimo schooner along this coast on a hot early summer day, I was disconcerted, time and again, to see our captain head straight into what appeared to be an island. Some were so clear, I could see trees growing on them. And then, as we came closer, they began to shift, and float and shimmer, then disintegrated and vanished.

Famous explorers have been fooled by such visions. John Ross in 1818

Arctic Air

abandoned the exploration of Lancaster Sound, because he thought he saw mountains extending across it. Peary swore by a place he called "Crocker Land," to the northwest of Ellesmere Island.

Viewing it from a high mountain, he wrote, "My heart leaped the intervening miles of ice as I looked longingly at this land, and in fancy I trod its shores and climbed its mountains, even though I knew that that pleasure could be only for another in another season." Much effort was subsequently expended to find Crocker Land, but like all good mirages it simply did not exist.

Natives of the north were fortunate that their lands and seas had nothing to offer the European invaders but furs and sea mammal products. Natives of other regions were less lucky. Newfoundland's Beothuk Indians interfered with fishing and were exterminated. Indians in the United States who stood in the way of the white man's Manifest Destiny to seize and occupy their lands were shot or shunted into reservations. But while in the south few disputed General Sheridan's observation "The only good Indians I ever saw were dead," in the north the only good, or at least from the white man's point of view, useful Indian, Lapp, Eskimo, or Chukchi, was one that was alive and trapping, or providing whaling crews with labor or food.

If a northern native people resisted the occupation of their land, as did the Kamchadales and Koryaks, they were forced to submit because the invaders had superior weapons. In general, though, the conquest of the north, if exploitative, was reasonably peaceful.

One method of obtaining the furs was to exact them, under threat of reprisal, as tribute. An agent of the Muscovy Company noted that in 1570 "the Lappians pay tribute to the Emperour of Russia, to the King of Denmarke, and to the King of Sweden." In Siberia the tribes gave furs as yassak for the tsar (this was abolished by Catherine the Great). Other furs they sold, in the manner of the time, to the traders who established posts in their region, for trinkets, for guns and metal goods they

really needed, and for vodka. The promyshlenniki's reign of terror and oppression among the Aleuts was brutal but brief. The Russian-American Company's policy was one of trade, peace and profit (and keeping a vast number of the natives in perpetual indebtedness to the company).

The Hudson's Bay Company followed a similar policy, but in general paid the natives better for their furs, and made a fairly sincere effort to keep its dusky customers happy. This was in part dictated by the fact that its field representatives, by the very nature of the business, had to live in isolated northern posts, and the last thing on earth they wanted was a quarrel with cheated, irate natives, now well-armed with Hudson's Bay Company knives and guns.

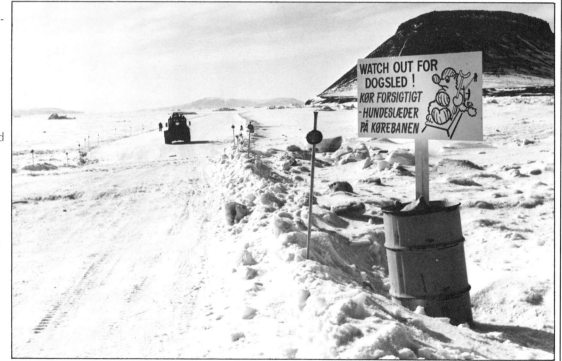

Commercial Development

The Sea

"... the pack is no place for a ship,
and however beautiful it may be from an aesthetic point of view, I wish
with all my heart that we were out of it."
George W. De Long. His ship, the "Jeannette" was crushed by ice on June 12, 1881 north of Siberia.
De Long and many of his men died in trying to return.

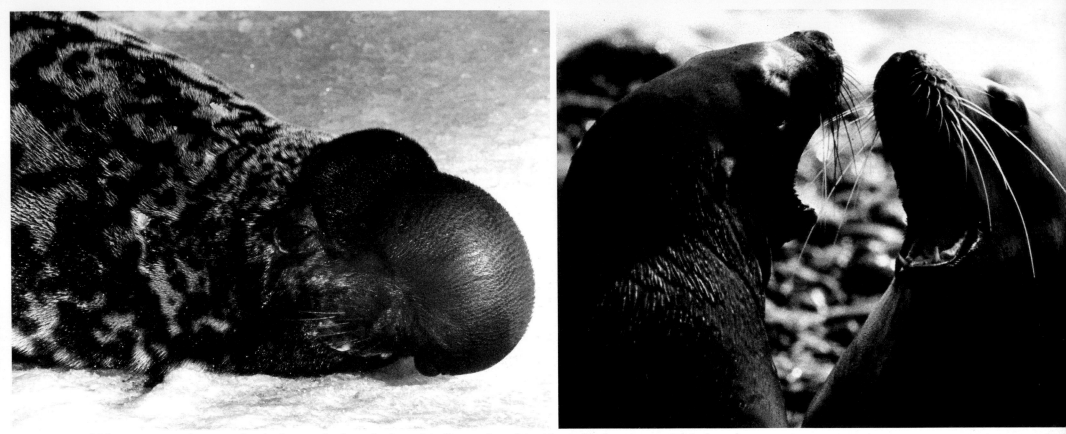

When angered or excited, the male hooded seal inflates the skin "hood" that covers his head.
Mouths agape, two Steller's sea lions threaten each other.

A massive walrus bull, its ivory tusks gleam in the light of the low sun. A harbor seal cautiously scans a beach for potential enemies before coming ashore.

"The ice was here, the ice was there,
The ice was all around:
It cracked and growled, and roared and howled,
Like noises in a swound."

Samuel Taylor Coleridge
The Rime Of The
Ancient Mariner."

Far to the north, the Vikings believed, in darkness and in cold, lay Helheim, the dreary land of the dead, and Nåstrand, the shore of corpses. In the same region, they thought, was Ginnungagap, the edge of the world. Bishop Adam of Bremen, wrote in 1070 the story of the Norse King Harold Hårdråde "who explored the expanse of the northern ocean with his ships, but darkness spread over the verge where the world falls away, and he put about barely in time to escape being swallowed in the vast abyss."

But the Norsemen were a hardy and adventurous people and undeterred by their own gloomy legends in the 10th to 14th centuries they ventured far into the northern seas: to Iceland; to Greenland and up its west coast at least as far as glacier-girt Melville Bay and perhaps even farther north. In the centuries since the Norse colonies in Greenland flourished and died, the northern seas have been explored in breadth and depth and courageously and ruthlessly exploited.

The landlocked Arctic Ocean with its crushing cover of drifting ice presents an obstacle to shipping only slightly less formidable today than it was when Norse and Elizabethan adventurers first encountered it. But despite the hazards, sailors continued to penetrate the ice year after year lured by the rich harvest of sea mammals, and the fame and wealth that awaited the discoverer of a northern passage to the orient.

Neither the Arctic Ocean nor any of the adjacent seas is totally or permanently covered by ice. Currents, winds and tides shift and rift the immense ice masses. The floes are forced together until they rear up into high pressure ridges, or they are torn apart, creating wide leads and lakes of open water. In the high arctic seas and bays there are extensive areas of permanently open water that never freeze over, not even in the severest winters. These sea areas are called "polynyas," a word derived from the Russian "polyi" — open.

The great polynya of northern Baffin Bay is about twice the size of Lake Superior. Nineteenth century whalers knew it well and called it the "North Water." Racing currents and upwelling water keep Hell Gate, between Ellesmere and North Kent Islands, open, and even the severest cold will not bridge all of Fury and Hecla Strait, between Melville Peninsula and Baffin Island, or the adjoining area of Foxe Basin.

When travelling across sea ice, one can see open water a great distance away. A dull greyish cloud hovers over it near the horizon, the reflection upon the sky of the sea's dark color. Sailors called it "water sky," as opposed to "iceblink," the whitish glare in the sky that indicates extensive icefields, or "landblink," the sulphurous reflection of a distant snow-covered land. A skilled ice-captain can read this projection upon the sky of ice or open water far ahead.

In fall, when the temperature has dropped below the freezing point of water, crystals of fresh-water ice begin to form in the sea. They grow, link with other crystals and enclose within themselves minute pockets of salt water. The sea, now filled with crystals of "slush ice," is smooth and looks oily. The wind no longer ripples its leaden surface. The cold increases, the crystals coalesce and squeeze part of their enclosed salt content towards the surface of this "young ice," so that it is covered with brine, grey and tacky. This ice is elastic and, when broken, razor-sharp. It will zip open a kayak in a trice, and can cut through the planking of a wooden boat in minutes.

The limit of landfast ice is the floe edge. It is a sinister place in winter and early spring. When the air temperature is −40°F the sea water is about 68 degrees warmer than the surrounding air and it literally steams. Dark grey clouds roll menacingly over the water and hover above it in a perpetual pall. Peary, coming upon open water in fifty below weather, wrote that in the bitter cold there rose from the sea "inky clouds of vapor which gathered in a sullen canopy overhead."

The floe edge is not permanent. A storm can break it and roll it back hundreds of yards. And on a calm, intensely cold night it can "grow" out into the sea for a mile or more. While slowly freezing sea ice has a salinity of about 2 per mill (parts per 1,000 by weight), fast frozen sea ice may have a salinity of 20 per mill.

Increased salinity gives ice greater elasticity and at the fast-freezing floe edge the sea ice's tensile strength may be twice that of fresh-water ice.

One early spring, I lived with Pewatook, an Eskimo hunter, and his family on Jens Munk Island in northern Foxe Basin. Every morning, fair weather or foul (mostly foul), Pewatook readied the great sled to make the two-hour trip to the floe edge. It was a rough ride. Pressure ridges, jumbles of upturned iceblocks, ran parallel to the floe edge and to reach it, we had to hump across all of them. Near the last pressure ridge Pewatook picked up a sealskin-covered plywood punt and lashed it onto the sled. From then on we rode in the boat on the sled, a commendable precaution since the ice was often thin and a dip at 40 below could result in death from exposure. (It doesn't have to. You may not even get wet. The outside layer of your clothing is so cold, water turns to ice the moment it touches it. So you may emerge quite dry but sheathed in ice and stiff as a statue.)

We travelled along the floe edge, looking for a good hunting place. Much of the new ice was thin but Pewatook's trained eye could spot weak areas from a distance. A call to the dogs and we neatly skirted the dangerous region. But once we had waited in vain for seal for many hours and when we left to look for a better place, the dogs were cold and eager to run. They streaked across the smooth ice, so thin (two or three inches) one could feel it bend underneath the weight of the sled. Suddenly Pewatook saw a particularly weak wedge, some 30 yards wide, and called to the dogs. But they were in full gallop and kept on going. They yelped with fear when the film of rubber-like ice buckled beneath them, but it held, the dogs kept running and the speed carried the sled across as well. When I looked back, black water was bubbling up in our tracks.

Near the floe edge, Pewatook picked a reasonably solid stretch of ice and there we waited for seal. He scratched the ice with his harpoon handle. The grating noise travels far in water and will attract curious seal.

When he shot a seal, we unlashed the punt and he paddled out into the ominous, grey, swirling frost smoke to retrieve his prey. And then he waited for more seals to appear, with the infinite patience of the true hunter.

Life in the sea, as on land, is a vast cycle. With the help of the sun, through the process of photosynthesis, the plants of the sea convert inorganic nutrients into organic substances and produce most of the oxygen we need to live. Without the sea plants, mankind and animals would die of anoxia — lack of oxygen. The tiny animals that graze upon this microflora of the sea are the food of bigger predators, who in turn are eaten by others still larger in size, and thus the conversion of food and energy continues along the sea's chain of life to sharks and seals and whales. They die, the tiny diatom and the mighty whale, and slowly drift down to the ocean floor, food for the bottom-dwelling scavengers and predators. But in their death there is new life. Bacteria break down the remains of animals and plants, and reconvert them into the nu-

trients needed by the sea's flora. The cycle of life beg anew.

The amount of nutrients in any given sea area, as in a area of land, at a given time is finite. But the waters of sea move; surface layers sink and are replaced nutrient-rich waters from the deep; currents swirl wards, carrying fertilizing minerals to the plants near surface.

Wherever two ocean currents meet, especially if th differ sharply in temperature and salinity, there are fou marine zones of great turbulence and unrest, with wa sinking or rising up from the depth. And wherever cold currents well up, the sea is prodigiously rich marine life. Arms of the warm Gulf Stream and its co tinuation, the North Atlantic Drift, probe northward wards Newfoundland and Labrador, where they meet icy Labrador Current, and their mineral rich mixture is basis for the immense fish-wealth of the Grand Bar They reach towards southern Greenland where they m and mix with both the East Greenland Current com south from the Arctic Ocean and the West Greenla Current sweeping north into Baffin Bay; they touch l land and give it warmth, and give its sea an abundar of fish. In a final surge, they reach towards Spitsber and the Barents Sea, mingle with the cold waters currents flowing down from the north, and their un gives birth to the stupendously rich marine life of th regions.

The pattern repeats itself in the North Pacific. Here warm current is the Kuroshio (or Japan Current) and prolongation, the North Pacific Drift, carrying warm w ers east and north. The cold water it meets is the Oyash rushing icy, arctic water south through the Bering St and wherever these mighty currents converge in viol depression and upheaval of water masses, they bre fog above the sea and within it a superabundance of l

In addition to the currents, there is in the north a v seasonal interchange of water layers. In spring, winter-chilled and heavy surface water sinks down an replaced from the deep by warmer, lighter layers of wa

The tropics are lavish in producing vast numbers species and often dress them in gorgeous colors. Mu hued finches flit through the air like dazzling jew Northern birds, in comparison, look dowdy, particula most sea birds in their formal suits of black and wh And, compared to the glittering variety of warmer clim

e are few species. But if the north does not encourage
ety, and dresses its creatures simply, it produces them
n prodigal abandon.

n his monograph on the murres, Dr. Leslie M. Tuck,
ada's foremost authority on sea birds, writes: "There
approximately fifteen million thick-billed murres and
million common murres in the Polar Basin; five
ion thick-billed murres and five million common
rres in the eastern North Atlantic; ten million thick-
ed murres and half a million common murres in the
tern North Atlantic; and some twenty million of both
cies in the North Pacific . . . I do not think the world
ulation can be less than fifty million. I do not think it
eeds one hundred million." Plus about two million
nars, twenty million puffins, eighty million dovekies,
at least a hundred million auklets.

ropical seas have warmth, variety and color, but their
le water layers lack the wealth of nutrients found in
grey and frigid churned-up northern seas which are
ne to the plebeian putty-colored cod, the grey Green-
d halibut, the dull brown tomcod and the silver-sided
elin. And though the northern seas are chill and dis-
and their denizens often drab, the number of fish is
on and it is they who feed the whales, the largest
atures that ever lived on earth, and the sea elephants,
seals and the walruses.

he bases of the sea's mighty pyramid of life are micro-
pic unicellular plants. Most numerous in the northern
s are thousands of species of diatoms, each species
tly encased in a jewel-like external silica skeleton of
own specific design.

In spring and summer, under near-constant daylight, the diatoms multiply with awesome speed. Soon these plants, so minute that millions float in a gallon of water, permeate the sea's surface regions in immense numbers, coloring it a deep blue-green. The meadows of the sea are in bloom. On this phytoplankton or plant-plankton graze the tiny herbivores of the sea, the zooplankton, hordes of little animals, among whom the copepods, each about the size of a rice-grain, are the most numerous.

Bigger planktonic animals prey upon the herbivores and are, in turn, eaten by larger predators. A blue whale scoops from the sea each day two tons of planktonic animals and they, to live, obtained that day through the sea's chain of life, the food energy of five trillion sea plants. Yet so vast is the microscopic plant life of the northern and far southern seas, it provided food in abundance for the millions of whales that existed before men hunted them almost to extinction.

The northern seas were (and are) rich enough to support a great sea mammal wealth. Before their systematic slaughter by commercial whalers, sealers and walrus hunters, the north was home to about 100,000 ribbon seals; 200,000 bearded seals; 400,000 sea lions; one million hooded seals; two million fur seals; five million

"The great sea
Has set me adrift,
It moves me as a weed in a great river,
Earth and the great weather
Move me,
Have carried me away
And move my inward parts with joy."
**Uvanuk, a woman shaman of the Igloolik Eskimos.
Quoted by Knud Rasmussen.**

ringed seals; 20 million harp seals; 800,000 walruses; tens of thousands of narwhal; hundreds of thousands of white whales; 100,000 grey whales; and 100,000 Greenland (or bowhead) whales. In the aggregate, this not only represents an awesome number of big animals (Greenland whales weigh up to 60 tons each), it also promised predators, including man, an apparently limitless supply of meat. (It is one of the sadder ironies of today's north, that Canada's Eskimos, at least those in the larger settlements, now live on meat imported from the south — if they can afford to buy it with their welfare cheques. Most Eskimos, whose very name means "eaters of raw meat," now have no meat, raw or cooked, and live on an exclusively carbohydrate diet ruinous to their general health and to their teeth. According to a report of the World Health Organization, Eskimos now suffer the worst tooth decay of all the world's people.)

The coastal peoples of eastern Siberia, the Chukchi, Eskimos and Kamchadales, and the Ainu of the Kuriles, looked to their chill and fog-shrouded seas for life. In the North American Arctic, a few Eskimo groups, the Nunamiut of Alaska's Brooks Range and the Caribou Eskimos of Canada's Barren Grounds lived nearly exclusively on caribou. But for the Aleuts and the vast majority of Eskimos, scattered along more than 10,000 miles of arctic coastline, the sea and its animals were the basis of their existence. They travelled across the frozen sea by dog team in winter and spring, hunting seals at their breathing holes or at the floe edge, and in summer and fall when the ice was gone, they travelled and hunted with their boats, the strong seaworthy, capacious oomiak and the sleek, swift, graceful kayak, perhaps the most efficient and elegant hunting craft ever designed by man.

Life at the narwhal hunting camp at Kangerdlugssuaq on the south coast of Inglefield Bay where I spent a summer, was quiet. The women made clothes; they scraped sealskins, steeped them in water and then sewed them together as cover for a new kayak. The men carved ivory harpoons and shaped, with infinite care, ivory-inlaid throwing boards. But whatever the people were doing, a part of the mind of each was tuned in to the nearby sea. Let a seal poke up his head a mile away, or a narwhal or white whale blow in the distance, and instantly a joyous alarm rang through the camp and men and women raced down to the shore to carry the kayaks

to water. Nimbly the hunters slipped through the manholes into their boats and paddled rapidly out onto the bay, while on shore women and children watched the hunt like fans at a major sporting event, keeping up a loud commentary and shouting encouragements and advice to men far beyond earshot.

If it was a single whale, the hunt was usually brief. The hunters either got it or, more often, the whale detected the stealthily paddled kayaks and vanished and the men returned. But if a pod of whales was scattered over the bay, the men tried to anticipate their path, and lay in wait near concealing ice floes, hoping a whale would surface in striking distance. And when one man harpooned a whale, the others paddled quickly to assist him and thereby, by ancient custom, share with him the whale. Together they killed it, and tying their kayaks in tandem, they hauled their prize, food for many people for many days, towards camp.

They returned once, triumphant after an all-night hunt, just as the sun rose above the mountains bordering the bay, the light a soft orange, broken into golden-edged patterns in the water. Skirting the big icebergs, the men paddled through the glowing water, their dark kayaks aligned in a row, the paddles flashing in smooth cadence. On the bluff above the sea the women and children stirred with anticipation, waiting, as women and children waited in ages past for their men to come home from the kill.

Walruses like togetherne
Here they cro
chummily on the rocky bea
of an isla
off Alaska's west co

The Eskimo uses his myriad skills to reap his harvest from the arctic seas.

arp seal
aces among the floes
he ice pack.

To Eskimos, Aleuts and Chukchi the great whales of the northern seas were once of vital importance. The hunt was dangerous, wildly exciting, socially prestigious and, if successful, immensely rewarding. One large bowhead whale provided them with a food supply equivalent to nearly 1,000 seals. They ate the vitamin-rich skin and part of the high-energy blubber. Surplus fat, rendered into oil, gave their homes light and warmth. The meat was food for the people and their dogs and helped them to survive long, lean winters. Cleaned whale intestines were sewn into waterproof clothing and into bags to preserve oil. Whale sinew was used as thread, braided into ropes, and made into snares. Whale ribs became house rafters; vertebrae served as stools. The jaw bone was ideal for sled runners, because snow does not stick to it. From baleen they made cups and thread, weapons and tools, and an ingenious, though cruel, coil device, used from Siberia to Greenland, to kill wolves and even polar bears.

The great whales were numerous.

In 1609 Henry Hudson attempted to sail beyond Spitsbergen across the top of the world to China. Ice stopped him, but his glowing reports of infinite number of great whales, "the best of all sorts," started arctic whaling on a large scale. Soon 500 to 600 ships sailed north each year, with 20,000 men or more, warships accompanying the fleets of each nation. The Dutch built a town at the northwest tip of Spitsbergen in 1622, and gave it the apt name "Smeerenburg" — Blubberburg. There, at nearly 80° north, they had taverns and a church, bakeries (the baker blew a bugle when the buns were ready), and a bordello.

The whales are practically extinct now in the Spitsbergen region. Only one or two forlorn stragglers, perhaps searching the great ocean for a mate, are seen each decade. In Hudson Bay, in 1631, the explorer Luke Foxe watched whales near Marble Island. "We saw some 20 playing," he wrote. There are now probably less than twenty bowhead whales left in all of Hudson Bay. In northern Baffin Bay in 1818 John Ross saw "vast numbers of whales." The Polar Eskimos still have a name "Arvik" for the bowhead whale, but only two men remember having seen one in their youth. Both men are now in their seventies.

Arctic whaling by Europeans and Americans lasted for three centuries. Thousands of ships and hundreds of thousands of men went north to bring the wealth of the arctic seas to the markets of the south. They took from the north much of its sea mammal wealth, the food basis of native life, and they took to the north diseases to which the natives had little resistance. Arctic whaling off Alaska started in earnest about 1850. Within one generation, from 1850 to 1885, the Alaskan coastal Eskimo population declined by 50 percent.

Natives of the Eastern Arctic also suffered.

In 1830, twelve years after Sir John Ross discovered the long-isolated Polar Eskimos, whalers visited a Polar Eskimo camp near Cape York. "Grouped around an oilless lamp, in the attitudes of life, were four or five human corpses, with darkened lips and sunken eyeballs; but all else preserved in perennial ice . . . The child, stark and stiff, (was) in the reindeer hood which enveloped the frozen mother." Since there was ample food, it was assumed that "an epidemic had stricken them. Some three or four huts that were near had the same melancholy furniture of extinct life."

Disease brought by whalers annihilated in the winter of 1902-1903 the entire Sadlermiut tribe of Southampton Island.

The bowhead whales of the ice regions were huge, lumbering animals, each 40 to 60 feet long, with a gigantic bulbous head, a mouth the size of a large living room, and flukes twenty-four feet wide. They were wrapped in a blanket of blubber nearly two feet thick. There were 30 tons of blubber on a large bowhead, and four tons of it rendered into three tons of valuable oil. From the roof of the cavernous mouth hung 600 to 800 triangular baleen plates, 10 to 13 feet long and spaced at quarter-inch intervals. The whales swam slowly along the ice front, scooping up "brit," as the whalers called the myriad tiny crustaceans and pteropods that form their food. When they had a mouthful, the one-ton tongue moved up, the water gushed out through the lattice-work of baleen, and the retained animals were pressed back and swallowed.

In the days before plastics, baleen, a tough, resilient, keratinous substance, had many uses. Shredded and colored, it was made into the panache of knights' helmets, or used to stuff chairs and bolsters. Ramrods were made of it, and fishing rods, shoehorns, umbrella ribs and the springs of the first typewriters. Most important, "whalebone" was needed for women's stays, corsets and busks, and the hoops of their voluminous skirts. So valuable was baleen, that at one time a single bowhead whale could pay for a two-year whaling voyage. The bowhead was thus the ideal whale: very slow, very timid, very fat, with a ton or more of baleen in its mouth, worth at one time $6 a pound.

The Norsemen had hunted the great whale. The "King's Mirror," a 13th century Icelandic document, says of the bowhead: "This whale is as thick around as it is long. He has a head so large, it is more than a third of his length . . . He does not rage against ships; he also has no teeth and he is a fat and perfectly edible fish."

The English weren't interested in eating the whales, they wanted to turn them into soap, and into oil for the lamps of the realm. This was an age of elegance, when the Tudor and post-Tudor dandy wore shirts of cambric with ruches at the wrist, immaculate collars, lace and ruffs. All had to be washed, the demand for soap soared, and the soapmakers' guilds clamored for whale oil. Women, hitherto encased in hard-leather and steel corsets, fell instantly in love with the elastic, more yielding and moulding busks made with baleen. Demand was high, arctic whales had been discovered, the great hunt was on.

In 1610, the first English ships went whaling to Spitsbergen. Two years later, Dutch ships joined the fray, and then came the Germans and the French. All hired at first Basques, master whalers since medieval times who, a contemporary document notes, "are cleverer than any other nation in the civilized world at shooting or catching whales." English shipowners, in particular, enjoined their captains that these experts were "to be used very kindly and friendly."

The whales were quickly decimated. By about 1630 the "Bay Fishery" in the fiords and inlets of Spitsbergen was nearly finished. The fleet then moved to the "West Ice," the enormous crescent of pack ice between Greenland and Spitsbergen. It was not unusual to see a hundred whaling ships moored to the edge of the pack, while their boats roamed among the floes, trying to "fasten" to the whales which each year became scarcer and more elusive. With fortunes invested in ships and material, it was time to look for new whaling grounds.

In 1719, two adventurous Dutchmen eased their tubby, blunt-bowed, high-pooped whaling vessels round Greenland's Cape Farewell and sailed up its west coast into Davis Strait. All along the edge of the shifting pack, whales lolled in the water, their twin fountains of exhaled breath hanging like plumes in the frosty air — a promise of wealth. Four years later, 350 ships, mainly Dutch, German and Basque were hunting whales in Davis Strait.

Dovekies wheel and circle ab
the frozen
of northwestern Greenl

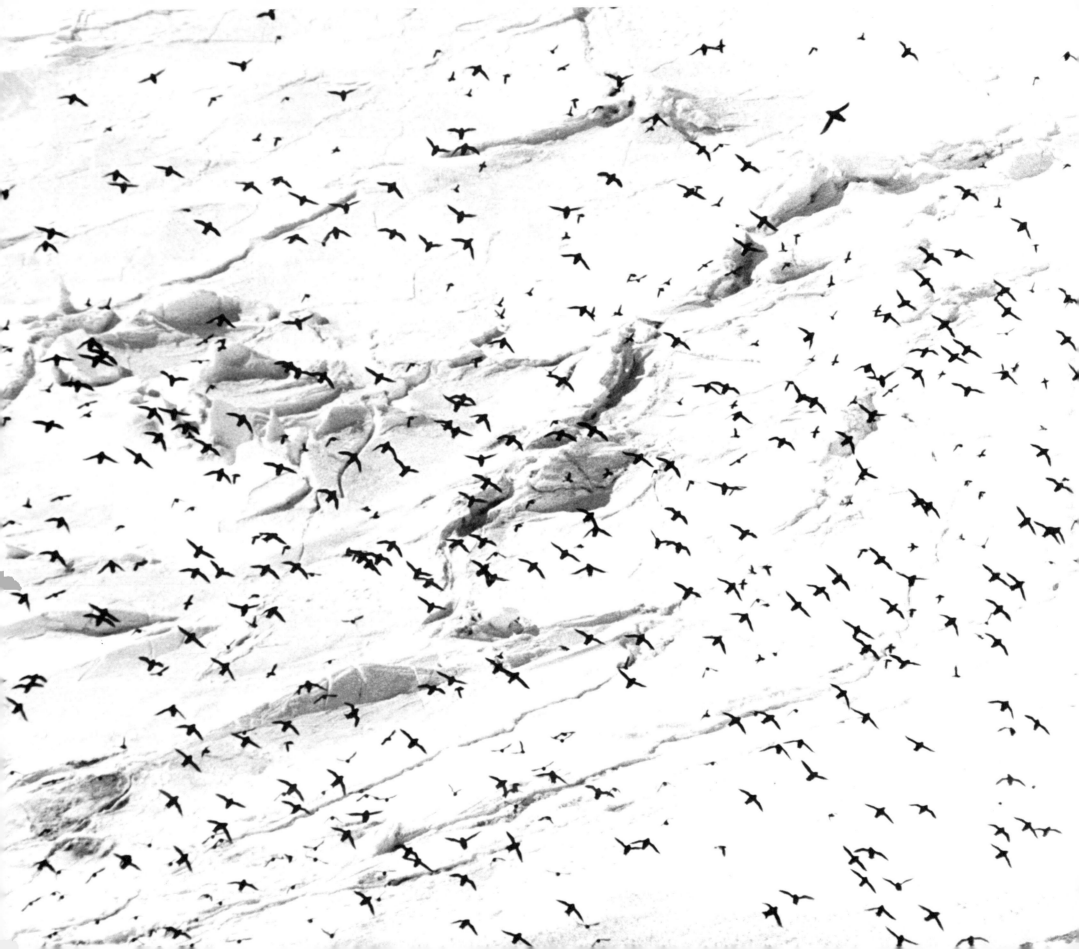

Top: Puffins, one with a successful catch of capelin.

Middle: Parakeet auklets on an island in the Bering Sea. A crested auklet perched on a rock ledge high above the sea.
Arctic terns breed in the far north, then migrate as far south as Antarctica.
Common murres on a favorite roosting ridge above the sea. Fulmars paddle industriously, searching for food.
An arctic tern scans the water for the glint of fish.

Bottom: A kittiwake on its nest built on a tiny cornice above the sea. The golden plover nests on the arctic tundra, winters in Argentina.

Low on the water, swift and silent,
the Eskimo in his kayak is nearly as much a part of the sea as the sea mammals he hunts.

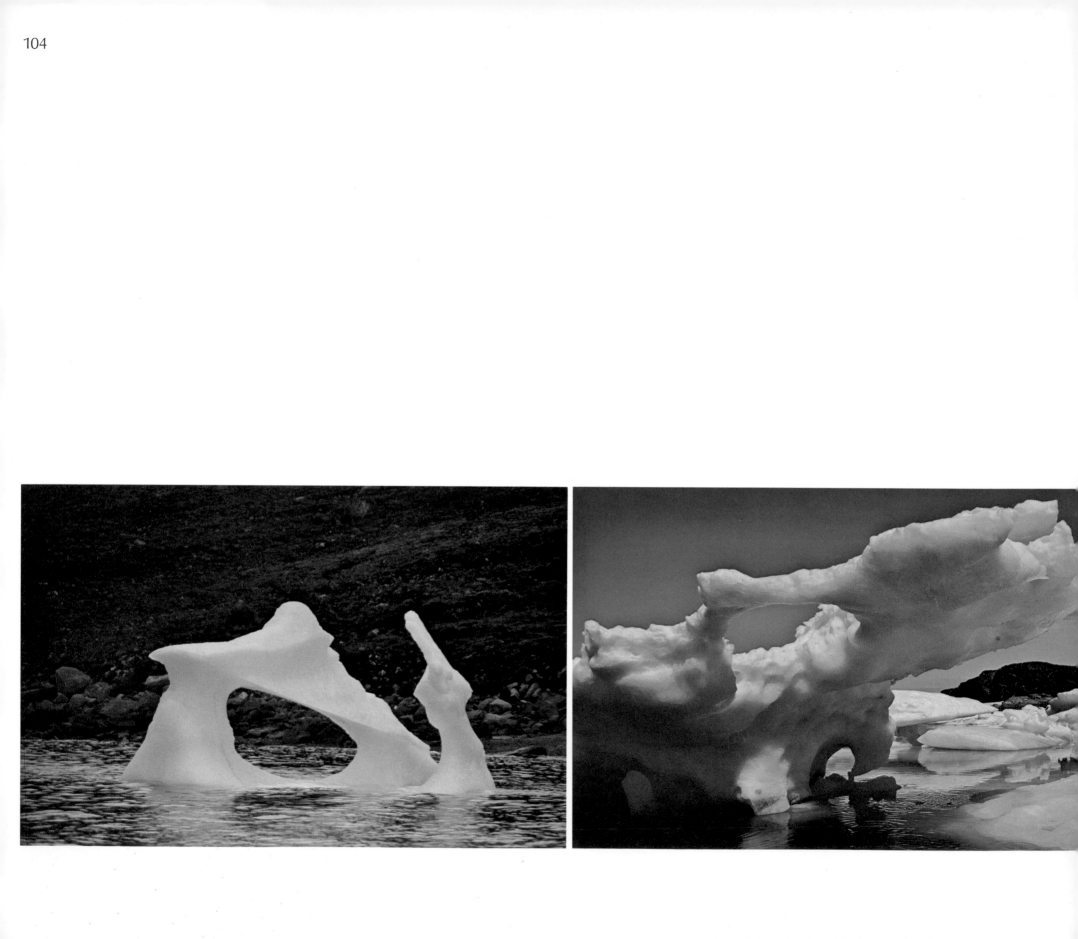

The wind, waves and currents carve fanciful shapes
in the floes and pack ice of the Arctic.

he great fur seal bull sniffs
e females of his harem,
rtly in territorial recognition,
ainly to ascertain
e state of their sexual responsiveness.

While the Dutch made fortunes in Arctic whaling, the English at first were lucky if they broke even. In 1725 they sent twelve ships to Davis Strait. They took 25 whales (the same year the Dutch took about 1,000), hardly sufficient "to pay for the expense incurred by the fitments and the hire of foreign harpooners." But they persevered. By 1756, they had 83 ships whaling in Davis Strait. The Scots, too, became interested in whaling and soon the tradition developed for both English and Scottish ships to recruit a good portion of their crews in the Shetland and Orkney Islands.

One New England ship went to Davis Strait in 1732. It brought back one dead whale and one live polar bear. Five years later, Provincetown sent a dozen hundred-ton ships north, crowded with so many whaler-sailors that only 14 men were left in town.

The ships from many nations (Danish, Dutch, German, British, French and New England) headed for Greenland's west coast, patrolled the pack, and poked into bays and fiords until north of Disko Island they were stopped by the "Middle Pack," a vast barrier of ice. Contact with natives seems to have been minimal, probably just as well, since the whalers were a rough lot. How rough can be gathered from an act passed by the Dutch States General in 1727 forbidding "the robbery and murder of the native populations."

The American Revolution and the Napoleonic wars enforced a slowdown of arctic whaling, but when the wars ended the hunt was resumed with new vigor. By now it was almost exclusively a British and American enterprise.

In 1817, the famous English whaler-scientist William Scoresby, Jr. informed Sir Joseph Banks, president of the Royal Society, that beyond the "Middle Pack," the vast barrier of ice stretching across central Baffin Bay, there lay the "North Water," an extensive region of open sea. Here, Scoresby suggested, the long-sought-after Northwest Passage might be found.

The British Admiralty, approached by Sir Joseph Banks, agreed to explore the North Water and Captain John Ross and Lieut. W. E. Parry sailed on June 17, 1818 in HMS Isabella and HMS Alexander, each ship having a whaling master and mate aboard as "experts." (This became standard procedure for most subsequent expeditions.)

North of Disko Island on the west Greenland coast, Ross came upon 45 whaling ships, huddled near the edge of the Middle Ice. He pushed north, ramming his way through the pack, and the whalers followed until they came upon new pods of whales in the North Water. Ross sailed on to the north where he encountered the Polar Eskimos in the world's farthest north human habitation.

The whalers were quick to take advantage of this breach of the hitherto impenetrable Middle Ice barrier. In 1819, they pushed through the ice, but eleven were caught in its terrible nip and crushed.

Undaunted, they returned and in 1820 Captain John in the Cumbrian sailed into Lancaster Sound and found the rich whaling ground near Pond Inlet, the "West Water." From then on, the voyages to the North Water and West Water became so regular that the Polar Eskimos called the whalers "upernagdlit" — the bringers of spring — since they arrived in June with spring in Melville Bay.

Fortunes were made in the new whaling grounds and the North Water fleet grew until in 1829 ninety-two ships from Britain worked their way through the ice. The next year ice closed in on the fleet. One by one the ships crumpled, as westerly gales drove the ice masses against their hulls. Finally 19 ships were in splinters. Freed from the iron discipline aboard ship, more than 1,000 sailors looted the wrecks, got rip-roaring drunk and camped on the ice until rescued by other ships. All survived and the year was long remembered as "Baffin's Fair." The owners were less amused. Their loss was £142,000. Altogether, more than 500 ships are known to have been wrecked in the arctic regions west of Greenland.

The mid 19th century was the golden era of American whaling. In one year 735 American (and 230 British and European) vessels were hunting whales around the globe. In 1854, the best year, 10,074,866 gallons of bowhead oil and 3,445,200 pounds of baleen were brought home from whaling voyages to the arctic seas. Between 1840 and 1860 the average annual gross value of the United States whale catch was $8,000,000.

In the 1840s, Nantucket and New Bedford whalers discovered the Bering Sea-Kamchatka coast whaling grounds and in 1848 Captain James Royce of Sag Harbour sailed north through Bering Strait into the whale-rich Chukchee Sea and returned with a full ship. The rush was on. By 1852, 278 vessels were scouring the North Pacific and adjoining arctic seas for the great whales. In 1889, seven steam whalers squeezed between the polar pack and the Alaska coast and emerged into the Beaufort Sea, last sanctuary of the harried and fast-vanishing bowhead.

The next year two ships wintered in the north and after hunting from July to September, one of them, the Mary D.

Hume, sailed for San Francisco with a cargo of oil and baleen worth $400,000.

The pattern had been set. The fleet sailed in March from San Francisco. In Bering Strait the whalers bought clothes from the Eskimos both on the Siberian and Alaskan coasts: 500 to 600 pairs of kamiks (sealskin boots) per ship at 50 cents each in trade goods; "deerskin" (caribou) coats at two dollars each; and squirrel-skin shirts at one dollar. They also bought dogs, 30 to 50 per ship. From open seams on the Alaska coast they mined coal, and took Eskimo helpers along from various coastal settlements. American whaling crews at this period were a mixed crowd: Negroes from Africa's west coast, Portuguese and Cape Verde Islanders, Japanese, Chinese, Arabs and, especially in the Pacific-Arctic fleet, an assortment of Hawaiians, Polynesians, Malays and Filipinos lumped together under the name of Kanakas. (Traces of this multi-national heritage are still discernible in the faces of Eskimos of both eastern and western Arctic. While in the eastern Arctic the Mediterranean influence is most striking — one of the finest Eskimo hunters I've known was the son of a Portuguese whaler — some Eskimos in the western Arctic have strong Polynesian features.)

The fleet wintered in the Arctic, and Eskimos supplied it with meat at six cents a pound in trade goods, at the rate of up to 50,000 pounds of caribou, moose and Dall sheep meat each winter, consisting only of saddles and hind-quarters of the animals. The rest was eaten by the Eskimos. To feed the whalers, the vast wildlife herds were quickly decimated.

Whales rapidly decreased and the whalers, to maintain profits, slaughtered the western walrus as well. Between

1860 and 1880, they killed more than 200,000. In ac tion, trade with the Eskimos was brisk. Most ships took to 30 tons of trade goods along to barter for clothes, m walrus ivory and, increasingly, fox pelts. Then, in 190 substitute for baleen was found, its price fell from m than five dollars per pound to less than two dollars, western arctic whaling was finished. It had lasted a sc 60 years. More than 5,000 ships had taken part in it, v at least 150,000 men. They had taken out $30,000, worth of whale products. They left a land and sea spoiled, a native people decimated and wracked by ease (especially consumption and venereal disease), a dependence upon white man's trading goods am the survivors.

The pattern repeated itself in the eastern Arctic. Th the impact was more prolonged and, if not quite as c clysmic as in the west, it was nonetheless a cumula disaster for the native people. As in the western Ar wintering whalers equipped Eskimos with guns and munition to procure fresh meat for them. The mainl muskoxen were hunted to near extinction, and vast n bers of caribou slaughtered.

As whales became increasingly scarce, the sl roamed farther afield, probed into bays and inlets, or their boats "rock-nosing," working close to land far f the ships. They set up shore stations, where whalers v tered and hunted, fed and assisted by Eskimo crews. S risks were great and returns precarious, sealing added to insure profits. The whalers' annual seal fluctuated between 30,000 and 300,000 annually addition, the Newfoundland sealing fleet was busy ki seals: 687,000 in 1831, their "best" year.

Between 1800 and 1914, whalers and sealers k more than 35 million harp seals and hooded seals.

Like arctic whaling, sealing was hard and dange work. Hundreds of ships were crushed by the shi pack over the years; thousands of sealers maroone crashing, crumbling floes. It has been estimated that r than 20,000 Newfoundlanders have died in the pursu seals.

Within a decade, in the 1890s whalers all but stroyed the once-vast walrus herds of the eastern Ar Polar bear rugs came into fashion. Every proper Victo baby had to have his picture taken lying on a polar skin. Between 1905 and 1909, Dundee whalers a killed more than a thousand polar bears off Greenla east coast. Thousands more were killed in Hudson and Baffin Bay.

owards the end of the 19th century, only the Scots some American ships continued whaling in the east-Arctic. The Scots were now using exclusively steam s, 300-to-400-ton vessels, built of hardwood, mainly throughout and sheathed with greenheart. Between interior timber and the shell was a layer of rock salt, to ion the crushing blows of the ice, bringing the hull's l thickness to 18 to 24 inches. Even this was not ugh protection for a vessel caught in the ice and each one or more ships failed to return. Some ships, ugh, seemed to have a charmed life. The "Truelove," t in Philadelphia in 1764, sailed the world's oceans 120 years, including 72 years of arctic whaling. While the American and Scottish whalers were scour-the Greenland coasts and the eastern Canadian arctic he last remnants of a sea wealth that once had seemed mited, the Norwegians were busy at Spitsbergen and her north and east, at Franz Josef Land and Novaya lya mopping up the remainder of wildlife that could urned into money. In 1906, a fairly typical year, 31 wegian sloops returned from the north with 131 white les, 135 walrus, 6,000 seals, 296 polar bears, 2,888 deer, 61 blue foxes, 80 white foxes and 1,000 pounds iderdown.

y the time the invention of plastics, particularly Cel-id and Bakelite, sent baleen prices plummeting and alled an end to Arctic whaling, the whales had nearly n exterminated. There were probably only 500 left in he arctic seas. (Today, more than fifty years after ling has ceased, bowhead whales are thought to ber about 1,000); the walrus herds were decimated; koxen had vanished from much of their range. In 3 two whalers, the "Morning" and the "Baleana" left dee. Both came home clean. The next year the ler "Active" returned without seeing a whale. After years, arctic whaling, which had brought wealth to y but death and disaster to more, was finally and ocably finished.

rom this three-centuries-long rapine the mammals of arctic seas have never recovered. But with proper ection and management, perhaps some of them will e back. The fur seals of the North Pacific, once re-duced to 200,000, now, with careful management, number again nearly 2,000,000, despite an annual "har-vest" of from 30,000 to 80,000 animals. Most arctic sea mammals now receive some degree of protection, if only in the form of "kill quotas," which, in the case of the harp seal, may still be excessively high.

Now other, more insidious dangers threaten the life of the arctic seas. For years, scientists on the Pribilof Islands have made "forecasts" of possible annual fur seal kills. Fur seals are polygamous. A relatively small number of mature bulls controls the breeding territories and the females on them. Surplus bulls who will never mate are killed by man. Since scientists know the number of pups born each year, and in decades of data gathering have established normal survival ratios, they have been able, until recently, to forecast with considerable accuracy the number of bachelor bulls that would be available each year for "harvesting." Lately, something has gone awry. The scientists' prognoses have been too optimistic: there are not the number of harvestable seals expected. Evidently a new and fatal factor has entered into the fur seal's life.

One guess is that it may be overfishing by man. The fleets of many nations, particularly Japan, Korea and the Soviet Union, crisscross the Bering Sea fishing grounds. Although fur seals probably eat primarily such non-commercial species as the ugly but abundant abyssal lantern fish, enough of their food fish may be taken from the sea by man to tip the balance of life just slightly against them. Lactating females may have to swim a bit farther, hunt a bit longer to obtain enough fish to sustain themselves and produce sufficient milk for the pups who hungrily await their return on shore. Because of this, pups are just a bit weaker when they finally enter the sea, their fat reserves just a bit thinner than in former times, and their ability to survive the winter in a cold and stormy sea is slightly diminished. And in future years, fewer of them will return to their ancestral islands in the northern sea.

"The moot point is,
whether Leviathan can long endure
so wide a chase,
and so remorseless a havoc;
whether he must not
at last be exterminated from the waters,
and the last whale,
like the last man, smoke his last pipe,
and then himself
evaporate in the final puff."
**Herman Melville, 1851,
from "Moby Dick".**

Only a century ago, the famous English biologist Thomas Henry Huxley could say with confidence: "I believe probably all the great sea fisheries are inexhaustible; that is to say nothing we do seriously affects the number of fish."

When Huxley wrote that, the world's population had not yet reached one billion. It increased to 1.5 billion in 1900, to 3.5 billion in 1970 and is expected to reach 7 billion in the year 2000. Protein is desperately needed for this spiralling population. Much of it must come from the sea. The world fish catch has doubled every ten years during past decades. In 1970 it reached 60 million tons. Many biologists believe this is near or already above the sea's regenerative ability. Yet it is planned to increase the harvest from the sea to 100 million tons a year, and fishing fleets are looking towards the wealth of the northern seas, to the immense schools of capelin and tomcod, to fill their gaping holds. But tomcod and capelin are also the principal food of some northern seals and many sea bird species.

Overfishing, however, has a built-in check, that of diminishing financial returns. Long before the northern seas will be totally exhausted, their exploitation will cease to be profitable, and sufficient animal stocks will presumably be left to regenerate at least in part their former wealth.

A more serious potential threat to the Arctic is the discovery of vast quantities of oil and gas in the far north. On June 18, 1968 it was announced in Dallas, Texas that drilling operations near Prudhoe Bay on Alaska's North Slope had confirmed great deposits of oil and natural gas. Since then, other oil deposits and, particularly, gas deposits have been discovered on Canada's arctic islands. The market for these fossil fuels is the energy-short south. To bring them to market, either tankers, pipelines or both will be employed.

In warmer seas, the more toxic parts of crude oil evaporate first and, though damage may be extensive and prolonged, the sea does eventually cleanse itself even of a major oil spill. But in a northern sea the process of oil decomposition is very slow or stops entirely at freezing temperatures. The foundering of one oil-laden supertanker in the far north could turn an immense area of the Arctic sea into a biological desert.

"The single most imminent threat to the Arctic at this time is that of a large oil spill," said Prime Minister Pierre Elliott Trudeau in 1970, at the time the giant tanker "Manhattan" made her famous trial voyage through the Northwest Passage to Prudhoe Bay. "Such a spill would be more dangerous than spills in temperate or tropical waters. Oil decomposes in warmer climates but it would be permanent in the frigid Arctic. The disastrous consequences which the presence of oil would have upon the marine plankton, upon the process of oxygenation in Arctic North America, and upon other natural and vital processes of the biosphere, are incalculable in their extent."

Long ago, the Eskimos believed that all animals had souls. "Life's greatest danger lies in the fact that man's food consists entirely of souls," an old Igloolik shaman told Knud Rasmussen. Therefore, when an Eskimo killed a seal, a walrus, or a whale, he did his best to placate the animal's soul. He would thank the animal for allowing itself to be killed, and would take care to explain that he had only done so because he, his family and his dogs were in need of food.

He would pour a bit of water into the seal's mouth in case its soul was thirsty. The Eskimo reasoned that if he showed proper gratitude and respect, the seal's soul would be pleased, and would allow itself again to be killed in a future reincarnation. But if the animal was wasted or otherwise treated with contempt, the soul would bring its plaint to the sea goddess, whom the Eskimos called "Sedna" — she down there, or "Imapukûa" — mother of the sea, and she, in anger, would withold from ungrateful man the bounty of her realm.

The air is filled with flyi
        common mur
    above a great colc
        of brooding bir
Overleaf: A harp seal p

Our plane from Anchorage to the Aleutian Islands and the Pribilofs was, not surprisingly, late in leaving. Weather conditions at our destination ranged, as usual, between bad and awful. When we finally left, I sat next to a tall, lanky man who informed me in a soft southern drawl that he was by profession a cowboy, bound for the island of Umnak, where a horse and job were waiting for him. Sheep ranching on a large scale, he told me, has been developed on the island in the post-war years.

We landed briefly at Cold Bay, near the western end of the volcano-studded Alaska Peninsula, then turned northwest for the 325-mile flight across the Bering Sea to the Pribilof Islands. We broke through the clouds low above St. Paul Island, the green, rolling land beneath us crisscrossed by brick-red scoria roads.

While the two-day tourists were shepherded to the island's only hotel, I searched for cheaper and more interesting lodging and was finally rented a room by a charming old Aleut couple, Sergie and Nadesda Shaishnikoff.

Sergie, now retired, had been a heavy equipment operator. Nadesda, also retired, had once been cook at the hotel. They, like the other people I met, seemed strangely tricultural: the core is Aleut, surrounded by a layer of Russian custom, and covered with a patina of more recently acquired Americanism.

Their spacious home was furnished in middle-class American style: wall-to-wall carpets, solid plush furniture, hi-fi set, refrigerator, freezer, large range, and washing machine and, in the absence of telephones, a walkie-talkie from which flowed an uninterrupted stream of local gossip. An icon hung in the corner of the living room, and Sergie and Nadesda crossed themselves devoutly in front of it, in the morning, at night, and before meals. We ate American food, but also kittiwake stew, basted roast of seal, and marinated murres. They were sorry, they could not serve me their once-favorite delicacy, fried seal liver because it contains excessive amounts of mercury.

Like the Aleutians, the Pribilof Islands have evil weather, and had once an immense wealth of sea mammals. Unlike the Aleutians, the Pribilofs were uninhabited by man, prior to their discovery by the Russians in 1786. Aleut legends tell of men who went to islands, far, far away, where seals covered the beaches for miles, but if in fact they visited the islands, they never settled on them. The Russians, and later the Americans, plus sealers and whalers of many nations, took part in the mass killing of animals. The walrus disappeared, whales are only rarely seen nowadays, the sea otters vanished, and at one time, only 200,000 fur seals were left, where once there had been 2,000,000 who "came and went in the legions that darkened all the shore," as Kipling said in his poem "Lukannon." (Thanks to careful management, the seal herds have now increased again to nearly their original numbers.)

During my stay on St. Paul Island, I went nearly every day to Lukanin Beach (or Lukannon, as Kipling called it), to watch and photograph the seals. The weather was fairly mild, occasionally foggy and it rained frequently; St. Paul has, on the average, 200 days of rain a year, and in winter it snows. It is usually not a heavy rain, just a dismal drizzle. The sky is almost always overcast; the light is a soft, diffuse grey; it is a land without shadows.

Yet though the island seems at first so triste, it is beautiful and full of life. Just past the cemetery with its neat white Russian Orthodox crosses, a fox family had its den. The male, a blue fox, was shy and to get pictures of him required patience and a long telephoto lens. But the vixen was tame. She was a white fox, now in her summer coat of brindled grey and brown and tan, who had arrived the previous winter on an ice floe from some land to the north, perhaps Siberia, where she had presumably never known people. When I sat near her den, waiting for the kits to appear, she came to talk or to see what she could beg or steal, and since my camera bag was too heavy to lug away, she tried to establish her claim to it by urinating against it.

It was early summer, whole acres of the island were deep blue with lupine, and a myriad water droplets sparkled on their furry leaves. Indigo-colored monkshood nodded among the lush green grass. Long ago, Aleuts had dug up this plant, and prepared, in secret ceremonies, a deadly poison from its roots, to smear on lances used to kill the great whales. Road sides and ridges were aglow with golden arctic poppies and the clusters of moss campion were spangled with tiny blooms. In some places the grass stood particularly thick

St. Paul Island

and green. These were the "killing fields," to which the seals are driven for slaughter, well-fertilized with their blood. "Ungisxalgeq" the Aleuts call them, "the place without hope."

The island cliffs were dotted with breeding or resting birds. Black-legged kittiwakes screamed and squabbled and the rare red-legged kittiwake, which breeds only on the Pribilof Islands, flew past the coast. Red-faced cormorants, like rows of heraldic birds, sat on a rock ridge, their wings spread to let their feathers dry. Auklets argued and jostled on favorite perches, and horned puffins looked on, their small, black, erectile horns giving them a supercilious, mock-satanic appearance.

Sea lions lazed on the beach, their fur golden brown against the black lava rocks. More than a million fur seals crowded the rookeries. They had swum thousands of miles through a stormy ocean to this small island hidden in a foggy sea, the island where they were born and where they now, in turn, would renew the eternal cycle of life.

The fog rolled in from the sea and wrapped the island in its grey and clammy shroud.

From afar came the rhythmic surge of the sea battering against the rugged coast; the shrill bleat of a seal pup calling its mother; the throaty roar of an angry sea lion; the warning snarl of a fur seal bull defending his territory; the plaintive mewing of the gulls; the whistling of the auklets; the yapping of a fox. Directionless and all-pervading in the fog, the island's voices blended together into a symphony of life, a life that for all came ultimately from the surrounding sea, the chill and dismal Bering Sea whose "waters bring forth abundantly the moving creature that hath life."

Sea Mammals

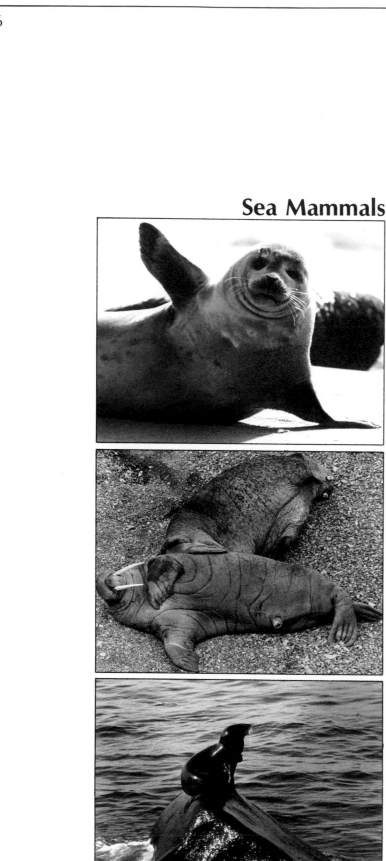

The bowhead exploits the sea's upper layers. The somewhat smaller grey whale takes most of its food from the sea's bottom. It plows along the ocean floor, scooping up, somewhat indiscriminately, whatever there happens to be, such as shrimps, worms, crabs or clams, surfaces vertically, and, while water and silt gush out between the lattice-work of baleen plates in its mouth, the solid contents rattle down into the first of the four chambers of its cavernous stomach.

The arctic seas are far more hospitable to animals than is the arctic land with its extreme and often violent climate and long seasons of scarcity. The waters are always chilly, never warm in summer, never colder than 28° F in winter. They are stupendously rich in nutrients. In summer there is an abundance of plant plankton and zooplankton and the food supply in winter, though not as rich, is nevertheless sufficient to sustain millions of sea mammals.

Nature has providently divided this wealth of food among the animals that inhabit the northern seas.

The bowhead whale, weighing as much as 60 tons, swims leisurely along the ice fields of the northern seas, scooping up tiny crustaceans and pteropods, winged, pelagic snails, at the rate of about a ton a day.

Grey whales spend summer in the shallow, cold but food-rich Bering and Chukchee Seas, and winter in the even shallower but warmer lagoons along the coast of Baja California, an annual migration of nearly 10,000 miles.

The strangest of all whales and the most truly arctic is the narwhal, long hunted and prized for the single, tapered, twisted ivory tusk carried by male. Exactly to what use the narwhal puts this tusk, which looks like an eight-foot corkscrew, no one really knows. Eskimos say it employs it to poke up Greenland halibut, flat, bottom-dwelling fish, and the narwhal favorite food. Scientists contend it is merely an ornament of the male, a secondary sexual characteristic, like the mane of a lion. Medieval man cherished the tusk as the horn of the mythical unicorn, and ascribed to it miraculous properties. It could detect and neutralize poison, it was believed and narwhal tusks were worth seven times their weight in gold. Modern man may be less credulous, but he still covets the strange tusk of the arctic corn, is willing to pay highly for it, and thus creates a demand which may threaten the narwhal's survival in the near future.

While narwhal feed, by preference in deep water, their closest relative, white whale or beluga, likes shallow water, at least in summer. It swims in large schools into bays and inlets of north, or spends the summer in the estuaries of great rivers, such as the Churchill and Nelson Rivers flowing into Hudson Bay, and the Mackenzie River delta. There they catch fish, primarily the small polar cod, capelin and cisco. They are pure white (but are born a deep slate blue), gregarious and garrulous.

All whales, according to scientists, "vocalize" a great deal. (The "song" the humpback whale has been recorded and serves as basis for the "concerto whale and orchestra," produced by American composer.) Of all the whales the belugas are probably the most chatty. They squeak and groan and (sailors used to call them "sea canaries"), and they can grunt and chortle in a most self-satisfied way. narwhal, when surfacing, are usually quiet, but occasionally one of them makes a strange sound, like a deep, resonant, rather melancholy t note, ending in a gurgle as the whal dives.

The seals of the north also divide sea's wealth amongst themselves. T

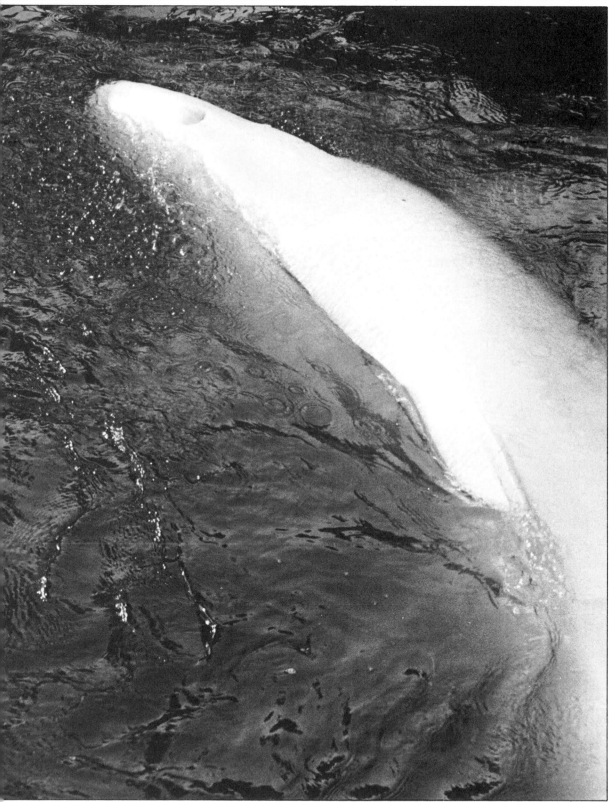

little ringed seal, now the most numerous of all seals, eats some polar cod, but its main food consists of little shrimp-like crustaceans, primarily the spindly Mysis and the fatter, long-legged Parathemisto. The great bearded seal uses its luxuriant and highly sensitive whiskers to locate and perhaps collect food on the sea bottom: whelks, cockles, crabs, sea cucumbers, and shrimps. Walrus, too, feed from the sea's floor, but their main food is clams, which they rake up with their long ivory tusks. The harp seal eats polar cod, squid, and crustaceans, but its favorite food is capelin. The hooded seal's range coincides, in some regions with that of the harp seal. But while harp seals exploit the ocean's top layer and do most of their hunting from the surface to a depth of 50 fathoms, the great hooded seals prefer fish from deeper ocean regions, and do most of their hunting at depths between 50 and 100 fathoms. And the harbor seal, who is the stay-at-home type, rarely ventures far from land, content to exploit the off-shore fishery which the other seals neglect. To every species, according to its niche and its need, the sea supplies ample food.

Inglefield Bay is about 60 miles long and 20 miles wide. In summer, for perhaps 70 days, about 2,000 narwhal and 500 white whales inhabit it, plus thousands of seals. The whales, it is believed, come into the bay partly because among the extensive ice fields near the glaciers they can find refuge from marauding killer whales, and partly because the bay is rich in food. During their 70 day stay, the whales eat about 10 million pounds of fish.

Each harp seal requires approximately 3,000 pounds of food annually, and the 30 million of them that lived in the northern seas in the days before commercial sealing would eat each year 90 billion pounds of fish, squid, and crustaceans; a bounteous and everlasting banquet, since the law of sea and land is balance between predator and prey. The seals could not deplete the sea's wealth without bringing ruin upon themselves.

Many sea animals dwell year-round in the Arctic.

Others are migrants.

The homing instinct, as compelling in many sea animals as it is in birds, brings them north each year in their appointed seasons.

For seven months of the year, the two million fur seals range in remote parts of the Pacific. But in spring, responding to an ancient, imperative summons, the seals swim north, thousands of miles, to five small, fog-hidden islands. There the most powerful males establish their territories, and the females come ashore to bear their long-flippered, glossy-black pups. Most pups will die. Some will be crushed shortly after birth by raging bulls rushing to repel rivals from their territories. Hookworms will sap the strength of many pups, and they will succumb in the icy, storm-whipped sea when they head south in early winter. Sharks and killer whales will eat them. But the balance between life and death will be maintained; the surviving pups, in time, will return to their ancestral islands, and eventually they will breed on the broad beaches whose dark lava rocks are worn smooth and shiny by millions upon millions of fur seal flippers through eons of time.

The Plants

"During the long, cold Siberian winter the snow lies
in a thick mass over the tundra; but no sooner does the sun get the better of it
than hosts of tiny northern flowers burst their way up through the snow . . . and open
their modest calices, blushing in the radiant summer day
that bathes the plain in splendor."

Fridtjof Nansen, 1893.

120

Top: Lousewort blooms on an island in the Bering Sea. Carmine cap of a mushroom among dwarf willow leaves. Delicate grasses sway in the wind near the tundra's southern edge. Male catkins of dwarf willows. Frail blossoms of the hardy broad-leaved willow herb.

Middle: Dwarf willow leaves in early fall. Purple saxifrage, the first flowers to bloom in the arctic spring. Cinquefoil on an island off Alaska's west coast. Monkshood and goldenrod on a far northern meadow. Cottongrass loves the moisture of an arctic marsh. Tiny hairs protect the stems of the arctic poppy. The vivid red of bearberry leaves on the fall tundra.

Bottom: Kamchatka lily on Marmot Island, off Alaska's west coast. Arctic chamomile, the daisy of the north.

here soil has accumulated
nutrients are sufficient,
sses often grow
lush profusion in the Arctic,
en where
nmer lasts only a month.

In most circumpolar regions plants are neither cultivated nor cropped. They provide man with little direct nourishment. Yet upon their stunted, precarious, incredible cycle of survival in conditions hostile to every form of botanical life, depends the balance of nature in an area of about five million square miles, roughly one-tenth of the earth's entire land surface.

It is winter and the tundra beyond our camp at Bathurst Inlet, near the northern edge of the central Canadian arctic mainland, stretches towards the far horizon, dead and desolate. The Eskimos with whom I live ignore it. Their life now comes from the frozen sea, where they hunt seals at their breathing holes, or from the caches of fish and caribou meat laid up during the preceding fall. The land holds no interest for them. "Nuna hiniqpoq," they say, the land sleeps.

The wind sweeps down from the hills and packs the snow into dells and depressions. It lies deep beneath the cliff that borders a valley a mile from our camp, and nearly buries an extensive patch of dwarf willow. The snow protects the willows and other plants that huddle underneath it from the icy desiccating wind of winter. It is an excellent insulator. The temperature under two feet of snow may be 40° F higher than the temperature above it.

The Eskimos visit the valley at least once a week to dig a sled-load of willows cut from underneath the snow. It is their main winter fuel for cooking food. The willows lie gnarled and twisted close to the ground. They may be centuries old. Plants grow slowly in the Arctic; the winter season of dormancy is exceedingly long, the summer season of growth desperately short. A thumb-thick willow trunk may have 400 or more annual rings, so closely spaced they can only be counted with a powerful magnifying glass.

There are ptarmigan in the valley. Willow buds and twigs are their staple winter food. When the Eskimos kill a ptarmigan, they slit open its gizzard and part of the intestine, take out the partly digested buds and eat them. I find them rather bland, but the Eskimos consider them a delicacy. They are extremely rich in ascorbic acid, the vital, scurvy-preventing Vitamin C.

The creek that meanders through our valley comes from a distant range of hills. One hillside, swept nearly clear of snow, is covered with boulders and rocks. Here one can usually find arctic hares. They are large and white, only their ear tips are black. When alarmed, they sometimes stand on their hind legs, like furry gnomes among the dark boulders, and they run in a most peculiar manner: after a short burst on all fours, they rise on their long hind legs and hop along in huge, erratic bounds, like someone on a pogostick. They like the boulder fields. There they find shelter from the searing wind, and with their long incisors they snip off the fallow grass that remains from last summer among the rocks, nibble the twigs of the creeping willows in the lee of the boulders, and add to this meagre fare by eating some moss and lichen.

Grasses that slowly wilt and wither in fall lose nearly their entire nutritive value. But on the hills, fall's first frost can quick-freeze plants before they are entirely wilted, and their slightly higher nutritive value may be of vital importance to the hares.

The hares forage on the sparse exposed vegetation and become, themselves, a reluctant ingredient in the cycle of plant subsistence. They have many enemies. The Eskimos shoot them or catch them in snares and eat the lean, sweetish meat larded with snippets of blubber. The hares' worst enemy arrives without warning. The great white arctic owl glides in on silent wings.

"Oogpik," the Eskimos call the arctic owl, or, in the language of their poets, "nangeqahijaq" — the always upright. It sits straight and stern on a favorite perch and looks at the white world around with yellow-glowing eyes. It prefers high boulders, as do the rough-legged hawks who will arrive in spring. One can see these traditional perches from afar. They are capped and streaked in brilliant vermilion by the lichen *Caloplaca elegans*, which the Polar Eskimos, less elegantly, call "sunain anak" — the sun's excrement. Jewel lichen is its common name and, like several other lichens, it is nitrophilous. It loves nitrogen and thrives only in its presence. It marks the nesting sites of arctic raptors with such brilliant splashes of color, one can easily spot them from a low-flying plane, and coats the rocks at arctic bird colonies in flamboyant profusion.

Every lichen is really two plants, a partnership between a fungus and an alga. The usually blue-green alga contains chlorophyll and is capable of photosynthesis; it can use the sun's energy to manufacture nutrients which it shares with its fungoid mate. The tough, gelatinous fungus envelops the frail algal cells, gives them protection and provides them with moisture which it absorbs, sponge-like, from rain, fog or melting snow. In times of drought, it coats the algae with hard, moisture-conserving layers, and both lie dormant until conditions improve.

This mutually beneficial relationship of two plants produces an entity of great hardiness and adaptability. Lichens are the pioneering plants of the Arctic. They exist as far north as there is land, in regions so harsh, growth may be possible during only one or two days in a year. And lichens don't ask for much: a touch of warmth, a bit of moisture, and they awaken from death-like dormancy, breathe, metabolize and grow. While other plants wait for higher temperatures to begin photosynthesis, lichens shake off their suspended animation the moment the temperature rises above the freezing point. Their growth is slow. The rocks near our camp are speckled with map lichen. Now, in winter, they are pale and lustreless, but in spring when they absorb some moisture, they shine in vivid, nearly fluorescent green so that one can see them, despite their minuteness, from a considerable distance. Although they are tiny, they may be extremely old. They grow three-eighths of an inch in a thousand years. Some lichens in northern Greenland are estimated to be five thousand years old.

The French scientist Becquerel subjected the lichen *Xanthoria parietina* "to temperatures within a fraction of absolute zero (−459.6°F), using an adiabatic demagnetization technique in high vacuum. Some of these (lichens) had been under vacuum for eight years and had been for two weeks in liquid air. They survived . . ." Not surprisingly, the lowly lichen thrives where other plants can barely exist.

Many of these lichens, only a few inches in diameter, and believed to be thousands of years old, are, perhaps, the oldest living things on earth.

Not all lichens are small. Large black foliose lichens *Gyrophora* and *Umbilicaria*, encrust many tundra boulders with their splayed and leathery growth. Now, in winter, they are puckered up and dry; they are firmly attached to the rock and if you try to pluck one off, it will probably crumble in your hand. But if a sudden spring rain floods the boulder, these lichens absorb water with such speed, they writhe and bloat visibly. They are rock-tripe lichens; "tripe de roche" the voyageurs used to call them. They were the food of starving explorers. (Sir John Franklin, after a hunger-plagued journey in 1821, not far from where we were camped, noted: "Hepburn, the servant, daily collected all the tripe de roche that was used in the officers' mess . . .")

The nutritive substance in lichens is lichenin, a carbohydrate akin to starch. But, in addition, lichens contain acids that raise havoc with the human digestive system, they taste vile, and a U.S. Air Force manual advises: "Lichens should not be considered an important survival food" and adds, significantly, "they are not eaten by any native peoples."

Indirectly, though, lichens are of vital importance to most circumpolar peoples, since they are a major food of caribou and reindeer. Farmers in northernmost Scandinavia collect *Cladonia*, the reindeer (or caribou) moss, which really is an immensely abundant lichen, as winter fodder for their cattle, but they must neutralize its noxious

usnic acid with potassium bicarbonate, usually in form of wood ash.

Few animals are able to stomach the acid lichen, caribou can. It is the secret of their immense succ There are millions of domesticated reindeer in Eurasian north, and millions of caribou once brow over the vast area of the North American taiga and tun

Most caribou spend the winter in the northern fores spring they become restless. Small groups begin to m north, others join, the herds grow, the dilatory dav becomes an urgent, purposeful march, and like a g living tide the caribou stream northward towards tundra. "La foule," the host, the voyageurs called th In summer and fall they scatter over the immense tun pasturing on its great verdant meadows of sedges grass. The Eskimos at our camp near the arctic c eagerly await their coming. They are our main foo summer and fall, and cached caribou meat and slab back fat form a vital reserve for the lean months of e winter. When the Eskimos kill a caribou, they open paunch and eat its partly digested, slightly ferme plant content. It has a sourish taste, like spinach sprin with vinegar.

In late fall, the caribou return to the forest. The gra wither and lose most of their nutritive value, but lic do not, and they enable the caribou to survive the wi Studies made by Soviet scientists show that Clad lichens form up to 95 percent of the reindeer's w food. They dig them out from underneath the snow their broad, sharp-edged hoofs. The word "caribou" Micmac Indian origin. It means "the shoveler." *Cladonia* lichens are rich in sugars and starches. Sw once used them to distill a potent brew called li brandy.

Desiccated in winter, the lichens crackle and crun when we walk over an exposed patch on a hillside. It them little harm. The broken parts will be blown ove tundra, settle on snow or bare land and, as soon as the sufficient warmth and moisture will establish thems as tiny new lichen colonies. *Cladonia*, and many o lichens, can multiply by fragmentation. They also ex their realm by branching out laterally, as vegetativ tensions of a parent plant until they cover square r with a silvery-green carpet. In addition, they sen billions of minute spores to reproduce their kind.

When conditions are unfavorable, the lichen *Cet richardsonii*, which resembles miniature caribou an

itself into a ball. Winds trundle it across the tundra
it reaches a better spot. There it unfurls and clings to
ground to start a new and happier existence.
has been estimated that in the south it takes a century
rm an inch of soil. In the north, where both growth
decay are exceedingly slow, it takes infinitely longer.
dreds of years pass before a lichen dies and its re-
ns are transformed into a minute bit of earth. Some
ns produce chemicals that leach and disintegrate the
s upon which they grow and, over millennia, these,
are turned into soil.
increase their nutrient supply, lichens avidly absorb
es of dust that float in the air. In recent years they have
garnering more sinister substances out of the atmos-
e: the radioactive fall-out products of atomic explo-
s, particularly Strontium-90 and Cesium-137.
ou and reindeer eat the lichen, the substances be-
e further concentrated in their bodies and are passed
their main predator, man. And Eskimos, whose
uage does not even contain a word for "war," have
found to be contaminated by these atomic fission
ucts at levels barely considered "safe."
April, winter loses much of its sting. It can still be
rly cold. One night, in early April, when we return
the seal hunt, it is 40 below. A bluish, diaphanous
haze fills the air. Dogs and sleds, like dark dots and
es, rush swiftly through the icy gloom. But in the
part of the month, the days are long, the sun intense.
calm days, evaporation vapor flickers and dances
e the dark ridges. The white snow reflects as much as
ercent of the sun's incident energy, but anything dark
rbs its warmth. Pebbles, twigs or ptarmigan drop-
s begin to sink into snow and ice. Later, in May and
a sun-warmed, marble-sized hare pellet can "burn"
e a foot across and two feet deep through solid ice.
shore, where the ice is covered by wind-driven
s, it becomes as pitted and holed as a Swiss cheese.
e land remains dry and dead. Frozen and rock-hard,
ground cannot absorb any moisture. The sun's
nth vaporizes the snow. Captain Thomas James, who
ored Hudson Bay and its southern appendage, James
named after him, noted in 1632: "The snowe does
nelte away here with the Sunne . . . but it is exaled up

by the Sunne, and suckt full of holes, like honeycombs, so
that the land wheron it lyes will not be at all wetted . . ."

In late April, early May, a strange restlessness pervades
the arctic world. Flocks of snow buntings fly twittering
from one bare patch of earth to the next, picking up last
year's seeds. The air is filled with the liquid lilting song of
horned larks. Female ptarmigan begin to moult, their
plumage piebald like the land, part winter's white, part
summer's brown. Ground squirrels awaken from eight
months sleep, poke up through the drifts that still cover
their burrows, run distractedly and rather foolhardily across the snow, and nibble at willow twigs, but their minds
aren't really on food. They are mostly males in search of
mates. The children at camp play through the luminous
spring nights. Visitors arrive from distant camps, and
some of the families who have lived with us all winter
suddenly pack up and go: inland, to intercept the approaching caribou; to visit friends at other camps; or to
fish through the ice of a distant lake.

We are happy in camp. We laugh a lot and tease each
other. We haven't really all that much to laugh about,
because we're nearly out of food. Seal hunting is finished,
and the caribou have not yet arrived from the south. We
eat ground squirrels, lean after their long hibernation, and
the little tomcod the children catch in a lead. It doesn't
matter. Soon the caribou will come. The sun is warm, the
air as clear and liquid as champagne, and we feel bubbly
and buoyant, and a bit high with spring and life.

Yet the land still looks stark and stern, in white and
black and dun. We will have vicious snow storms well
into June, but now there is a subtle difference. When the
sun comes out again, it does not vaporize all the snow. A
bit soaks into the top layer of soil, and moistens, however
briefly, the clusters of last year's vegetation. And suddenly, in the middle of May, on a snow-free ridge, the first
flowers bloom, gay little rosettes of purple saxifrage.
Under little or no snow, they bore the brunt of winter's

"Bottle caps and metal cans
do not disintegrate
for at least a hundred years on the tundra.
Fifty to one hundred years
of plant growth can be snuffed out
by a beer can."
**Ann H. Zwinger and
Beatrice E. Willard, in "Land Above
The Trees", 1972.**

cold, its deadly desiccating winds, the threat of snow and sand abrasion. Incredibly hardy, they survived and now, while most plants still slumber under their blanket of snow, the ridge plants glow in the spring sun.

By botanical standards established in other latitudes, they shouldn't be growing. It is too cold. Photosynthesis can only take place at temperatures above 43°F; botanists are quite emphatic on that point. And it is not nearly that warm. Yet the plants grow, thanks to a miracle, in part of their own making; a private, cozy climate, the so-called microclimate, which can be considerably warmer than the ambient air temperature. The temperature within a dark, sun-warmed cluster of vegetation may be 20 and even 30 degrees higher than the air temperature a yard above the ground. Dark petals (relatively few arctic plants have white blooms) absorb and retain the sun's heat; their internal temperature can be five to six degrees higher than the temperature outside.

Stems and buds of many plants are covered with a fuzzy growth of minute hairs. They protect the plant's stomata, the pores through which it breathes, they reduce moisture loss, and they trap heat rays. Dark brown, velvety hairs envelop the buds of arctic poppies, they absorb long-wave radiation and warm the nascent flower within. The stems of most arctic flowers are hollow. The tubular construction is notably strong, less energy and plant-material are required than for the pith-filled stems of southern species and, in a sort of greenhouse effect, the plant gathers so much warmth within the hollow stem, its interior temperature may be 36°F higher than the air temperature outside. Such microclimatic increases in temperature prolong by weeks the season of growth for arctic plants, and make it possible for them to survive in the farthest north. In the Thule region of northwestern Greenland the average temperature of only one month, July, is above the freezing point, yet in a year I lived there, the first purple saxifrages were already blooming on the 30th of May.

In the south, plants prudently await the assured, continuous warmth of spring before they bloom, avoiding the risk of a belated nip. With a growing season of three months or less in the low Arctic, and only some forty days in the high Arctic, northern plants cannot allow themselves the luxury of waiting for optimum conditions. They begin to grow as soon as warmth and moisture permit. Buds swell, sap courses through stems and leaves. And then a sudden cold spell freezes them solid, so they snap, like icicles, at a touch. Renewed warmth awakens them, unharmed, and they can thus oscillate in the fickle arctic spring, between icy, death-like dormancy and burgeoning growth, conditions that would be instantly fatal to southern plants.

For the plants emerging first, on ridges and hillsides, rapid growth is imperative, for soon they will have to face another threat: drought. In spring the earth absorbs the moisture of melting snow, but in late June and in July the ridges will be dry and dusty. Many arctic plants are xerophytes, desert-adapted, with small, leathery leaves, often covered with fine fuzzy hairs that help to prevent moisture loss. The average annual precipitation for much of the tundra is about ten inches. Ellesmere Island received 1.6 inches annually, and Peary Land, at the north tip of Greenland, less than an inch; they have a climate drier than the Sahara. The permafrost beneath the thin top stratum of earth that thaws in the brief arctic summer contains rain and meltwater within reach of the shallow root system of arctic plants. And thus in a land that without permafrost would be a giant, icy desert, the plants flourish: there are more than 900 species of flowering plants in the Arctic, 2,500 species of lichen and 500 of mosses. Greenland is home to 496 species of flowers, including several orchids; 356 species grow on Siberia's Chukotski Peninsula, the northeast end of Asia; the rugged, wind-seared Taimyr Peninsula, the northernmost part of Siberia is briefly aglow with the blooms of 118 species; 115 flower species grow in the vicinity of Lake Hazen, on northern Ellesmere Island; and even Peary Land, the northernmost land in the world, arid and cold, supports 90 species of flowering plants. Antarctica has three species, and the tropics 100,000!

"The vegetati
. . . is superior to anyth
that I could have expec
in such a latitu
. . . patches of several acres . . . of as f
meadow-la
as could be seen in Englan

Captain William Scoresby
1822, northeast coa
Greenl

Arctic chamo

On left: Isopod husks on lichen-encrusted rock.
Lichens form delicate filigrees and patterns with infinite slowness,
sometimes forming dense growths that almost cover boulders.

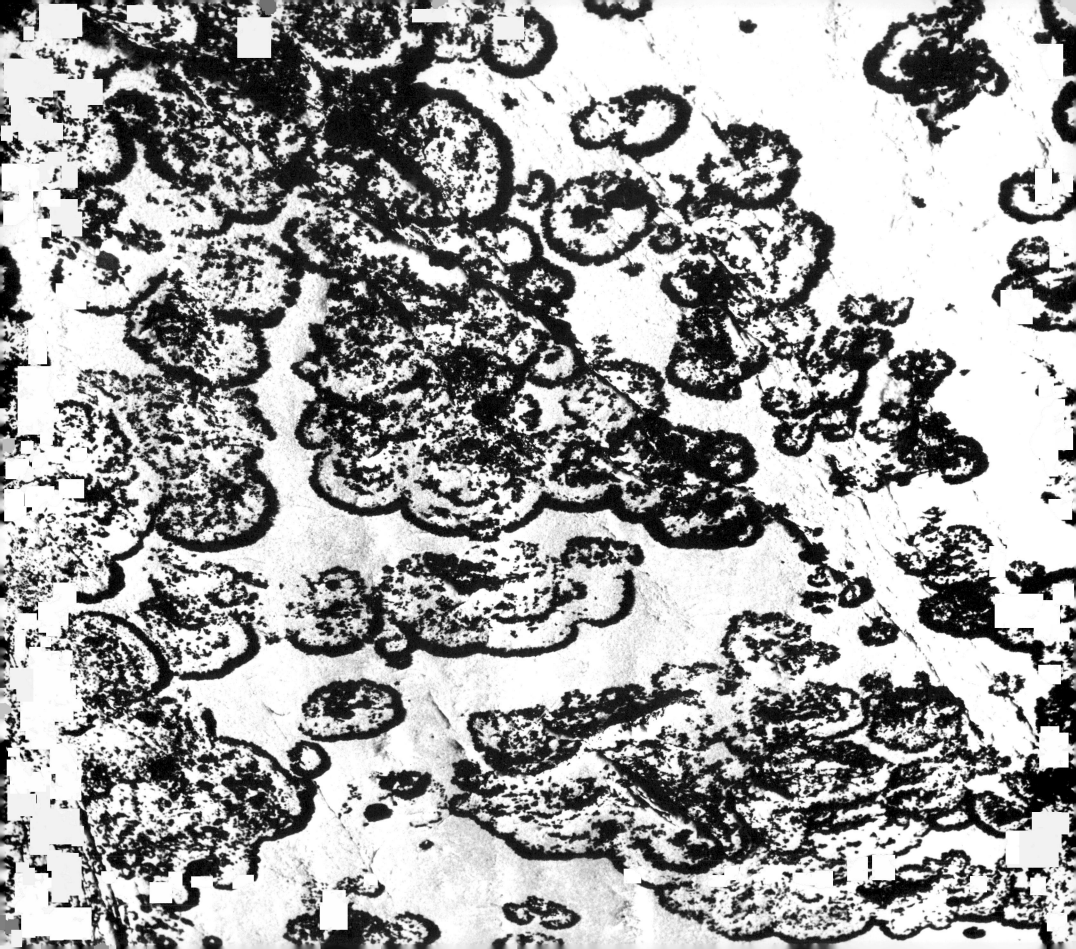

"We found in many places
such angelica.
We suppose the people (Eskimos) eate
the roots thereof . . .
for we have seene them have many
of them in their boats.''

**William Baffin, 1612,
on the coast of Greenland.**

A tracery of black lichen
on quartzite rock.

In early June, our camp at Bathurst Inlet, so clean and white in winter, becomes distinctly messy. The snow-block walls that protected our double-layered tents from winter winds, sag and crumble. The accumulated debris of winter soils the mushy snow.

On June 8, we cache our bulky winter clothing, the seal hunting equipment and all the other paraphernalia of winter life on top of a rock pile, and move to our summer camp on the bare, dry shoulder of a hill overlooking the sea. It is a festive occasion. The children discover long-lost treasures. The huskies snitch anything remotely edible and have some glorious fights. They are beginning to shed their warm winter wool, and the fur is flying. We load the sleds high with our possessions; the broad runners glide silently through the moist snow. Golden plovers swoop and dive in the sky in the exuberant gyrations of their courting flights. They have just returned from the Argentinian pampas where they spent the winter, and now fill the air with their clear, slightly melancholy fluting. The land is vibrant with a sense of urgency, of resurrection and of life.

The leesides of valleys and dells remain buried by thick drifts. But wherever the snow has vanished, on hill and plain, the ground is covered with a profusion of flowers. The tiny bells of arctic white heather nod in the breeze; moist spots glow with the purple blooms of Lapland rhododendron; and the delicate, feathery blossoms of Labrador tea, white with a blush of pink, shine among the dark leaves. Arctic travellers never fail to be amazed by the "Barrens bursting into bloom"; one day, it seems, the land is wan and wintry, the next it is spangled with the blossoms of a myriad tiny plants.

The plants' secret is preparedness for that magic moment of new life. During the preceding summer, they have hoarded food reserves: sugars, starches and lipids. Arctic plants, though their growth, in comparison to southern regions, is sparse, are nutritious, and in fall the plant eaters of the north are sleek and fat. When winter approaches, the plants store their carbohydrate reserves in roots and rhizomes underground, or in the wintering leaves of the evergreens. They also prepare, beneath the soil or at the surface, protected by decaying vegetation, next year's buds and shoots, often in an advanced stage of development. Thus they go into winter's long sleep, ready to jump into rapid growth, drawing on their nutrient reserves the moment warmth and moisture awaken them.

Less than one percent of arctic plants are annuals, completing life's cycle from germination to the production of ripe seeds within one season. Theirs is a risky existence. One bad season in a certain region can wipe them out. The perennials play it slow but safe; their success in the Arctic is due to hardiness and adaptability, tempered by caution. Many take two and some as long as 12 years from germination to first flowering. An exceptionally harsh year is not fatal, it merely delays their growth. Their seeds, encased in tough, moisture-preserving shells can survive decades. Buried in permafrost, they can sustain the spark of life through millennia. A lemming's cache of lupine seeds, hidden an estimated 10,000 years ago, was discovered within the permafrost of the northern Yukon. Given light and soil and moisture, the seeds sprouted, after a sleep of one hundred centuries.

Many arctic plants do not bother with seeds. Others go through the motions of seed production as if it were some ancient, hallowed rite, but are so laggardly about it their seeds never ripen and mature. Such plants reproduce vegetatively: through rhizomes, subterranean stems that send up shoots at intervals; or turions, root-like runners that surface at a distance to produce a new plant. Some prefer adventitious budding. They grow bulbils, often in their leaf axils, that drop to the ground and quickly take root. And many plants take out an all-risk policy against the hazards of arctic life by reproducing both vegetatively and through seeds.

Those plants dependent upon pollination, make themselves as attractive as possible to insect visitors. Some exude a faint but seductive odor; they supply nectar to their visitors; and a few are heliotropic, a tracking mechanism keeps their flowers turned towards the sun, their petals act as parabolic reflectors and insects, easily chilled in the Arctic, seek out such blooms to bask in the warmth which can raise their body temperature by 9°F to 27°F above the ambient air temperature.

The most common pollinators in the Arctic are many species of flies; the most beautiful — the colorful and incredibly fragile-looking butterflies of the far north; the most conspicuous — the plump and hirsute bumblebees that drone ponderously from bloom to bloom. To be rotund has definite advantages in the north. Since surface area in relation to body volume is small, it is easier for a big, round animal to conserve warmth. There are many species of bumblebees in the Arctic, the further north, the hairier and plumper they become, until, in the highest Arctic, only one species persists, big, round and furry, to whom scientists have given the fitting name *Bombus hyperboreus.*

In the latter part of June, the spring thaw is in full swing at Bathurst Inlet. Meltwater rushes down the hills and across the meadows in a glistening network of runnels and rills. It can still freeze at night, and when we walk across the tundra in the morning, paper-thin ice tinkles into splinters. But winter's long reign is broken. Flowers are everywhere. Arctic poppies turn their golden heads towards the sun and sway in the wind on six-inch, deceptively frail-looking stems that bend easily and gracefully, but rarely break, even in a storm. The poppies grow fast. They are among the few arctic plants capable of rushing through life's entire cycle, from germination to flowering to ripe seeds in slightly less than a month.

Lupines cover a small plateau, their blooms sky-blue, the rosettes of their long, lanceolate leaves glittering with water droplets after a rain. Their name comes from the Latin "lupus," the wolf, since the Romans believed that lupines, wolf-like, ravished the earth. In this assumption they were unfair to both wolves and lupines. Far from despoiling the earth, lupines enrich it. Like some other plants, particularly the mountain avens, they are hosts to

nitrogen-fixing bacteria, which form nodules on their roots and busily collect and bind atmospheric nitrogen, thus fertilizing the Arctic's nitrogen-starved soil.

By late June the anemonies come into flower in our valley and under the midnight sun the brief growing season is near its peak in all the polar regions. The importance of its produce for human comfort and survival varies between regions.

The Aleuts were among the most dependent on vegetation. By arctic standards the Aleutian Islands are relatively mild. Precipitation is abundant and plant growth luxuriant. It is therefore hardly surprising that the Aleuts used plants much more extensively than the Eskimos, to eat, to heal, and to kill.

Their favorite plant is cow parsnip. The outer layer of its stalk is noxious and, when eaten, produces cankers. But peeled, the young stems taste like celery. The Aleuts used the juice of yarrow leaves to stop bleeding; the root of iris as a laxative; and poultices of aven leaves to heal a festering wound. Less kindly, they'd slip a shot of buttercup juice into an enemy's drink, in the belief he would then waste away and die. Monkshood, with cowl-shaped blooms of a deep indigo color, gave them their deadliest poison. From its roots, in secret ceremonies known to only a few initiates, they extracted aconite and smeared it on their long whaling lances made of slate. Driven into a great whale, the lance broke off in its body, and the poison killed it, usually within three days, while the hunters studied winds and currents to determine where its carcass would be washed ashore.

Siberia's Chukchi, to an even larger extent than the Aleuts, systematically collected vegetables, the edible roots, leaves or stems of vetch, sorrel, fernweed, roseroot, coltsfoot and fleabane, preserved them and ate them in winter with meat and fat. All other arctic peoples make only incidental use of the vegetable products their lands have to offer. But this use can be quite varied.

Sphagnum moss, soft and highly absorbent is used by Lapps and other arctic people as disposable diapers, and by Eskimos as wick for their sealoil lamps. Lapps cut sennegrass in summer, dry it, and stuff their reindeer skin boots with it in winter, in lieu of socks. Similarly, the

Eskimos of Greenland put dried lymegrass between inner boot of hare skin and the outer boot of sealskin. American army tries to achieve the same effect with t nylon-mesh insoles. They are not nearly as insulativ the Eskimo's lymegrass or the Lapp's sennegrass, no cheaply and easily replaced.

Eskimos in Canada and Greenland love to eat leaves and stalks of sorrel, which looks like minia rhubarb and has a tart taste. In Greenland they eat it meat or blubber, and when mosquitoes bite, they themselves with crushed sorrel leaves, to ease the s ling and the smart. Scurvy grass, that Vitamin-C rich e of scurvy-wracked arctic whalers and seamen is eate many Eskimos, usually mixed with meat and fat, a fairly acceptable tea can be brewed from the fresh le of Labrador tea. They are also used to dye sealski bright ochre color, while from arctic white heathe infusion is prepared to induce vomiting and relieve upset stomach, and dye sealskins yellow.

The Greenland Eskimos' favorite vegetable is ange They call it "kuaneq," a name derived from the N "kvan," a linguistic heritage from the Vikings who, were fond of angelica. It was a favorite plant in medi Europe: its roots, it was believed, saved the eater f poison and plague; stalks speeded digestion; and le protected from sorcery and enchantment. *Angelica changelica* is its scientific name. The pragmatic Eski just eat them because the leaves have a pleasant f taste (they are rich in Vitamin-C) and the stalks are c chy and sweet. William Baffin visited the west coa Greenland in 1612 and noted: "We found in many pl much angelica. We suppose the people eate the r thereof . . . for we have seene them have many of the their boats." And the Eskimos of East Greenland ar fond of seaweed, particularly the bluish shoot bladder-wrack, and eat it in such quantities, scien believe they obtain from it a major portion of t Vitamin-C requirement.

At Bathurst Inlet, we eat no vegetable food, with exception of some berries, casually picked in fall. central Canadian Eskimos and the Polar Eskimos are all the world's people, probably the most exclusi carnivorous. Their diet consists nearly entirely of m and fish. The vitamins they require they obtain by ea parts of seal, caribou and fish raw. Having been raise the standard western precept that, like them or not, " etables are good for you," I had some misgivings ab living on meat alone at Bathurst Inlet and took vita

ts along. I never used them, never needed them. By
g what the Eskimos ate, I remained as healthy as

July, the snow is fast disappearing. From the hills
nd our camp, we look down on the rich green sward
xtensive arctic meadows. From this distance, they
smooth and even, but they are really composed of
sands of foot-high, tousle-headed tussocks which
ists, ungallantly, call têtes de femmes. Each tussock
ists of a core of frost-heaved earth, capped with an
ating layer of decayed plant matter and a luxuriant
th of new sedges and grasses. Walking across such a
ptively even looking arctic meadow, you have your
ce of teetering from tussock to tussock, or trudging
ugh the mucky troughs that separate them. Either
od is guaranteed to tire you out in a short while.
here the meadow slopes down to a pond, it is shim-
ng with the white bolls of cottongrass. The cotton-
ses like it wet; their roots creep through the water-
red ground, their leaves and stems are a rich green,
silken heads a glowing white. Long ago, Eskimos
cted the tufts of cottongrass, and the gossamer fuzz
illow catkins, and used them as tinder, to catch the
ks produced by striking chunks of pyrite against each
r.
mid-July, the great snowdrift below our valley cliff is
ly yielding to sun and rain, and from beneath it the
of the summer's plants emerge. In years with excep-
ally cold summers, they may never emerge. They are
ared for this eventuality, and most species can re-
buried for several years without dying. When their
mer finally begins, all conditions for plant growth are
eir optimum; they have warmth, continuous daylight
ample moisture. But they must hurry. Just as their life
ns, the brief arctic summer passes its zenith. Within a
th, the first chill autumn storms will sweep over the
.

Life at our camp is quiet in July. After the long travels
and exertions of the spring caribou hunt, the people relax.
We have an ample supply of dried lean (and leathery)
caribou meat, and our nets provide us with fat char and
whitefish. The men carve or repair hunting implements.
The women scrape skins or sew. The children play
through the long bright summer nights, and then sleep
most of the day. They collect big bags of arctic white
heather, so rich in resin it burns with a hissing sputtering
flame even when wet. We boil big pots of char, and eat
and talk, and swat mosquitoes, and sleep whenever we
feel like it. Eskimos are capable of prolonged, nearly
super-human effort when the hunt requires it, and are
equally good at enjoying, totally relaxed, long periods of
indolent leisure.

To pass the time, I visit the valley each day. Arctic
ground squirrels, called "siksiks" by the Eskimos, have
their burrows in the dry river bank. They spot me from
afar, spread the alarm with loud and raucous cries, and
zip down into their burrows. Special plant communities
grow in the vicinity of the siksik holes, purple Pallas'
wallflowers and the sky-blue Jacob's ladder. They like the
well-drained, well-manured soil near the dens of foxes,
wolves and ground squirrels. Their seeds stick bur-like to
the fur of animals and are thus transported to new locations.

The snow-bed plants grow with desperate urgency.
Some are in bloom a mere fifteen days after the snow
receded. The waxy petals of snow buttercup gleam
golden in the sun. The petals have an oily substance in the
outer epidermal cells and they contain, as well, layers of
cells of pure white starch that reflect the light, and give the
petals their special, intense glow.

"...on a little island,
we found great abundance
of the herbe called scuruie (scurvy) grasse,
which we boyled in beere,
and so dranke thereof, using it
also in sallets,
with sorrel and orpen, which here
groweth in abundance;
by meanes hereof, and the blessing
of God, all our men within
eight or nine dayes space were
in perfect health."
**William Baffin, 1616,
Greenland.**

In the high Arctic some snowdrifts never melt. They are too thick, the summer too short. No plants can persist beneath this perennial blanket, but occasionally minute plants will grow right on the snow. They are tiny algae, usually encased in tough rose-red coats, and where they are numerous, they can tint an entire snow field. John Ross, sailing along the coast of Melville Bay, in north-western Greenland in 1818 saw immense snow fields that "presented an appearance both novel and interesting, being apparently stained, or covered, by some substance, which gave it a deep crimson colour." A boat was sent ashore to collect some of the red snow. It "was immediately examined by a microscope magnifying 110 times, and the substance appeared to consist of particles resembling a very minute round seed, all of them being of the same size, and of a deep red colour . . . It was the general opinion of the officers that this was a vegetable substance." As officers and men crowded around to stare at the strange red snow, it slowly turned into water the color of "muddy port wine." This part of the Greenland coast is known to this day as "Crimson Cliffs."

In August, the arctic summer draws to a close. Flower petals fade and fall. Plants are busily storing up food reserves for the next year. Ground squirrels gather supplies in their winter burrows. The birds begin to leave for the south. We travel far in late August and September, searching for caribou, fat now after pasturing all summer on the rich arctic meadows. Their meat and the tallow-like slabs of backfat will be cached to provide the Eskimos with food during the lean months of early winter, until seal hunting is possible again.

As we travel by canoe along the mainland coast, into inlets and through island groups, my Eskimo companions point out to me the former camp sites of their people. Some were used until recently, others are centuries old. They are easy to spot, oases of lush green in drabber surroundings. The Arctic is one of the few places where archaeologists commonly use aerial surveys to find pre-historic settlement sites.

Early September brings the first frost to Bathurst Inlet. Delicately-veined ice glazes the smaller ponds. The caribou begin their long migration toward the south, to the boreal forest where they will spend the winter. The Eskimo men hunt far inland. The women and children remain at the coastal camps, take captured char from the nets and collect berries on the tundra: bilberries, juicy and sweet; crowberries, glossy-black, watery and sourish; and the golden-yellow cloudberries. Barren

Ground grizzlies, nearly ready to retire to their wintering dens, shuffle across the berry patches munching contentedly; foxes take time off from chasing lemmings and feast on berries; and even the pure-white, grey-mantled glaucous gulls fly inland and gorge on berries until their immaculate plumage is daubed with blue.

The caribou move south and we follow them across a tundra aflame in the colors of fall: the scarlet of bearberry leaves; the brick-red of dwarf birch; the glimmering gold of dwarf willow; and, peeping out among the fallow grass of fall, the carmine caps of mushrooms. We walk for days, the pack dogs follow us with lolling tongues; the tundra is infinite and still. We carry no tent. At night we stretch out on beds of dry lichen and grass; a velvety black sky vaults above us, aglitter with stars. The caribou the hunters have shot are cut up and cached under rock piles on prominent ridges. Later, in winter, the Eskimos will come by dog team to pick up the vital food. On some ridges, our task is eased by finding piles of stone; perhaps centuries ago other Eskimos had used them to cache their winter supplies.

In late September, snow mantles the land and snuffs out the flamboyance of fall. All is white and very quiet; the Arctic becomes a land of solitude and silence. Most birds have gone, only the ptarmigan, the owl and the raven remain. The siksiks retire to their winter burrows, eat their hoard of food, curl up and fall into the deep, eight-months sleep of winter. The plants that knew in three brief, intense months the fullness of life are dormant. "The land is again asleep," say the Eskimos at our camp, and their thoughts turn to the sea that will soon freeze, and whose seals will give them food and life during the long months of winter.

A decaying bowhead whale b[...]
provides nutrie[...]
for a cluster of arctic flow[...]

One summer I lived for some weeks with the Naskapi Indians at Davis Inlet on the Labrador coast.

The Naskapis have always been an isolated people. The late Diamond Jenness, Canada's foremost authority on Indian tribes, felt the Naskapi were the least affected by whites, partly because the region they call home "is so rugged and inhospitable, that even today (1955) it has not been fully explored."

The widely-travelled Finnish geographer Vaino Tanner met the Naskapis, "probably the most isolated Indians in North America" at Davis Inlet in 1939, "thin, supple men, with unbelievably long legs, slim women with flashing glances . . . and shy children. From the first moment it was clear that I was meeting a fragment of mankind who had to a great extent been preserved from the influence of Europeanizing culture . . . Never before have I had so overpowering an impression that I stood face to face with people of the Stone Age . . ."

Only a few Naskapis lived then at Davis Inlet. Most of them came merely to trade and vanished again into the vast forests of the interior.

The American engineer W. B. Cabot had visited the Naskapis inland at Mistinipi Lake in 1906. "The men appeared well fed and easy . . . They had speared no less than twelve or fifteen hundred deer [caribou] in a few weeks. In such times of plenty the Indian life is peculiarly attractive . . . The people are lords over their fine country, asking little favor, ever, save that the deer may come in their time."

But later the caribou no longer came and the people died. John James Audubon, travelling in southern Labrador in 1833, had seen the beginning of disaster. "For as the Deer, the Caribou, and all other game is killed for the dollar which its skin brings in, the Indian must search in vain over the devastated country for that on which he is accustomed to feed, till, worn out by sorrow, despair and want, he either goes far from his early haunts to others, which in time will be similarly invaded, or he lies on the rocky seashore and dies.

We are often told rum kills the Indians; I think not, it is oftener the want of food, the loss of hope as he loses sight of all that was once abundant . . . Nature herself seems perishing."

Long ago, the land had been rich. Nearly a million caribou roamed across Labrador's vastness of forest and tundra. Black bears gorged on the rich fall harvest of berries, and near the coast polar bears captured salmon in crystal-clear rivers. Millions of ducks and geese nested along the innumerable lakes of tundra and taiga, and in fall, migrating Eskimo curlews arrived at the coast in

such numbers they reminded Audubon of the million-bird flocks of passenger pigeons. The curlews were so fat they were commonly called "dough birds" and so tame people could kill them with sticks.

But slowly nature perished and with her the northern Indians, dependent upon her animal wealth. A. P. Low of the Canadian Geological Survey estimated that between 1870 and 1900 half of Labrador's forest was destroyed by fire.

With it vanished the slow-growing lichen, main winter food of the caribou. Overhunted, much of their range devastated by fire, the caribou declined to a few thousand. Polar bears vanished from the Labrador coast. The Eskimo curlew is now classified as "practically extinct." When Dr. Jacques Rousseau, director of the Botanical Garden in Montreal, crossed Labrador in 1947, he found the land empty. Travelling north on the George River, Dr. Rousseau followed the starvation route of the Barren Ground Naskapi: "j'ai suivi sa lente migration vers la mort" (I followed their slow migration toward death) he wrote. He saw only 20 caribou on the entire trip. The remnant of the Barren Ground Naskapi were resettled at the mining town of Schefferville in the interior of Labrador. A group of senior social scientists, making a 10,000 mile tour of northern Canada, saw them there in 1967: ". . . the squalor of the Indian village at Schefferville was probably the worst sight on the tour," they reported.

The Naskapis of the forest region moved to Davis Inlet. They were encouraged to fish cod. Being a people of the land and the forest, they did not like it. Fishing was women's work. Man was a hunter. "In accordance with the idea that hunting is a holy occupation and that game animals are holy as well, we see how the entire aboriginal life and being of this people is held in a holy light," the American ethnologist Frank G. Speck noted in his book about the Naskapi. But the Davis Inlet Naskapi had little choice. Since the ravished land failed them, perhaps the sea could provide. They set cod traps near the off-shore islands. Once the coast of Lab-

Naskapi

rador had been among the richest fishing grounds on earth. Now the highly mechanized, efficient fishing fleets of many nations scooped up fish in millions of tons far out at sea. Fewer fish came into coastal water, and the Indians' simple inshore fishery faltered and died. The ravaged sea, too, had failed them.

Now the Naskapi eke out a living by fishing trout in summer near Davis Inlet, but in winter most of them return to the great, silent forests of Labrador to hunt caribou. A few years ago, Thomas Noah left with his family for the interior in October. It was eleven months before he showed up again at Davis Inlet. "Hunting was good," he said, when I asked him why he had stayed away so long.

With his deep-set eyes, gaunt face and whispy beard Thomas Noah looked stern and aloof, and at first I felt shy in his presence. But he was kind and generous, invited me often for meals, with that delightfully spontaneous Naskapi hospitality, and took me along on his fishing and hunting trips inland. Alone, I had been afraid of the forest. One day, I had walked far inland, skirted some lakes, crossed a small river and suddenly, with sickening abruptness, it struck me that I was lost. The forest was sombre and silent. Its very vastness awed me. It took a long time to find my way back, and I arrived late in the evening at Davis Inlet, tired and subdued.

Travelling with Noah was different. He did not fear the infinite forests. They were his home. They spoke to him with a thousand signs I could not see. He knew a story or legend about each lake and river. In the past, his people had believed that all things had spirits, or souls; the rocks, the rivers and the lakes, the animals, the trees and man. And thus they felt as one with the land, the forest, and the animals linked to them in mystic, spiritual kinship.

We camped at night on a spur of land jutting out into a lake, where the evening breeze kept the mosquitoes away. We built a small fire and boiled the trout we had caught. The wind soughed through the pines and the balsam firs near the lake. The fire crackled, and the wild, eerie laughing of the loons quavered across the black water. We ate and drank tea and smoked and talked, and after a while we were silent and stared at the glowing coals, the lake, and the great dark forest. And then Noah began to sing.

I had heard him before, during a drum dance one night in the village. He had played the great Naskapi snare drum, and sung. The rhythm was monotonous. We danced to it, hour after hour, around a fire, a strange, shuffling, jerky dance, and gradually most drifted off into the magic twilight world of trance. Now Noah sang softly, long, dirge-like chants, of caribou and hunts and of travels through infinite forests. His eyes were closed; the fire light flickered across his dark face. And the night wind moaned gently through the tall pines.

Samson Koeenagnak

Samson Koeenagnak's camp was at the narrows between Beverly and Aberdeen Lakes in the central Barrens. His tent stood near a bluff, presumably the spot from which Tyrrell looked over the lake he had discovered in 1893: ". . . we landed at a bluff point on the north shore and from it gazed over the solitary but beautiful scene . . . We were undoubtedly the first white men who had ever viewed it."

In 1966, when I went to live with Koeenagnak and his family, they were the last Eskimos on the Barrens, five people, the sole and solitary occupants of a land vaster than France. One hundred and fifty miles east of us was the village of Baker Lake, an increasingly community-centred cluster of humanity. But all around us the land rolled away to the horizon, vast and empty of all humanity. It was early summer and the tundra was magnificently alive.

Only two weeks before, the tundra had looked sombre in its mantle of last year's vegetation, all russet, brown and fallow. Now a green luster spread over the valleys, as the tender shoots of grasses and sedges sprouted. Whole acres were covered with the tiny bells of arctic white heather. On the slopes the white and gold mountain avens burst into bloom, and in marshy hollows glowed the purple flowers of Lapland rhododendron.

Snow buntings flitted across the rock ridge where they had their nests; Lap-land longspurs were busy lining their cup-shaped nests hidden in tundra tussocks with feathers and silky fox hairs, and the air was alive with the liquid lilt of the horned larks. Lemmings dug holes and homes into the spongy ground, arctic foxes were busy trying to catch them, and near their burrows in a dry esker sat the ground squirrels, sentinel-straight, and cussed all passers-by with loud and raucous voices.

At the narrows between the lakes, caribou had crossed and Eskimos had watched for them, since time immemorial. Now the caribou herds had moved north, but some stragglers remained behind and Koeenagnak spent his days stalking them. We travelled far in all directions, on foot or by canoe, and never did we see another person. But wherever we went, we saw the signs of men who had once lived on the tundra: the stone circles that had held down the lower flaps of their tents; the low stone breastwork of ambushes in the caribou's migration path; the ingeniously constructed stone fox traps.

Walking across a ridge and down to a river, we came upon an ancient alignment of inukshuks, stone men keeping guard over a land from which living men have vanished.

In August, the caribou returned. The herds were marching southward, a long, straggling, brown-grey throng that flowed past our camp for three days and four nights. Where single caribou had been wary and hard to approach, the herds showed little fear. Often the animals came to within 30 yards of our tent and the tethered dogs, intent on moving and apparently oblivious to their surroundings. Koeenagnak shot as many as we could cut up and dry on the meat racks and rocks near camp.

With his family well supplied with food, Koeenagnak set out for Baker Lake to buy ammunition, flour, tea and sugar. We crossed Aberdeen and Schultz Lakes, shot the long foaming rapids of the Thelon River, which had frightened even Tyrrell's famous Iroquois Indian canoemen, and then cruised down the great river.

On either side the tundra stretched toward the horizon, a land as vast and lonely as the sea. Immense, billowy cumulus clouds sailed across the sky, and below lay the land, green and brown in sunlight, grey and sombre in shade. From its nest on a cliff high above the river rose a rough-legged hawk and circled above Koeenagnak in his boat, its wild and mournful cry echoing the mood of the Barren Grounds.

Equipment

Man needed amazingly little equipment to survive in the Arctic.

The explorer I. I. Hayes listed, in 1861, all the possessions of the Polar Eskimo Kalutunah: "The entire cargo of his sledge consisted of parts of two bear skins, the family bedding; a half-dozen seal-skins, the family tent; two lances and two harpoons; a few substantial harpoon lines; a couple of [stone] lamps and pots; some implements and materials for repairing the sledge in the event of accident; a small sealskin bag, containing the family wardrobe [that is, the implements for repairing it, for the entire wardrobe was on their backs]; and then there was a roll of dried grass as lining for the boots; some dried moss for lamp wick; and for food they had a few small pieces of walrus meat and blubber." The whole cargo was covered with sealskins and lashed firmly to the sled with thong. These few belongings, plus ingenuity, courage, hardiness and a superb sense of self-reliance enabled a man like Kalutunah to live successfully in a land that to most explorers seemed hostile and desolate.

In 1971, one hundred and ten years after Hayes, I made the inventory, not of all the possessions of a Polar Eskimo, since they now have houses and possessions are numerous, but of things my friend Masautsiaq took along when he, his wife Sofie and I went on a hunting trip in early May. On his sled, pulled by nine strong huskies, he carried: a kayak, to retrieve seals shot from the floe edge; three rifles (an old army carbine, a .222 with scope, and a .22); a heavy-shafted walrus harpoon, the harpoon head filed from a piece of aluminum; a stout, steel-tipped pole to ram into the ice and hold a harpooned walrus or narwhal; a lighter harpoon, for seal and narwhal, its point and fittings carved of ivory, and equipped with an ivory-inlaid throwing board; several harpoon lines, of sealskin thong and nylon; a sealskin float; an ice chisel; steel hooks to catch Greenland halibut, plus several hundred yards of nylon line; a long-handled bird net to catch flying dovekies; a tent; caribou sleeping skins; a great bearded seal skin, a large tarpaulin and a sheet of plastic to cover the sled load; sealskin thong and nylon rope to lash the load; six knives; a jerry-can of coal oil; two Primus stoves plus repair kit; pliers; screw drivers; four cooking pots; an enamelled chamber pot; ammunition; a sewing kit; dried narwhal sinew as thread; dried grass to line the boots; binoculars; comic books (Donald Duck in Danish); an electric (battery-operated) razor; dental floss; two whet-stones; vitamin-B tablets; spare sealskin boots; aspirin; a bag with fur pieces to repair clothing.

Thus equipped, Masautsiaq was ready to take any animal his region offered: birds, fish, walrus, seals, narwhal or white whale. He could travel where he wished and as long as he wished. Land and sea, and his skill, supplied us with food.

The Animals

"The valleys and hillsides
for miles appeared to be moving masses of caribou.
To estimate their number would be impossible. They could only be reckoned
in acres or square miles."

**The explorer J. W. Tyrrell
on crossing the Barren Grounds
in 1893.**

Successful Eskimo Hunters . . .

A Bathurst Inlet Eskimo spreads caribou skins on the snow to let them dry. Baffin Island Eskimos pull a killed walrus to shore to cut it up and cache its meat.

Eskimos with shot caribou bull on Coats Island in Hudson Bay. From a long snare line, a Polar Eskimo removes an arctic hare.

...htning-quick,
...spite its lumbering appearance,
...odiak bear grabs
...almon ascending a rushing river.

The Arctic, Vilhjalmur Stefansson once remarked, "is lifeless, except for millions of caribou and foxes, tens of thousands of wolves and muskoxen, thousands of polar bears, millions of birds, and billions of insects."

This is true but slightly misleading. You can travel across the Arctic at certain times in certain areas for days without seeing a single animal. You could then be forgiven for assuming that the Arctic is indeed the harsh, hostile, barren land of popular fancy. Yet, by choosing a more propitious time and place, you can see, within a day, wildlife in such profusion, you may feel the Arctic is a true Eden and arrive, by extrapolation, at totally erroneous conclusions.

The famous writer and naturalist Ernest Thompson Seton visited the Barren Grounds in 1907, saw "unlimited wild herds" of caribou, did some fast figuring and decided that the caribou "may number over thirty million, and may be double that."

The weakness in his reasoning was that Seton happened to be in the midst of a major caribou migration. Had his travel route been a hundred miles further east or west, chances are he would have missed the mass of migrating caribou; he would then probably have seen only a few dozen and could have arrived, with equal logic, at the conviction that caribou were rare.

Similarly, if you go to Churchill on Hudson Bay, in October, charter a small plane and fly east and south along the coast, you may see, with a little bit of luck, 100 polar bears within an hour. Right place, right time. Make the same trip in February or in June, and you'd be lucky to see one or two bears. Right place, wrong time. Spend a year at Bathurst Inlet along the central arctic coast, and you will most probably not see a single polar bear. Wrong place, any time.

Devon Island is about twice the size of Belgium and exceedingly rugged and mountainous. If you were to land on its north coast, near Cape Sparbo, you have a good chance of seeing, within a day, some fifty muskoxen. If you go home and say: "There are lots of muskoxen at Cape Sparbo," you are right. But if you say: "There are lots of muskoxen on Devon Island," you are wrong. Aerial surveys have shown there are only about 200 muskoxen on the whole island. You just happened to land at the one spot which, for a number of environmental reasons (primarily food supply and snow depth in winter) is favored by the muskoxen.

Fur seals are among the most numerous sea mammals of the north. They number about two million. Yet few people see them. They spend the winter at sea, usually far from shore, and the summer breeding season on some of the most remote islands of the north: the Commander Islands and Robben Island off Siberia's east coast, and on the American-owned Pribilof Islands far out in the Bering Sea.

These seasonal agglomerations of some arctic animals in certain areas have led in the past to greatly exaggerated estimates of animal numbers, and to the ruthless slaughter of some animal species, once it had been found when and where they congregate.

The Arctic is a harsh and exacting environment. Only those plant and animal species adapted to its special rigors and demands can exist in the far north. And their number, compared with the number of animal species in more temperate parts of the world, is small.

Of 340 North American land mammal species, only 20 inhabit Canada's immense Northwest Territories and while the small country of Ecuador is home to 1,500 bird species, only 80 breed in the Canadian Arctic, and of these only six spend the entire year in the north. And of the world's 750,000 insect species, only 600 are found in Greenland. Yet the number of individual animals of a successfully adapted arctic species may be large, because in their chosen ecological niche they have little competition from other species.

The Arctic is a land of feast or famine, or, to put it into today's scientific jargon, a land with a brief season of "high energy input" followed by a long season of "low energy input." But the energy requirement of animals remains the same throughout the year. Thus their ability to survive that low-energy season is the most vital factor in the existence of all arctic animals.

Most arctic birds solve this problem by being temporary residents of the north. They arrive in spring and early summer, just prior to the north's peak period of food productivity, mate, raise their broods and leave for the south where food is plentiful. They partake of the north's bounty during its brief season of plenty, and wisely leave it during its long season of penury.

Caribou, too, multiply their potential food supply by migrating, and by eating different plants in summer and in winter. In spring, driven by millennial instincts, the caribou, who spent the winter in the boreal forests, begin to move north. Small groups coalesce and merge with others, even larger. As thousands of herds join, their march towards the north becomes urgent and purposeful. As an Eskimo told Knud Rasmussen, "The whole earth seems to be moving."

Winter has been hard on the caribou, and the strain of the long northward march depletes their last energy reserves. To the Eskimos at Bathurst Inlet who hunt the caribou when they reach the northern limit of the arctic mainland, the animals yield only lean meat. The caribou are weak and vulnerable. A winter-starved pregnant female, who has just completed a long migration, will "last only about half a mile before aborting or dying" when chased by a helicopter, warns an Alaskan biologist in a report.

During summer and most of autumn, the caribou spread over the tundra, to graze on sedges and grasses of the lush arctic meadows, and in fall they are sleek and strong. A large buck is padded with layers of tallow-like backfat weighing as much as 30 pounds, energy reserves for the strain of the approaching rutting season and for the lean months of winter.

In winter, the caribou return to the taiga, the northern forest, which is carpeted with a thick growth of lichen, the caribou "moss." It forms between 80 and 95 percent of their winter food. With their broad hoofs they shovel the snow aside to browse on the lichen below.

Where lichen are plentiful, each caribou digs about 50 dish-pan-sized craters through the snow to obtain the 10 to 12 pounds of lichen it requires each day. But when lichen are sparse, due to overgrazing or forest fires in the past, each caribou may have to dig 100 craters for the same essential amount of food.

Like the caribou, the muskox doubles its range through migrations. But while those of the caribou are in a north-south direction, and span, in some instances, more than a thousand miles, the muskox usually moves only a few miles between hill and valley. In summer muskoxen feed in valleys and in the plains, on grasses, sedges and, wherever available, on their favorite food, dwarf willow. When the winds of winter sweep the snow off the mountains and pack it into valleys and swales, so hard the sharp rim of the heart-shaped muskox hoof leaves only a faint imprint when an 800-pound bull walks across it, then the muskoxen move to the wind-swept hills. There the vegetation is scant but covered by only a thin layer of snow, and the muskoxen can easily reach it.

Instead of migrating like the muskox and the caribou, the Barren Ground grizzly and the arctic ground squirrel have another method of satisfying their winter energy needs. They go to sleep.

Only some 500 to 1,000 Barren Ground grizzlies are believed to inhabit the entire tundra region. Lighter colored than his southern cousins, his fur frequently a mel-low honey blond, the tundra grizzly is solitary, s tempered and shortsighted. Eskimos call him "the k bear." One charged a Canadian biologist, appare under the impression that he was a caribou, realize mistake at a distance of a few yards, veered off galloped on across the tundra, leaving behind h badly shaken scientist.

Summer is good to the grizzlies. They stuff thems with roots and grasses, eat carrion when they fin capture fat char in river shallows, root out ground s rels, and fatten up on the fall's berry harvest. By Oct they are swathed in fat three to four inches thick, ro relaxed, and content. Stefansson saw an old male Ba Ground grizzly "lying on his back, pawing the air l fat puppy." Since he considered it "the rarest of the l land carnivorae of the world," Stefansson shot it museum specimen, as well as eighteen others he during his years of arctic travel.

The bears do not hibernate. Deep in their sn covered dens, they sleep. Breathing and heartbeat down, but their body temperature remains near nor Isolated from the rigors of the arctic winter, they sub into placid dormancy, living off the fat accumulated ing the feast months of summer and fall.

The arctic ground squirrel, or "siksik" as the Esk call it in imitation of its alarm cry, is a perky, exci animal. It emerges from its burrow in spring, lean famished after eight months of hibernation. For the si summer on the tundra is lush but risky. Foxes and wo stalk it, rough-legged hawks, arctic owls and gyrfal swoop down with silent speed. In Alaska the siksik stitutes 90 percent of the golden eagle's summer food mighty Barren Ground grizzly will excavate an e burrow system with the frenzied power of a steam sh gone berserk in pursuit of a single squirrel.

Being prominently on the menu of such an arra predators makes the ground squirrel understand nervous. It leaves its protective burrow with infinite tion. A dark, twitching nose appears, the head inches bit farther, the black, slightly protuberant eyes look riedly about, and slowly, with great care, low mutter and many feigned retreats to provoke a hidden en into betraying himself, the siksik finally emerges, upright near its burrow and inspects the countryside and carefully. Scientists who have completed a time motion study of siksiks, report that they spend four percent of their active time in observation.

alanced against all these precautions, is the ground
rrel's urgent need to forage for food. The arctic sum-
is short. In four months they must raise a new genera-
of siksiks, accumulate provisions for early winter
above all, store up energy for the foodless winter
ths in the form of a thick fat layer. They eat day and
t, and carry surplus food home in bulging cheek
ches.

late fall, the ground squirrels prepare their winter
ows. Ideal locations become the objects of acrimoni-
territorial fights. The females, wooed and welcomed
ring, are now competitors. The males turn upon them
ely, chase them from their territories, and force
to hibernate in unsuitably shallow dens where their
nergy supply is not equal to energy loss. As a result
females than males die during winter. The strongest
s take the best locations: dry, sandy regions, where
permafrost layer lies well below and they can tunnel
, preferably in the lee of a hill, so a thick insulating
blanket will cover their winter home.

e sleeping chamber is thickly padded with grass,
by September an energetic siksik may have stocked it
four pounds of assorted foods. They are fat now,
, furry; they have doubled their weight since spring.
n the chill winds of late September sweep over the
, and ice glazes the tundra ponds, and a snowy
tle wraps the hills, the siksiks retire from the hostile
to their cozy chambers.

r a few weeks the squirrels nibble away at their
d food, then, as October's frost creeps through the
, they curl up on their soft beds and subsist for the
months on their fat reserves. To stretch out this
ed energy supply, they keep their body motors barely
g. They breathe only once or twice every minute;
body temperature drops from a normal 98°F to near
ing, and their heartbeat slows from more than 200
s per minute to only five or ten, and thus they hover
early eight months in that mysterious borderland
een life and death.

Like many predatory birds and wolves, the white arctic
fox prospers in times when there are plenty of lemmings
and voles and, unlike the migrants and sleepers, foxes are
year-round hunters, protected from the cold by their thick
downy fur.

Arctic foxes are dimorphic; nature produces a white
and a blue edition. For some reason, which scientists
have not yet been able to explain, arctic foxes living
mainly on sea birds (as on northwestern Greenland, the
island of Jan Mayen or the islands in the Bering Sea) are
usually a dark smoky blue while those living primarily on
lemmings are usually white.

Lemmings are cyclic animals and white fox populations wax and wane in rhythm with the lemming cycle.
Even in low lemming years, summer and fall are feast
seasons for foxes. The tundra is alive with birds; ground
squirrels, despite all their precautions, can be caught by a
patient fox, and the fall berry harvest is always abundant.
But in winter most birds have left; the vast, snow-covered
tundra is silent; lemmings and voles live in their world
apart deep below the snow. Digging them out requires a
lot of energy, not always repaid by a successful hunt.

As the snow becomes harder, and lemmings and voles
nearly impossible to reach, some of the famished foxes set
out in search of a provider. They follow wolves at a
respectful distance, hoping to inherit the remains of their

"(We frequently saw)
many herds of them (muskoxen)
in the course of a day's walk, and
some of those herds
did not contain
less than eighty or an hundred head."
**The explorer Samuel Hearne,
crossing the Barren Grounds
in 1771 - 1772.**

kills. But wolves, too, are frequently hungry in winter, left-overs tend to be scanty, and furthermore wolves are liable to look upon a fox as a potential meal. Polar bears make more promising, and less risky, hosts. When hunting is good, polar bears are fussy feeders. They strip a seal's carcass of blubber, their favorite food, and leave the rest to their retinue of foxes. Where man feeds them, the little foxes quickly become tame. Long ago, when lonely Scandinavian trappers still inhabited the northeast coast of Greenland, they often befriended the hungry little foxes in fall. They came to their huts and took meat scraps from their hands. This idyl, unfortunately, always ended on a sour note. Once the foxes were in full winter fur, the trappers killed and skinned them.

For the blue foxes living near sea bird colonies, such as the great scree slopes of northwestern Greenland where millions of dovekies nest, summer is one glorious feast. But their seasons, too, are sharply divided into one of plenty, from May to the end of August when the dovekies are there, and one of dearth, from September to April when they are not. So in summer the provident little foxes lay up stores for the winter ahead. The Danish scientist Alwin Pedersen found a foxe's cache. "It contained thirty-six little auks (dovekies), two young guillemots, and four snow-buntings, as well as a large number of little auk eggs. The frozen bodies of the birds were neatly arranged in a long row . . . and the eggs were heaped in a pile . . . The whole store would have provided food for a fox for at least a month . . ."

Although their caches are buried by snow in winter, the foxes seem to have no trouble finding them. Most of the dovekies in these caches have their heads bitten off and the Polar Eskimos who seem to have an appropriate legend concerning nearly everything, explain this with the following story: "Long ago a fox cached dovekies. But one of the birds wasn't quite dead and when fall came and it got cold, it awoke and cried: 'It is cold! Let us fly south!' Since the dovekie had returned from death, its cry had magic power, and all the cached dovekies revived and flew away, and the foxes spent a very hungry winter. Ever since, the foxes bite the heads off all dovekies they catch and cache."

If the arctic land is a land of extremes, the Arctic's second realm, the sea, is considerably less mercurial. The temperature of its waters varies little from summer to winter, and while food is more plentiful in summer, it is still quite adequate to feed millions of seals in winter, particularly the small ringed seal and the big bearded seal, the two species most specialized in spending the entire year in the far north. They made life possible for Eskimos in former days, and they are the main food of the one arctic land mammal, the polar bear, whom evolution has chosen to exploit this particular niche.

The polar bear's domain is vast: more than five million square miles of circumpolar land and ice-covered sea. He roams as far south as Moosonee, at the south tip of James Bay, nearly on the latitude of London, and when the U.S. atomic submarine "Skate" surfaced near the North Pole in 1959, a polar bear ambled over, probably to determine its food potential. I have seen polar bear tracks half-way up Newtontoppen, Spitsbergen's highest mountain, rising above its extensive icecap, and the odd polar bear has been known to cross the infinitely vaster, totally foodless icecap of Greenland.

The sly and adapta
red fox has in recent ye
moved far north into the realm of the sma
arctic f

polar bear walks
ng the edge of a tree-ringed lake
a gloomy day
early winter, in the forest region
uth of Churchill.

Such far-flung travels are exceptional. Most polar bears live in regions where an abundance of seals and favorable ice conditions promise hunting success. In such areas polar bears were in the past, before they were ruthlessly decimated by white men's guns, quite numerous. Seven Dutch whalers spent the winter 1633-1634 on Spitsbergen. A few bears visited them in November and early December. But the real rush started around Christmas, and from then until spring "the whole of the day and night we had many bears around our tent, making a . . . terrible noise by their growling." The bears went about "in troops, like the cattle in the Netherlands," and one day "we saw fourteen or sixteen bears together on the coast who were having a great fight." Three hundred and twenty-nine years later, in the summer of 1962, a group of ornithologists spending the summer in a hut on Kong Karls Land, the eastern-most island of the Spitsbergen archipelago, where polar bears are protected since it is one of their most important denning areas, sent out a frantic radio message: "Want to be taken off soonest. Surrounded by nine hungry bears. Dare not go out."

Along the Manitoba shore of Hudson Bay, where polar bears may not be hunted, Dr. Charles Jonkel and Dr. Ian Stirling of the Canadian Wildlife Service counted 126 bears along a 40-mile stretch of coastline during an aerial survey in November 1970.

Essentially, though, the polar bear is a lone wanderer. High-rumped, low-shouldered, massive and immensely powerful, he shuffles across the ice in a slow, smooth, rolling gait, testing the breeze with his large black nose. His eyesight is poor; his hearing average; but his sense of smell incredibly acute. He lives in a world of smells; each shift of the breeze brings him new messages. If the wind is from shore and tells him that muskoxen are near, he will ignore it. When faced by an enemy, the muskoxen stand shoulder to shoulder in a defensive circle, a sharp-horned array that no bear dares to breach. If it tells of caribou he is equally unmoved. Caribou are too fleet of foot. There is one smell, among all others, to which the polar bear reacts and which pulls him onward like a magnet. It is the scent, however faint, of seal.

Superbly adapted as they are to their sea environment, seals have three weaknesses. They are mammals and, at about ten minute intervals, they must surface to breathe; they must bear their young on the ice; and in spring and summer, particularly during the moulting season, they like to haul out onto the ice and sleep. On these three basic traits of their main prey rests the hunting success, and the survival, of polar bears and, in former days, of most Eskimos.

In early winter, when the sea begins to freeze over, ringed seals gnaw breathing holes through the ice. As the cold increases, they keep the holes open, vital vents to the air above, sometimes through ice five feet thick. Covered by snow, they are invisible. The Eskimo hunter finds them with the help of specially trained dogs. The polar bear is guided to them by his keen sense of smell. The Eskimo inserts a thin sliver of wood through the snow into the breathing hole below. When the seal surfaces, he will push against the stick, the motionless man above will see it move, and drive his harpoon through the snow into the seal with one smooth, powerful motion. The bear's method is to scrape the snow away from the hole, crouch down beside it and wait. When the seal surfaces, a lightning-swift swipe of the bear's paw crushes his skull; in the same instant the bear grabs his prey and hauls it out of the constricted hole. But each seal has many breathing holes, and by using those of a neighbor he further enlarges his range. It may be hours, it can be days before the seal will surface in the hole where the hunter waits. Yet the hunter persists in the bitter cold of arctic winter, motionless, in total concentration, for the seal, to Eskimo and bear, is life.

152

In spring and summer the seals like to sleep on the ice. They choose a flat place alongside a hole in the ice or open water, with a clear view all around so, they hope, no enemy can sneak up on them. And they sleep fitfully. Each minute or so, the seal awakes, looks carefully in all directions and, satisfied that all is well, goes back to sleep. It seems like a foolproof system, but it has, for the seal, two fatal flaws. The sleep period of each individual seal tends to be of the same length, nearly to the second, and the same internal alarm clock that awakens the animal at such regular intervals causes a faint, telltale muscular movement in the still sleeping animal an instant before it opens its eyes.

Bear and Eskimo synchronize their stalk towards the seal to its sleep-wake periods. The moment the seal goes to sleep, the bear creeps slowly, softly across the ice. An instant before the seal awakes, the bear freezes into a motionless, limp, yellow-whitish pile of fur. The Eskimo crouches behind a white portable shield, once made of sun-bleached sealskin but now usually a framed square of canvas, or in the Thule region of Greenland he advances on his belly pushing a tiny sled with a white sail. The seal's vision is poor. He can detect motion a long distance away, but the motionless whitish bear, the hunter hidden

behind his white screen, both, for the seal, blend with their white surroundings. Slowly, with infinite caution, Eskimo and bear advance. The bear must come to within a few yards before, in a blur of smooth, co-ordinated motion, he pounces upon the sleeping seal and with one blow breaks its skull. For the Eskimo, now with a gun, the stalk is easier. In former days he, too, had to creep to within at least ten paces of the seal for a sure throw with his harpoon.

In the northern part of their realm, most bears roam the floating pack in summer, hunting seals. But in Hudson Bay, their icy world disintegrates in summer. Seal hunting is over, for while a polar bear swims well, he is no match for a seal. The bears must come ashore and lead a life that, in some ways, may be akin to the one their remote ancestors led, hundreds of thousands of years ago, before they evolved into the Arctic's specialized hunters of seals. The "ice bears" become "shore bears." They raid duck and goose colonies, rob the nests and eat as many of the brooding birds as they can catch. They hunt voles and lemmings, even if the energy expended on catching these tiny rodents barely equals the energy gained by eating them. A meal of two-ounce lemmings must be quite a come-down for an 800-pound polar bear who, given the chance, can devour 150 pounds of seal blubber at a sitting. Mainly, though, these shore-bound bears, the world's largest carnivores, with the possible exception of Alaska's Kodiak bear, turn into herbivores. About 80 percent of their summer and fall diet consists of plants: sedges, grasses, seaweeds and, in fall, great quantities of berries.

By October they mass at capes and wait impatiently for winter, for cold, for ice to form on Hudson Bay. As soon as it is strong enough to support them, they leave the land to resume their solitary wanderings in search of seals, in darkness and in cold, on their true realm, the ice of the arctic sea.

Summer in the low and middle reaches of the Arc fairly long and relatively mild, and there is a profusi insect life. The most numerous, probably, are earth-bound species, such as the millimetre-long sp tails, more than half a million of whom may inha single square yard of arctic sward.

The most noticeable, though, are the mosqu (Alaska, alone, is home to more than 40 species) an blackflies. On warm days they surround man and be a hungry, humming cloud, dense enough, I know personal experience, to make photography diff Dionyse Settle, who visited Baffin Island with Frobisl 1577, obviously got properly stung, because he that there were "gnattes, which bite so fiercely, tha place where they bite, shortly after swelleth, and ite very sore." But the assertion of the Hudson's Bay pany manager at Fort Prince of Wales on Hudson who wrote in 1743 "they have been so thick we been obliged to shovel them away before we could at the door!" is perhaps just a trifle exaggerated.

Insects need a certain amount of warmth for their muscles to function. At 50° F mosquitoes become gish, at 45° F they are torpid, and strictly earth-bo (Antarctica, nearly always chilly, has only one mos species, and it is wingless.) In the far north, where summer temperatures tend to be low, this prese special problem to insects. Some plants, anxious to a pollinators, are heliotropic; their blooms are a turned towards the warming sun and their petals parabolic reflectors, warming insect visitors. The b flies, whose caterpillars are able to survive such mu ous winter cold, also make use of the sun. Betwee to flowers to nip nectar, they bask in the sun. In or get maximum benefit of incident solar radiation, always sit with their heads turned towards the sun, wings wide-spread. If you disturb them, they fly a distance, and settle in precisely the same, sun-ori position as before. If, during their flight a cloud obs the sun, they settle on a patch of earth in any positio re-orient themselves instantly when the sun reap "Even in copulation they maintained the dorsal ba posture, although orientation was not precise," a server noted.

These butterflies, and all other high-Arctic inse close to the ground since the temperature there, heat reflection, is considerably warmer than one yards above the ground. This, for a casual huma server, creates the impression that there is very little

the far north. The birds know better. I once watched
ow bunting family for a couple of days in the Kânâk
n of northwest Greenland, an area that had struck
s being low in insect life. But the parent buntings,
ing within a radius of about 500 yards from the nest,
ed to have no trouble finding abundant food for four
cious, fast-growing nestlings. Male and female ar-
at five to ten minute intervals, with beaks full of flies,
s, caterpillars or butterflies, and often brought the
dibly delicate and fragile-looking craneflies, with
hair-thin legs and diaphanous gossamer wings, that
ar so out of place in the rugged Arctic, yet are
erous and obviously well-adapted to the demands of
harsh environment.

mmander James Clark Ross, wintering on Boothia
nsula in 1831, placed 30 caterpillars into a box in
ember. "After being exposed to the severe winter
perature of the next three months," he related, "they
brought into a warm cabin, where in less than two
s every one of them returned to life."

aterpillars of several high-Arctic butterflies eat
nously in fall as long as temperature permits. When
weather turns chilly, they creep to exposed ridges,
lapse into winter dormancy, hidden, perhaps, under
ne, or attached to a small clump of vegetation. There
are exposed to the full fury of the icy, desiccating
er wind; the temperature, in northern Ellesmere Is-
, for example, will be below 0° F from the middle of
ober to the end of April, and during this time, for a
of about 80 days, it will be 50° F below zero and
er, right down to -70° F.

ut in late spring, these exposed ridges are the first
es to benefit from the sun's increasing warmth; they
usually safe from the threat of meltwater flooding;
here the first plants of the season begin their new
vth. Warmed, the caterpillars return from nine
ths suspended animation, and continue life as if there
never been an interruption.

he secret of their ability to survive such awesome cold
t yet solved. Scientists suspect the answer may lie in
in the caterpillar's ability to produce for the winter,

within themselves, a form of anti-freeze. They convert
glycogen, a carbohydrate akin to starches, within their
bodies to glycerol, an alcohol-type, highly freezing-
resistant substance, and reconvert it to glycogen in spring.

It is not cold arctic animals fear since nature has magnificently equipped them to withstand it, but sudden
warmth in winter. This rarely happens in arctic Canada or
Siberia, where winters tend to be cold but stable. It occurs
occasionally in Alaska and, most frequently, in Greenland and the result can be catastrophic. Warm, dry foehn
winds rushing down the mountains in winter are the curse
of west Greenland. They can send the temperature soar-
ing, in hours, from 20° F below zero to 60° F above,
meltwater gushes down the hills, and snow evaporates
rapidly in the dry air. Then the frost returns and glazes the
country; caribou suffer, (lemmings do not exist in this part
of Greenland, since sudden thaw, destroying their insulating snow blanket, would be lethal to them) and
sheep farmers can lose hundreds of animals, whose
waterlogged fleece freezes to the ground when the frost
returns, so that the animals perish either from cold or
starvation.

Winter rain hit the Thule region of northwest Greenland several times in the last years of the 19th century,
and by 1900, where caribou had once been common, not
a single one was left.

The worst famine in the hunger-haunted history of the
Netsilik Eskimos on King William Island in the Canadian
Arctic occurred in "the year when winter did not come,"
sometime in the latter part of the 19th century. These
people hunted caribou in summer, fished in fall, and
hunted seal through the ice in winter. And then, in that
terrible year, winter did not come. In fall the migrating
caribou left. The birds left. In late fall char fishing ceased.

"When one is no longer able to go hunting
How beautiful the mountains seem to be.
Brooks with their crystal clear water!
A roast on a fire of moss!
It is summer — the mosquitoes are gone!
One is happy to live!"
**Poem of an old Eskimo
hunter from "I, Nuligak",
Maurice Metayer editor.**

And winter did not come. The people ate their stock of cached caribou and char. October turned into November, and still it remained mild, and continued mild into December. Seal hunting was impossible. The people ate all the food they had left; they ate much of their leather clothing, and then they began to die, and the survivors ate the dead. In January, finally, the cold came, ice covered the sea, men could hunt again, and the ancient rhythm of arctic life, so dependent upon winter cold, resumed.

Populations of some animals flood and ebb, in long or short-term cycles, and this periodicity affects, directly or indirectly, many other animals in the interrelated and interdependent community of arctic life.

Snowshoe hares increase slowly for some years. Then their populations begin to soar, and so do those of their main predator, the lynx. The hares reach their peaks in ten-year cycles; and just as the land seems overrun by the multitude of hares, their populations abruptly drop. The lynx hunt in vain, they weaken and die. Some roam far in search of other prey and are seen in regions where lynx are usually absent.

Rock ptarmigan populations, too, wax and wane in ten-year rhythms. But the animal whose spectacular rise and decline most profoundly affects the north, is the small and usually inconspicuous lemming. In a strange way a good portion of tundra ecology is linked to the lemmings' fluctuating libido.

Some Eskimo groups call the lemming "kilang-miutak," the one who comes from the sky, assuming that when they appear suddenly in great numbers, the animals have dropped like manna from heaven, a belief which, oddly enough, they share with medieval Scandinavian peasants who called lemmings "sky mice," and regarded them as a literally heaven-sent pest.

Lemmings kept in captivity have given stunning proof of their fecundity. Females produced as many as 16 litters in a year, each with four to eight young. Their precocious daughters mated at the age of 25 days and bore their first litters 20 days later. And within another six weeks granddaughters were procreating. In the wild, winter slows them down; nevertheless, they produce, in some years, the first litter as early as March, in nests below the snow, and five or six more litters can follow in the course of spring and summer.

After a population crash one sees few signs of lemmings. There may be only one to every 10 acres. The next year, they are evidently more numerous; their runways snake beneath the tundra vegetation, and frequent piles of rice-sized droppings indicate the lemmings fare well. The third year one sees them everywhere. The fourth year, usually the peak year of their cycle, the populations explode. Now more than 150 lemmings may inhabit each acre of land and they honeycomb it with as many as 4,000 burrows. Males meet frequently and fight instantly. Males pursue females and mate after a brief but ardent courtship. Everywhere one hears the squeak and chitter of the excited, irritable, crowded animals. At such times they may spill over the land in manic migrations.

Lemmings are small but voracious. Within a year, each lemming eats about one hundred pounds of plants. "Fat, busy, agile mowing machines," the British scientist Charles Elton called them. In their legions, they can denude vast areas of tundra, and riddle it with holes and tunnels. But by digging up the soil, they loosen and aerate it, and fertilize it with their droppings and their dead, ensuring luxuriant plant growth in a future season. A good lemming year is a bad year for phalaropes. They build their nests near ponds within the protective cover of high sedges. With the sedges eaten, the phalaropes, who flew to their arctic nesting grounds all the way from the sea off Argentina may return there without raising a brood. But while the lemmings' number and voracity may, momentarily, deprive phalaropes of cover, and caribou and hares in some regions of forage, they more than make up for it by assuming the tundra's burden of death.

Cautiously, an arc
ground squirrel pee
from its burr
to make certain no ener
is ne

rp-horned and powerful,
 lead muskox bull
ds ready to defend his herd
inst any enemy.

Wolves ignore the caribou, usually their main prey, and live nearly exclusively on the abundant lemmings. Foxes cease their search for the hare's fluffy-furred leverets and fatten on the easily caught rodents. The vixen, who in poor lemming years only had three or four cubs, may now have as many as fifteen and with food abounding has no trouble raising them. The sight of lemmings scurrying across the snow in early spring, stimulates, in some mysterious way, the ovaries of the snowy owl. Instead of the normal four, she will lay as many as nine eggs. She, her mate and their downy owlets eat 60 to 80 lemmings each day. Jaegers, gulls, ravens, hawks and falcons flock to the region where lemmings are abundant and the living is easy. They no longer bother to chase birds and rob nests; while the lemmings die in legions, the other tundra animals have a holiday from death. The predators' feast begins early in spring when the lemmings leave the cover of the snow and emerge on the surface.

I travelled once with the Eskimo hunter George Hakungak in April from Bathurst Inlet inland over the tundra, and everywhere the lemmings popped out of their holes. Our dogs rushed left and right to snap up the running rodents, and the sled slued wildly as we zigzagged across the snow.

Perhaps in their thousands, the lemmings have exhausted the food supply beneath the snow. They are high-strung, individualistic animals. Crowded into adjoining and overlapping galleries of tunnels and runways, they get on each others nerves. And in the globular grass nests, the first litters of lemmings are being born.

Later, in May or June, the stress becomes intolerable. Some animals leave. Others follow. Their irritability increases. The urge to move is contagious. The trickle becomes a swarm, all moving, more or less in the same direction, but never in serried, ordered rows, as paintings often show. They are a vast, irregularly scattered host, thousands, perhaps hundreds of thousands of scurrying, rushing animals. They swim across rivers and lakes, and char and trout surface and devour them. (Trout taste "mousey" in a lemming year, complained a visitor to Labrador.) Foxes, ermines, owls and other birds of prey follow the lemmings and decimate their ranks. Yet on they go, sometimes at the rate of ten miles a day. And if they do reach the sea, which rarely happens, they may swim out, chill and drown.

Since in nature there is reason in all that happens, the apparently suicidal march of the lemmings must serve some purpose of vital importance to the animals. Not all lemmings die on these migrations and one guess is that survivors may establish colonies in new locations. But even if there are no migrations, the lemming boom will inexorably be followed by a bust. Tense and hyperactive, their adrenal glands swollen, their sex drive diminished, their bodies weakened, the lemmings die in droves. When winter comes and snow covers the land, the larder is empty.

Foxes, immensely abundant after the rich years, wander famished over the silent land. Any food attracts them; hunger overcomes caution, the Eskimos will have a rich trapping season and orders will flow into the Hudson's Bay Company stores for new motor toboggans.

The owls hunt hares and ptarmigan or fly far to the south. In 1972 they were so numerous in the vicinity of Toronto airport, a region heavily populated by mice, they became a hazard to aircraft. People who feared for the beautiful birds live-trapped them and released them far away.

The year after their population has peaked, lemmings are rare. Owls and jaegers lay fewer eggs, and may be able to raise only one or two of their young. The phalaropes breed again among the luxuriant sedges near the tundra ponds. The wolves concentrate their hunting effort on caribou.

Unlike the fox and owl populations which rise and fall in rhythm with the ebb and flood of lemming life, the wolf population is relatively stable. Wolves were numerous once, because their main prey, the caribou, was numerous: about a million caribou lived in Alaska, three million, perhaps, on the central Canadian arctic mainland, and another million in Labrador. These were maximum populations, their numbers regulated by the plant productivity of their combined summer and winter ranges.

Caribou like to do things en masse. They migrate together, mass near the forest edge in late fall, come into rut together, mate rather abruptly together, and as a result bear their calves at about the same time in spring. If during this period a late blizzard whips over the land, or freezing rain chills the newborn fawns, mortality amongst them may be extremely high. In years with favorable weather calves constitute 25 percent of the herds, in bad years less than five percent.

After a few years with high calf survival, the herds would grow beyond their optimum number. To find enough food, this greater number of animals had to roam farther in summer, and dig more energetically through the snow in winter. The range suffered from overbrowsing. The herds weakened. The wolves had easy hunting and might increase for a while until their predation and perhaps another spell of adverse weather re-established the ideal balance between caribou and plant supply.

When white men invaded the north with fire and guns, this balance was, to a large extent, destroyed.

Inevitably, the caribou declined. Where once they had been so numerous that the explorer J. W. Tyrrell said in 1893 they could "only be reckoned in acres or square miles," the harried, hungry herds were now widely and thinly dispersed. By the late 1950s, throughout most of arctic North America, only 10 percent of their former numbers survived. Famine haunted the camps of those Indians and Eskimos who over millennia had become highly specialized caribou hunters, living largely, in a few cases almost exclusively, off this one animal.

Loath to admit responsibility for this catastrophe, man looked for a culprit, and found an obvious one in that ancestral arch-villain, the wolf. In six years, between 1953 and 1959 in northern Manitoba, Saskatchewan and the Northwest Territories, more than 10,000 wolves were poisoned, as well as untold thousands of other animals who had the misfortune to eat the poisoned bait.

Yet recent research points strongly to the conclusion that not only do wolves live in balance with caribou, but the presence of predators may be vital to the health of the herds. Caribou (or reindeer) released on predator-free islands off Alaska's west coast, have prospered for some years but these years have been followed by periods of sharp decline. The herd on St. Paul Island increased rapidly and then, for some still unexplained reason, crashed. Food was plentiful and other conditions appeared favorable. One guess is that in the absence of predators, sickness had a chance to spread among the animals. On some islands, after a brief period of glory, they died out altogether.

Wolves kill primarily sick and weak animals. Caribou are fleet-footed and to run down a healthy animal would require an arduous, prolonged and not necessarily successful chase, which wolves, wisely, avoid. Over the ages, wolves have evolved hunting techniques that achieve maximum success with minimum strain and risk. They "test" their prey. In the case of moose, wolves rush at the animal to see how vigorously it will defend itself. If its health is poor, its reflexes slow, its stamina waning, they will close in for the kill. If the moose lashes out with

sharp-edged front hoofs, powerful and quick, the w quickly leave it alone and continue their search more vulnerable victim. The biologist Gordon C. H who observed wolves in Alaska, reported one "tested" 113 moose, of which it killed ten.

Wolves test caribou in similar fashion. They ar winnowers of the herds. For the most part they co trate their efforts in culling out the halt, the feeble ar infirm and thus help to maintain the health and vi the herds.

In relation to their prey, wolves are thinly sp across the land. In Alaska there are now 600,000 car 160,000 moose, 40,000 Dall sheep, hundrec thousands of hares and ground squirrels, and milli lemmings and voles, but only an estimated 5,000 wo This, presumably, is not a natural ratio since the wol Alaska are still relentlessly pursued and often gu down from low-flying aircraft. But even in former the wolves were probably widely scattered over the since pack territories tend to be as large as 1,00C more square miles. This is the private hunting domai pack, its boundaries marked by squirts of urine, neighboring wolf packs respect it and will not tres

Like the wolf, arctic hunting man of former day thinly spread over the vastness of the north. The av population density was one person to every 250 s miles. Like the wolf, the arctic hunter had to li balance with his prey.

The population density of each region, in former was a direct reflection of the number and size of animals available in that region. Bering Strait, that maritime route of marine mammals migrating to and the Arctic Ocean, was a hunter's heaven. Here, each year, passed more than a million whales and ruses, prey for any man with the skill, the courage, ar equipment to hunt them. There were large villages c shores of Bering Strait and along adjacent coastal a

There were no whales in the sea of the Netsilingm the central Canadian Arctic. Only seals, and they neither numerous nor easy to catch. A good hunter kill 50 seals a year, plus perhaps 60 caribou in su and fall. It was barely enough. There were no larg lages. The population was small, scattered, prac infanticide, declined in famine years, and increas former levels in good years.

The Polar Eskimos of northwest Greenland be isolated from the rest of mankind near the beginn the "Little Ice Age," in the 16th century. They forg

f three vital hunting aids: the bow and arrow, the
, and the fishing leister. They survived because the
they inhabited was home to some of the world's
st sea bird colonies, a virtually inexhaustible source
mmer food. In winter they harpooned seals, walrus
occasionally, narwhal. They numbered about 200
they were "discovered" by John Ross in 1818, and
ought that this was roughly their number during all
enturies they had passed in isolation. After contact
whites, numbers gradually decreased, because
died of diseases: 140 were left in 1855, 110 in
. Then the population slowly rallied, to 302 in 1950
with a rush, to 611 in 1971. This, the Polar Eskimos,
still live primarily by hunting, decided, was the
mum number the regional game supply could sup-
They now practice birth control to keep the popula-
at that, or perhaps a somewhat lower level.

white men, the Arctic was a cold, miserable, alien
with but one attraction: a wealth of animals, and
set about exploiting this wealth with ruthless
mination. The more vulnerable or valuable an ani-
the faster it was destroyed. The bulky, dim-witted,
seless and edible sea cow was discovered in the
ow seas of the Commander Islands in 1741 and
minated by 1768. A flightless cormorant which also
ited these islands, quickly suffered the same fate.
eria's sable, of whom N. Spathari, Russia's first
ssador to China, said in the 18th century: "So pro-
the animal that it is regarded as inexhaustible," was
ed to the verge of extinction. Alaska's once abun-
sea otter was saved from imminent extermination
by an international treaty in 1911. Of the muskox,
Tyrrell said as early as 1893 that it was becoming the
of "a policy of systematic slaughter in quest of the
ely robes so much in demand by the fur traders." It
aved, in the nick of time, by protective legislation in
. Walrus were so numerous and killed in such num-
n the Spitsbergen region, their bleached bones lie in

huge mounds on the island of Moffen, looking from a
distance like snowdrifts. But in ten years of recent travel
among the islands of the Spitsbergen archipelago, Thor
Larsen, Norway's foremost polar bear expert, has seen
only five walruses.

Eskimo curlews were so numerous their migration
reminded Audubon, who saw them on the Labrador coast
in 1833, of the million-bird flights of the soon-to-be-
exterminated passenger pigeon. On their 9,000 mile migration from the Arctic to Patagonia, the curlews flew the
2,500 mile stretch from Labrador to the llanos of Vene-
zuela non-stop in 48 hours. They could fly so fast, they
had few enemies, and hence little fear. They were tame,
trusting, and fat. "Dough birds," New Englanders called
them; and in some years they were killed in millions. On
the Boston markets they sold for six cents apiece. They are
now virtually extinct.

The list of these victims and near-victims of greed is
long and sad. Belated protection safeguards at present
most arctic animals from direct, exterminative killing. But
other, more insidious dangers threaten their survival.

Tanker routes, pipelines, highways, railways, all are
proposed for the north; all will have some impact on
arctic wildlife. Five hundred moose a year are killed by
the locomotive of Alaska's Anchorage-Fairbanks train,

"On the 10th of August, 1860,
the (Eskimo) curlews appeared in great numbers.
We saw one flock which may
have been a mile long and nearly as broad
. . . their notes sounded at times
like the wind whistling through the ropes
of a thousand-ton vessel
. . . Fishermen killed them by the thousands . . ."

**A. S. Packard, traveller on
the coast of Labrador, 1860.**

along its 363-mile run. The Dempster Highway from the Yukon into the Northwest Territories had barely been finished before "hunters" began gunning down caribou near the road from the comfort of their cars, often abandoning the carcasses. Gravel for road construction comes from eskers and moraines, the most important denning areas of foxes, wolves, and bears. Exploration camps attract curious or hungry polar bears. They are regarded as a menace to human life, and shot. Low-flying aircraft and helicopters scatter caribou, calves are killed, adults frequently break legs in the sudden panic; breeding birds are abruptly flushed from nests, their eggs are destroyed, or their just-hatched young die of exposure.

Some mammals, such as the narwhal, are threatened with extinction by the relentless search for rare, expensive objects to satisfy yearnings of an affluent society running out of status symbols. The demand, and the price for narwhal tusks has shot up in recent years. Narwhal are now primarily killed for their tusks.

Walrus hunting in Alaska has largely degenerated into "head hunting." Whole herds are gunned down, the heads are cut off, the carcasses are abandoned. The tusks yield the valuable ivory for Alaska's thriving tourist souvenir business. Polar bear skins now sell for $1,000 to $2,000. Oil-rich Middle East sheiks are willing to pay $20,000 to $30,000 for each pure white gyrfalcon from the high Arctic, the ultimate in status symbols. Poaching of these rare falcons is already a severe problem, polar bear poaching may soon become one.

Aleuts can no longer eat their favorite food, fur seal liver. It contains 40 to 172 parts per million of mercury, far in excess of the "safe" limit of 0.5 p.p.m. established by the U.S. Food and Drug Administration. The meat of white whales in Hudson Bay contains 0.97 p.p.m. of mercury, the liver 8.87 p.p.m., the heart 1.35 p.p.m. The Eskimos still eat them.

The chlorinated hydro-carbons of DDE, a long-lived breakdown product of DDT, cause peregrine falcons (and other now fast-vanishing birds, such as ospreys and pelicans) to lay thin-shelled eggs that do not hatch. Dr. David B. Peakall of Cornell University has stated ". . . it is estimated that there are a billion pounds of the substance [DDE] in the world ecosystem." It has been found in the fat of polar bears in the highest Arctic, and in the penguins of the Antarctic. Peregrine falcons have already become extinct in eastern and central Canada and the United States, and are even threatened in their last stronghold, the north.

Keith Hodson, a student at the University of British Columbia, worked for three summers for the Canadian Wildlife Service studying the plight of the vanishing peregrine. He concluded his scientific report with some personal impressions after visiting a peregrine aerie where, in 1966, he had watched falcons raise their young above the Mackenzie River. Now the nest "was empty and lifeless . . . As I sat there overlooking the great river flowing beneath me and the wide expanse of Arctic tundra beyond, the outline of two falcons came into vision and I heard the wailing of the old hen, a sound I had heard so often that summer at other deserted aeries, and the two birds drifted slowly off into the Arctic summer's twilight. I pondered for awhile, wondering whether this was all man's progress was going to yield him, cold stone where once there had been birth and life, low wails where once there had been loud calls of love and of anger and of feeling, and only ghost-like shadows gliding into the sunset?

"It was not only what was happening to the peregrine that bothered me so much, but that this disease of pollution which man was spreading over the face of the earth in the name of progress was slowly growing within all living things. The peregrine or the brown pelican or the loon may be the first ones to succumb, but where was it going to end if man did not realize what he was doing until it was too late?"

A male snow bun
heads h
to its brood with a b
full of inse

Migrating caribou move across the vastness of the Canadian tundra. A caribou calf sleeps, exhausted after a long march. A varying lemming in its winter coat. An arctic ground squirrel on guard for predators. The great arctic hare in the far north keeps its winter white all year long.

On right: A ptarmigan nearly fully moulted into summer plumage blends with the tundra landscape.

The rare white gyrfalcons of the far north are threatened by poachers who sell them in the Middle East.
The arctic tern, an arrow of swiftness and grace.
Threatened by chemical poisons, the peregrine falcon is already extinct in most of North America; it only survives in fair numbers in the north.

Lapp Journey

Most Lapps today are farmers and fishermen, or work in offices and industry. But some of the 30,000 Lapps who inhabit the northern sections of Norway, Sweden and Finland (another 2,000 live in the Soviet Union), remain true to their ancestral pattern of life, and since between them they own 650,000 reindeer, it is at present a by no means unprofitable pattern in meat-short Europe.

I first met Nils Aslakson Siri and his family at church in the north-Norwegian village of Kautokeino. It was Easter, and Lapps from the entire region arrived for the service and subsequent festivities by reindeer sled and motor toboggan. They were dressed in flamboyant finery. Their clothes, beautifully ornamented with multicolored ribbons, and braidwork in vivid red and yellow on a deep-blue background, brought gaiety to the stern, wintry landscape of black and white.

The clothes reflected the flair and pride of the Lapps, as well as their practicality and their ability to absorb and adapt outside influences. The ankle-high boots of reindeer skin were of ancient Lapp design: warm, light and, with their turned-up points perfectly shaped for slipping quickly in and out of the Lapp-style ski binding. The soles were made of two sections of the tough, short-haired skin from reindeer heads, one section with the hair facing forward, the other backward. The hairs dig into the snow whether one walks uphill or down; on such skid-proof soles the Lapp can run sure-footed over the hard-packed, slippery snow of the fells. The hip-long, stiff-collared coat was of medieval European design, and ornamented to suit the Lapp's love for brilliant colors. The broad belt, studded with metal disks, was of even more ancient vintage, a heritage from the days of the Vikings.

Nils had agreed to take me along on the spring migration. Nearly all Lapps are bilingual, speaking one of the more than 50 dialects of the Lapp language, plus the language of the country they inhabit. Nils was quadrilingual, fluent in Lapp, Norwegian, Finnish and Swedish, plus a smattering of German and English, useful in his summer trading with tourists.

Now, in his spacious winter home a few miles from Kautokeino, he repeated in a mixture of all these languages the one point he wanted to make crystal clear from the outset: the trek to the coast would be long, cold and arduous, and no allowance could be made for any weakness on my part. "If we camp too early because you are tired or cold, the reindeer will move on and scatter," he explained.

Nils and his brother Per had spent days rounding up their combined herds. The reindeer were restless. It was time to move. The sleds were packed, the draft reindeer harnessed, and we left the valley, a long caravan of 14 sleds, and travelled upward through the birch forest in the blue-grey light of the northern spring night.

Flurries of snow eddied over the vast treeless vidda, the rolling inland plateau, an infinity of snow-covered moorland and fell. In the distance we could see the herd, a dark, amorphous blob moving slowly over an endless plain of white; 1,700 reindeer on their way to the summer pasture.

Nils and Per followed the herd on skis. Whenever some reindeer broke away from the main group, to browse or to wander off into another direction, they dispatched their superbly trained dogs, mixed-breed Pomeranians, who streaked off with intelligent enthusiasm, nipped at stragglers and returned strays to the fold, yet careful not to panic and scatter the main herd.

We lived by the whim of the herd. As long as the urge to move was upon them, any attempt to halt the reindeer was doomed to failure. The animals browsed restlessly and distractedly, the herd began to scatter, a few reindeer began to drift northwest, others fell in and the great march to the coast continued. Only when the urge had spent itself, and the reindeer were tired and hungry, did the herd settle down to feed and rest.

We unharnessed and released t draft reindeer. Nils unloaded the 12-foot tall tent poles, three forkec the end to fit into each other at the the others leaning against them to a wide circle.

We pulled the canvas over the cal "kota," leaving open a smoke at the top. Anna Christina, Nils' w spread a layer of birch branches to our reindeer sleeping skins off the The children dug dwarf willow an birch out from underneath the snc and Nils lit the fire in the centre of tent, using rolls of dry, hot-burning birch bark, taken along from Kaut keino, as kindling. The green, snc crusted brush sputtered and sizzle acrid smoke filled the tent, and we low on the pelts until the flames le up and the heat whisked the smok upwards out of the vent. Sacks wi possessions were carried in and la against the tent wall. Nils hung the cauldron from a chain above the f Anna Christina made dough and b a flat, pancake-like loaf of unleave bread in the big pot. The baby, wr in down-soft fawn fur and securel lashed into its "komsa," the cradl made of a split and hollowed out trunk, looked in fascination at the ing flames. Nils lugged in a large of dried reindeer meat and cut off ample slices for everyone, carving meat with his "buiko," the traditic Lapp dagger with a broad and slig upcurved blade.

Anna Christina ground coffee b and threw a generous portion into bubbling pot, blackened by the fir many past treks. We ate the cold meat and later when we were not so hungry, we roasted slivers impa on a pointed stick at the fire, dran coffee, and talked of reindeer. Wc they stay? How close were the co calving? One of the draft animals limping. Another one would have place it. How would the snow be children, full with food, yawned, up on the pelts and Anna Christin vered them with blankets and skir Nils pulled on his mittens and slip out of the tent to look after the he and Per slept little during the mor long trek. Anna fed the baby, cha its diapers, and pulled it next to h under the skins. The embers glow softly. The wind picked up, and moaned around the tent. Snow, a as dust, filtered in through cracks chinks and sprinkled the fur-cove figures with white frosting. Slowly fire died, and we slept.

he morning it stormed. The can-
llowed and clattered. The poles
ed and the tent swayed in the vic-
usts. I peeked out of the tent flap
whirling world of white. "Don't
t," Anna Christina warned. You'll
st." How about Nils, I asked.
Christina smiled. "He is with the
He doesn't get lost!" Nils ap-
d after some hours, a snowman on
He brushed himself off, ate a great
of meat, filled his beautiful
en mug, carved from a birch burl,
dozen times with strong coffee,
ll asleep nearly instantly after-
, the deep, heavy sleep of exhaus-
his first sleep in more than 50

er the storm, the temperature sud-
rose. Although we travelled
y at night when frost crusted the
the surface softened and even the
er whose splayed hoofs act as
shoes, began to break through the
y snow. It became foggy. Our
of reindeer-drawn sleds crept
gh the skim-milk bluish haze like a
al procession. Somewhere ahead,
eat herd was heading for the
The weather and the reindeer.
lked of little else.
e weather was usually bad. These
the erratic, capricious days of
g, icy, blinding snow storms fol-
l by equally evil soft soggy
her. But when the wind died down,
became cold and clear, it was
b: the sky aflame with the rays of
sing sun, the snowy dells a deep
, the hilltops tinted in nacre and
Ahead, the great herd travelled
he hills, bunching, scattering,
scing, the cows large with calf in
an, moving swiftly, urgently to-
s the coast.
hen we reached the coastal moun-
ange, Per remained with the herd
e inland fells, while Nils took the
es and sleds down into a valley,
r from a mountain road, where
would camp until he came to pick
up with a hired truck. He had
d, with considerable reluctance, to
e come along on the last and most
ult part of the drive, through moun-
alleys and over rugged passes
to the coast. I would be given a
eer, sled and provisions, to follow
st I could.

Driving a reindeer is not really that difficult. It is a herd animal, and will try to keep up with the herd. It runs willingly and tirelessly at a steady trot. "I have never been able to make a deer go slow — they never walk unless very tired," wrote the American Paul Du Chaillu who travelled in Lapland in the 1880s. The single rein, attached to a halter, is used to pull the animal's head either towards the left or right, and it will then perforce move in the desired direction. It does not obey shout or command, and if the driver falls off the sled, the reindeer's only reaction is to run all the faster, and neither calls nor curses will stop it. The surest means to avoid such a parting, and a long walk, is to tie the rein securely to one's wrist. If one falls off the sled, the dragged body of the driver acts as an effective break.

Nils and Per drove the herd towards the mountains. The reindeer were restless and skittish. Per skied ahead, leading a tame reindeer, enticing the herd to follow in the right direction. His dog guarded one flank of the herd, Nils and his dog the other, and I brought up the rear, shooing on the occasional laggard. The herd poured up a broad valley.

Side valleys beckoned. Again and again, groups of fifty or a hundred reindeer would suddenly break away from the main herd to head towards a branch valley, and Nils and the dogs raced to head them off. The night passed, and the day. It started to snow and blow. Per and Nils tried to contain the herd in a wide, open area of the valley. It didn't work. The reindeer browsed on fallow grass and lichen, began to spread, small groups suddenly bolted and vanished into the driving snow. The herd began to scatter in the snow storm, high in the mountains. This was the nightmare of Lapp life. Those 1,700 reindeer now rapidly disappearing into the white whirling snow were Nils' and Per's total wealth. Per took charge of what remained of the main herd and drove it on. Nils set out in search of strays. I huddled on the sled, blinded by the

wind-driven snow, hoping my reindeer knew where to go. It didn't. It walked absent-mindedly over the edge of a cliff. Fortunately it was a small cliff and the snow beneath it was soft. Nothing happened to the reindeer or me. Only the sled was knocked askew.

The storm dwindled to flurries. The herd was tired, and willing to rest. Per vanished into the mountains to look for lost animals. I dozed on the sled. Nils and Per returned in the morning, driving groups of reindeer back to the herd. The commotion of their arrival infected the main herd. The animals were restless again. The drive continued and day passed into night. Nils was gone again. About 200 animals were still missing. The valley narrowed and rose steeply. The snow was deep and soft. The reindeer broke through to their bellies, and labored up in awkward, humped jumps. The sled runners cut through the snow and the sled was stuck. When I jumped off, I was hip-deep in snow. The reindeer jerked forward, dragging me and the sled along. The herd moved slowly, no longer bunched, but strung out in long straggling file.

Nils caught up with us, driving 150 reindeer. He had found them in another valley. Fifty animals were still missing. There was no more time to search for them. The reindeer were tired now, less fidgety and more inclined to follow Per, the leader, with his reindeer. We reached the pass. The snow was thin, the going easy. The herd bunched again. Ahead was the sea. We plunged down, Per moving fast, Nils and the dogs urging on the herd.

The light northern night merged into another day. Everything became dreamlike and vague; I dozed on the sled. Falling off and being dragged through the

snow, perked me up from time to time. Per and Nils showed little sign of fatigue. The herd moved down through the forest. The sun came out; it was warm and the air fragrant with the smell of moist earth, and birch and spring. The corral was on a plateau near the sea. The reindeer were very tired now, docile, the great driving urge spent. They meekly followed Per and his reindeer into the great enclosure. Nils returned to the mountains to look for the lost reindeer. Per and I began to inspect and repair the corral fence. Per went to fetch some wire and I lay down on a dry grassy stretch to rest a bit. It was night when I woke up. Per had thrown a reindeer skin over me to keep me warm. He was still repairing the fence. Nils returned the next day with 40 of the missing reindeer.

After a few days of rest, the reindeer were herded into the sea, to swim to a nearby island, the ancestral summering place of reindeer belonging to Nils' family. The spring tide of animals and men had run its course.

They would ebb back to the fells and to the forests in fall, and the great annual migration cycle of reindeer and Lapp would be complete.

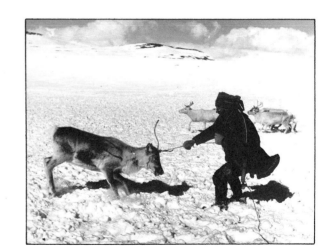

We tend to think of cold as inimical to life. This is the subjective view of an animal species whom nature originally designed for a warm climate. A naked human begins to loose heat at about 80° F; shivers and suffers severe energy loss at 40° F; and dies in about 10 minutes at 40° F below zero.

The body temperature of warm-blooded arctic animals is about 100° F (100.8° F in a polar bear, 101.2° F in a muskox). They can tolerate very little fluctuation in this temperature. Yet an arctic fox feels quite cozy at 40° F below, and so, incidentally, does an Eskimo wearing a fox fur parka.

Warm-blooded animals generate heat as a by-product of the process of converting food into energy. Heat is lost to the environment. In cold weather, naked man dissipates heat much faster than his body can generate it. The fox is wrapped in dense wool, covered by long guard hairs; hair cells are filled with air, and the total forms such a perfect insulating mantle around the fox that the heat his small body creates remains where it does the fox most good, right next to his skin.

Nature has helped arctic animals to adapt to winter cold by giving them decreased heat dissipating body surfaces and superb insulation.

Most arctic animals tend to be compact, and they usually have short appendages. The lemming is chubby, thick-furred, with tiny rounded ears and a mere snippet of a tail. The muskox is stocky and bulky, short-legged, short-eared and short-tailed. The foxes of hot lands, the kit fox of the southwestern United States or the fennec of North Africa, have huge, elongated, thinly-furred ears to assist in the dissipation of body heat; the arctic fox has small, rounded, densely-furred ears to avoid heat loss. Foxes, wolves and huskies have long tails, but they are thick-furred and bushy and serve as handy, portable blankets. In cold weather, a husky curls into a tight ball, legs tucked under his body, tail covering face and head, fur fluffed out, and sleeps blissfully even if it is 40° F below zero. But when they pull a sled on a warm spring day, huskies must cope with the opposite problem: excess heat. They run along with lolling tongues, and frequently scoop up gobs of snow, partly because they are thirsty, but also to cool their bodies.

Adult muskoxen are wrapped in a fur coat so thick, it renders them virtually impervious to the Arctic's worst winter weather, even the deadly combination of great cold and high winds.

Beneath an immense cloak of coarse guard hairs hanging nearly to the ground, the muskox carries a thick, dense layer of silky-soft wool, called qiviut by the Eskimos. In winter the muskoxen move to the windswept hills where they must endure the full fury of arctic storms, "a roaring, hissing, suffocating Niagara of snow," as Peary described it. In such a blizzard, the muskoxen stand in triangular formation, facing the storm, the lead bull at the apex and near it the herd's most powerful animals, while within this furry rampart the calves find shelter. Thus they stand, stolid, for however long the storm lasts, sometimes for days.

Insulation

The caribou has only a single fur layer of fairly short hairs. It lacks the downy underwool that protects musk-oxen, hares, foxes, and polar bears. Yet it is able to withstand searing cold and wind, and so is an Eskimo dressed in clothes made of caribou fur.

Caribou fur is one of the miracles of nature's design. Each hair contains numerous air-filled cells. The hairs are club-shaped, thicker at their tips than at the base. While the tips touch, there are tiny air spaces between them and the skin; the caribou is thus surrounded by a layer of warm air that cannot escape and since still air is virtually a non-conductor and offers near-perfect insulation, the caribou in its light, short coat remains warm no matter how cold it gets.

Sea mammals do not suffer fatal heat loss in the frigid sea because they are sheathed in blubber, an excellent insulator, varying in thickness from two inches on the small seals to two feet on a bowhead whale. The blubber is both insulation and energy reserve. Grey whales, for instance, after months of copious feeding in the northern seas, make a migration of nearly 5,000 miles to Baja California, eating little or not at all. The energy expended on such an enormous voyage must be fantastic; it is primarily provided by the whale's blubber which it converts into energy.

Seals and walruses periodically haul out on land, and have a dual heating problem: they must stay warm in the icy water, and not stew in their body-generated heat when they lie on land. They have a dense network of blood vessels leading through the blubber to the skin. In water, this vascular system is constricted; just enough blood passes through it to keep the skin healthy, and the seal is warm within its blubber blanket. On land, the blood vessels dilate, blood courses through and just underneath the skin, is cooled by the air, and flows inward to cool the seal's body.

Walruses, normally madder-brown, after long immersion in the frigid sea assume a peculiar bluish-white color.

When they lie on a beach, blood begins to pulse through their skin, and they gradually turn russet, brick-red or piggy-pink. If they are still hot, they may hold their two-foot long flippers in the air, to assist in cooling their massive bodies.

Two sea mammals have opted for a different kind of protection. To keep warm the northern fur seal and the sea otter rely on fur coats so dense that no water can penetrate to their skins. Some patient scientist has figured out that each sea otter is covered by 800 million fur fibres. Though technically a land mammal, the sea otter is really a sea mammal in the making. The female comes ashore to give birth to its young, but sea otters walk awkwardly and hunchbacked on land, and seem to feel happy only at sea. They are fussy with their fur and preen and clean it frequently. Soiled or matted fur, they know instinctively, loses its ability to hold an insulating air layer next to the skin.

The fur seal, with 300,000 hairs of a downy underwool to the square inch, covered by a coat of glossy guard hairs is equally well protected from the chill waters of the northern seas.

For its small, easily chilled denizens nature in the north provides a different, highly insulating blanket: snow. The temperature beneath two feet of snow on an icy arctic day may be 40° or even 50° F warmer than the temperature above it. Under the snow lemmings and voles spend the winter in the darkened world of their nests and runways, comparatively secure from their enemies — the owl, the fox, the wolf and the cold.

In the fall, before the snow comes, as the nights get longer and colder, the small mammals suffer. They moult into winter fur, but a sudden rain followed by frost can diminish, fatally, the insulation provided by their fur and by their nests. Both become wet, and heat-energy is drained from the rodents' tiny bodies faster than they can replenish it through metabolism. One sometimes finds them thus on the frozen fall tundra, tightly curled up, in a last desperate, pathetic attempt to reduce body surface and heat loss; dead, life and heat sucked out of them by the chill, sapping wind of approaching winter. In an Eskimo poem, a little lemming looks up at the icy, glittering sky and says:
"The sky's round belly
Is clear without clouds.
It is cold, and I am shivering;
A—aye!"

The People

''These people are in nature verye subtil, and sharp witted
. . . they delight in Musicke above all measure . . . they liue in caues of the Earth,
and hunte for their dinners . . . even as the Beare . . .''

**George Best, 1578,
description of Baffin Island
Eskimos.**

Overleaf: Tug-of-war players
string out on Baker Lake,
west of Hudson Bay.

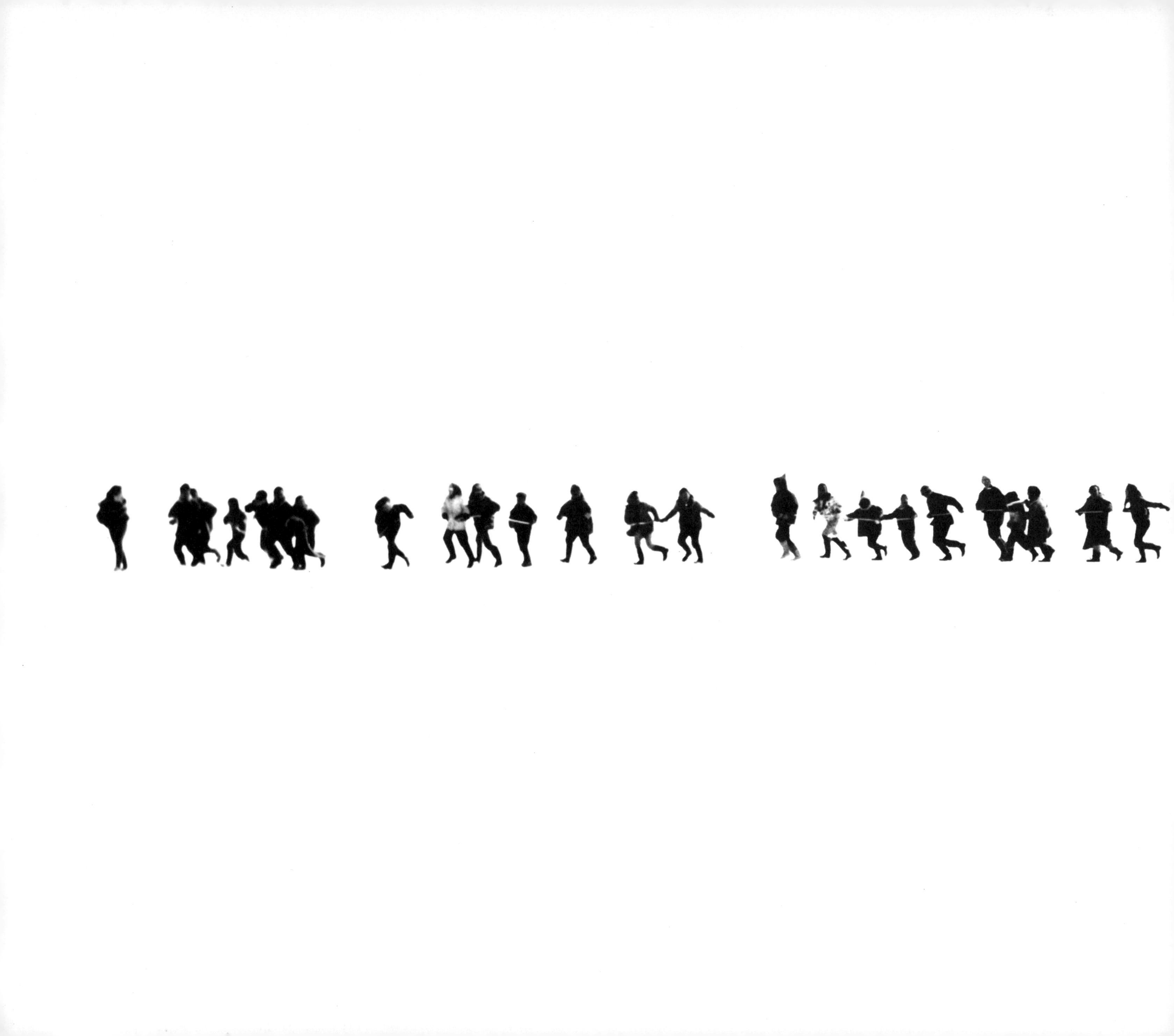

ped by family and friends,
olar Eskimo
ns the massive carcass
a walrus.

Man did not come to the Arctic. The Arctic came to man. As the descendant of warm-weather anthropoids, man, the "naked ape," was, physically, singularly unsuited for life in a cold climate. Populations were small, the world still infinitely big, and the chill and remote north exerted no allure.

But then the Arctic came south. After the long and relatively mild last interglacial period of the Pleistocene, cold and precipitation increased, glaciers began to form in the north and on mountains, grew in extent, merged into ice sheets, and, about 80,000 years ago, began to creep southward towards the haunts of man.

Early man, warm-blooded and as vulnerable to cold as are his modern descendants, faced the advancing glaciers by developing a cold-adapted culture. He learned to live and hunt in cold weather, and to use the pelts of cold-adapted animals to protect his easily-chilled naked body. And over millennia a few human groups developed some physical adaptations that help them to cope with cold.

Aborigines in central Australia, where days are hot and nights cold, sleep naked at an average nighttime temperature of 39° F. They keep warm in a manner similar to the one nature has evolved to keep seals warm in icy water. Blood vessels in their skin constrict. Their "shell" becomes chilly, but the vital core remains warm. The now nearly extinct Alacaluf Indians of cold and windy subantarctic Tierra del Fuego, and the arctic Eskimos keep comfortable through metabolic adaptation. When their bodies become cold, an internal thermostat increases

heat production. The metabolic rate of Alacaluf Indians is 160 percent higher at night than that of Europeans. Eskimos, too, have a higher metabolic rate than whites, and at night it will increase or decrease according to the requirements of the sleeper. Increased metabolism requires increased fuel and it is perhaps for this reason that Eskimos are able to digest and assimilate fat better than most Europeans can. Often at night, shivering and icy-footed in my double eiderdown sleeping bag (the heat production of a resting white person is roughly equivalent to that of a 100 watt lamp) have I looked with amazement and envy at Eskimo friends sleeping soundly and apparently warmly next to me in thin, kapok-filled bags or under a blanket or two, occasionally with a naked hand or foot sticking out from underneath the protective covers.

Such physical adaptations, while helpful, did not enable man to survive arctic cold; the invention of skilfully tailored fur clothes did.

The winter clothes of all far-north peoples, from Lapland through Siberia to arctic America and Greenland, although varying in appearance, are essentially of the same design and based upon the same principle. An Eskimo's winter suit consists of an inner parka, worn with the fur against the skin and an outer parka, worn hair outside. Both are tight at neck and shoulders, preventing warm air from escaping upwards. Attached hoods with ruffs of wolverine or wolf fur protect head and face. The pants are spacious, and tied at the waist, to keep warm air in. Footwear is usually double-layered: a sock of short-haired caribou skin, or downy hare fur, an intermediate layer of dried, and frequently replaced, grass, and an outer boot of durable sealskin. Parkas were made of caribou skins, or of bird or fox skins in areas without caribou such as the Belcher Islands in Hudson Bay, or the Thule region of northwestern Greenland.

The pants were of polar bear fur, strong and extremely warm, or of caribou fur. In the Eurasian north, reindeer skins were used.

This clothing is light. A complete Eskimo winter outfit weighs about ten pounds. Similar clothes made with southern materials weigh about three times that much, and are not as warm. The Eskimos' clothing is loose. When a man stands, warm air remains imprisoned near his body. When he runs, the clothing flaps, air circulates, he is cooled and does not sweat. Sweat-moistened clothes lose much of their insulating ability. "In this well-ventilated costume the [Eskimo] man will sleep upon his sledge with the atmosphere 93° below our freezing point," the explorer Elisha Kent Kane noted in 1853. Siberia's Yakuts, similarly dressed, can sleep at 70° F below zero in a lean-to. And a Lapp, sheathed in reindeer furs, is nearly impervious to the icy winds that sweep over the fells of his homeland.

To make the magnificent and ingenious fur clothes that enabled him to live in an arctic climate, man had to, first of all, invent the needle and learn how to make thread. Europe and adjacent regions to the east, was inhabited by Neanderthal man at the beginning of the last ice age and for much of its duration. He was small (average height about five feet), squat and powerful, big-brained and a skilful hunter but, despite the severe cold, probably poorly dressed because he (and his wife) did not know how to sew. No Neanderthal-made needles have been found. He probably wrapped himself in furs, using stone splinters as awls to make holes for lashings. At home, often a cave entrance, he was reasonably warm since he knew how to make fire.

Somewhere in that dim past, man had learnt that if you strike flint against flint, or flint against pyrite, catch the resulting sparks on a suitably inflammable material and blow, you obtain fire.

Arctic man used variations of this method for thousands of years. It was crude perhaps but effective. Using chunks of pyrite and cottongrass balls as tinder, Ekalun of Bathurst Inlet with whom I lived for many months, could produce fire in one or two minutes. A bow drill, which produces fire by friction, took longer, usually five to ten minutes. "I'm out of practice," said Ekalun. In his youth, before the advent of white men and matches, he could do it much faster. Either of these methods, one dating back to the dawn of man, gave the peoples of the north fire whenever they needed it.

It is almost certain that Neanderthal man did not have the bow drill, since he had not invented the bow. Nor did his immediate successor, Cro-Magnon man, who, in a manner yet unknown about 35,000 years ago eased the Neanderthalers off pre-history's stage. But then in a burst of creativity that probably spanned several thousand years man invented the harpoon, the spear-thrower, the oil lamp, the antler-bender, the fish trap, the fishing gorget and its improvement, the fish hook, the fishing leister, the eyed needle.

The harpoon, from the simple barbed harpoon of paleolithic hunters to its most ingenious refinement, the toggle harpoon of today's Eskimos, enabled man to exploit the immense sea mammal wealth of the north. It was the most essential tool of arctic hunting man. Without it, most Eskimos, Aleuts, and the sea mammal hunting tribes of Siberia could not have survived. A skilled hunter can throw a harpoon or spear accurately to a distance of about 20 feet. The spear thrower or throwing board, employing the principle of the lever, more than doubled the power of a man's arm. Polar Eskimo hunters who still use the throwing board, can hurtle a harpoon with high speed and deadly accuracy at a whale or seal surfacing 45 feet away. The throwing board, these Eskimos say, roughly trebles their chance of hunting success. In the past, for arctic man, this often meant a trebled chance of survival.

In the flickering light of oil lamps, paleolithic man painted magnificent animal pictures full of magic meaning on walls and ceilings in the deepest recesses of remote caves. Arctic man used the lamps to cook his meals, heat his home, and give him light during the long dark days of winter. Living primarily, in the case of some Eskimos, exclusively on meat and fat, arctic man ate much of his food raw, thereby obtaining life-sustaining vitamins. What he did not eat raw he boiled. "Boiled foods are more digestible than fried foods, and the juice gives you vitamins, minerals and needed water," advises a U.S. Navy polar survival manual in scientific acknowledgement of what, for eons, has been a basic tenet of native arctic cuisine. "They eate their meate all rawe . . . or parboyled with bloud and a little water, whiche they drinke," wrote Dionyse Settle of Baffin Island Eskimos in 1577.

When archaeologists began to unearth the posses of paleolithic man, they frequently discovered a puz stick-like instrument of antler or bone with a hole pie in it. Simple in Aurignacian times 35,000 to 27,000 before the present, these implements were often nificently ornamented by people of the subsec Magdalenian period and scientists, assuming them pre-historic versions of the swagger stick or mars baton, bestowed upon them the somewhat grandiloc name "bâtons de commandement." Any Caribou Es would have been mildly amused about this inte tation. He and his ancestors as well as other pe throughout the Arctic, had used this implement to str ten antler pieces softened in hot water.

Fish were abundant in the north. Several lake systems in the Canadian Arctic now give 100,000-p sustained-yield catches of char to commercial Es fishermen, and fishing in the lakes and rivers and the coasts of Siberia and Alaska is as rich if not ri Most arctic people were keen and patient fisher Some (among them the Eskimos at Bathurst Inlet) ingenious fish traps plaited from dwarf willow bran identical in design to fish traps used 15,000 years a Denmark, and still used in many parts of Europe t "They are known also from tomb-paintings of the tian Old Kingdom," writes Jacquetta Hawkes i superb book on the prehistory of man. Hooks were by most arctic peoples, usually barbed, and occasio barbless.

Because paleolithic man's hooks are usually bart archaeologists classify them as primitive. However nologist Diamond Jenness learned there was a reason for barbless hooks as well as a special techr for hauling in a fish. Jenness found out that the Es used his wrists, rotating them alternately against the so that the strain remained constant. A barb was not unnecessary, but a disadvantage, because, in jiggi fish is caught in the lip where the flesh is tender, barbed hook often tears loose where a barbless holds firm.

The leister, the trident-like fishing spear whose c prong impales while the notched or barbed fle side-prongs hold the prey, dates back to the Magdale period. Perfect in its initial conception, it has rema unchanged in twenty centuries.

An Eskimo bride's trousseau, Jenness noted, cons of four things: her ulu, the crescent-shaped won

, her sewing kit, a lamp and a cooking pot, and the latter items were not obligatory. Her groom might ~ly them. But a sewing kit she had to have; it was her : cherished and frequently used possession. The ~ Eskimos placed on needles, made of ivory or the wing bones of gulls and geese, can be judged from ovingly carved, beautifully ornamented tube-like ~ in which these treasures were preserved. Peter chen, a Dane who lived among Greenland Eskimos narried one said, "An Eskimo's wife is a necessity. If an loses his wife, he is immediately destitute." A ~l Eskimo seamstress could, with one look, take the ~sure of her man, cut the skins according to ancient ~stral patterns handed down from mother to daughter ~gh centuries upon centuries, and sew them into a ~with thread made of caribou or narwhal sinew, her ~es closely spaced.

~was such clothes that enabled the man to hunt ~essfully in cold weather, to sit on a snow block and ~r fish in a violent winter gale. And clothing based on ~ar principles and probably sewn with the same ~rtise with nearly identical bone or ivory needles kept ~lithic hunter warm as he stalked caribou or mam-~ across the icy winter tundra of Germany.

~us, about 20,000 years ago, or longer, the essential ~al of the arctic hunter was complete. Little was, or ~o be, added for survival in the far north. There would ~nprovements and refinements. The Eskimos would ~t that masterpiece of arctic architecture, the igloo. ~lomestication of the dog in mesolithic times and the ~tion of the sled would help man to travel farther and ~. Kayaks and similar skin, plank, or bark boats would ~him mastery over the coastal sea and enhance his ~ing success in summer.

~ man culturally adapted to cope with cold, the ice age was no disaster. It brought to central Europe an abundance of game animals. The ibex came down from the glacier-covered mountains, and the marmot whistled on the plains. Mighty mammoths stomped over the tundra, from France to Siberia and Alaska, and great herds of muskoxen and reindeer roamed as far south as the Danube, which was not blue then, but a turbid, silt-laden glacier stream. Arctic seals basked on the shores of the Bay of Biscay and the shaggy-coated woolly rhinoceros, one horn nearly four feet long, the second somewhat shorter, browsed on the lush vegetation of marshy regions (medieval man finding these horns thought they were the talons of the mythical griffin). Most important was the reindeer. Just as the herds of caribou, once millions strong, on North America's tundra and taiga provided inland Eskimos with nearly all the food they needed, so for nearly 10,000 years, from the Upper Périgordian to the end of the Magdalenian period did reindeer supply ice age man with 90 percent of his meat.

When the ice began its retreat, the reindeer moved northward and reindeer hunters followed. They waylaid the reindeer at river and lake crossings; they shot them with bow and arrow, once these implements had been invented in mesolithic times; and they drove them into defiles where hidden hunters speared the massed animals. An extension of the latter method, invented in extremely remote times, is to build a pound, a man-made

"Glorious it is to see
The caribou flocking down from the forests
And beginning
Their wandering to the north.
Timidly they watch
For the pitfalls of man.
Glorious it is to see
The great herds from the forests
Spreading out over a plain of white.
Glorious to see."

Eskimo poem; translated by Knud Rasmussen.

enclosure into which animals are driven. Giant pounds, called kheddas, are used in India to this day to capture wild elephants. North American Indians, from Labrador to Alaska, built pounds to capture caribou.

Samuel Hearne saw an Indian-built caribou pound in 1771 near the treeline in the region of the upper Dubawnt River. The pound consisted of a circular brush fence, about a mile in circumference with a narrow opening facing the caribou's normal line of approach. Outside the pound the Indians set out two long rows of brush clumps and brushy poles which formed two sides of an acute angle converging at the pound entrance. When caribou approached, they were driven toward the pound by the Indian women and children acting as beaters. Then, herded between the rows of poles and brush clumps which they mistook for more people, the timid caribou funnelled through the entrance and were caught in snares and killed by spearing or shooting with arrows.

In Hearne's diary for March 2-3, 1771, he observes, "This method of hunting is so successful that many families of Northern Indians subsist by it all winter."

In the remote northeast region of Alaska, the Loucheux Indians used such caribou pounds until the 1890s.

Pounds were used by the Eurasian reindeer hunters. But they went one vital step further. Instead of killing all the captured animals, they kept a few, tamed them and used them on subsequent drives as decoys to lure their wild brethren into the fatal enclosure. The idea caught on and grew. More and more reindeer were kept, not just as decoys but as an assured, year-round meat supply on the hoof. And thus the hunter became a herdsman.

We really don't know in which section of the Eurasian Arctic reindeer herding originated. Each scholar seems to have his own pet theory, tribe and region. One thing, though, is clear; wherever it originated, the idea spread far and fast. Reindeer herding became a way of life not only for most Lapps and Samoyeds, but for a multitude of northern Siberian tribes all the way to the Pacific. In an ancient Japanese painting, an Ainu with flowing beard is shown on skis herding reindeer; and a Chinese manuscript from the year 499 A.D. mentions that far to the north (in Siberia) there are people who milk reindeer, and use them as beasts of burden and to draw sleds. In the ninth century the Norse chieftain Ottar claimed he was the owner of "six hundred tame deer called rhanas."

Reindeer, like caribou, are migratory animals and their owners, by necessity, have to lead nomadic lives, north to

the tundra in summer, or up into the fells, and south again to the northern forest in late fall. To a Lapp, whether he has 20 animals or a thousand, each reindeer is an individual, often known by name. A quarter of all the words in the language of Swedish Lapps pertains to reindeer and reindeer herding. They have more than one hundred specific words to describe reindeer according to color and antler shape.

The Lapp's feeling, love and admiration for his reindeer are expressed in a song, a traditional Lapp "yoik."

"The many white-faced, white-faced,
reindeer with the white spots on their noses
the grey-white, the snow-white.
Reindeer with forward-pointing antlers,
reindeer with high and swaying antlers.
The slanting antlers,
the high, swaying antlers . . .
Many tall reindeer
they are mine."

In southern man, the far roaming reindeer nomads of the north inspired an odd mixture of fear, pity, envy and greed. They were feared, as Richard Johnson said of the Samoyeds whom he visited in 1556 because "they use much witchcraft, and shoot well with bowes."

"He (the shaman) picked up a swo[rd]
a cubite and a spanne long
and put it into his be[lly]
. . . in at the navill and out at the fundamen[t]
the poynt be[ing]
out of his shirt behin[d]
I layde my finger upon it
This I s[aw]
the fifth day of Janua[ry]
in the yere of our Lord 155[6]

**Richard Johnson, 1[556]
among the Samoy[eds]**

A Lapp wedding in Kautoke[ino]
arctic Norw[ay]

182

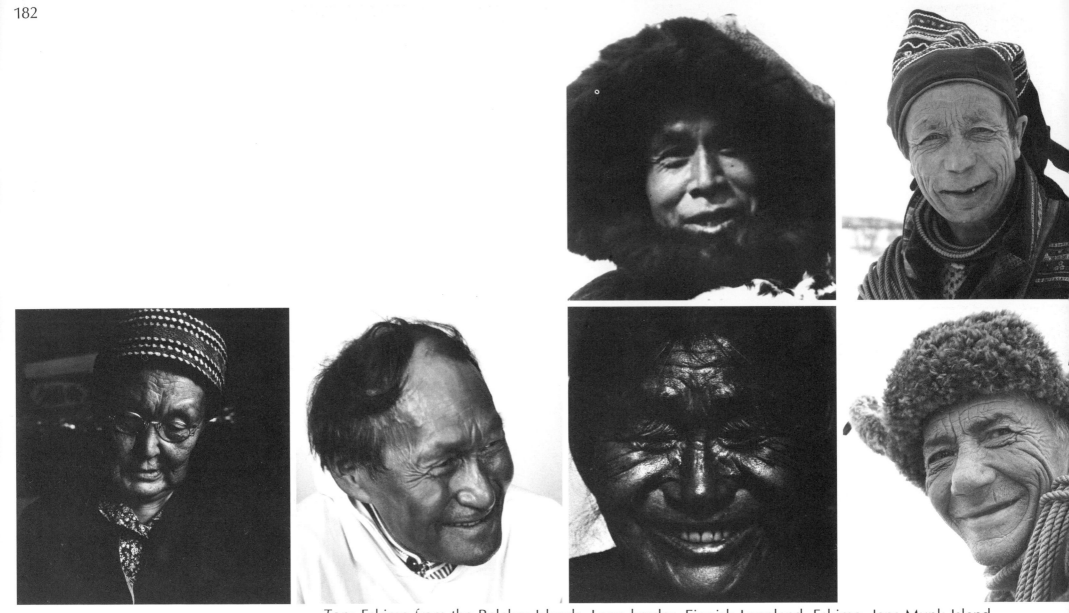

Top: Eskimo from the Belcher Islands. Lapp herder, Finnish Lappland. Eskimo, Jens Munk Island. Eskimo from Igloolik, northern Foxe Basin. Eskimo, Bathurst Inlet.

Middle: Old Eskimo woman from the Hudson Bay area. Polar Eskimo from Kânâk, Greenland. Polar Eskimo woman from northwestern Greenland. Lapp herder, Finnish Lappland. Lapp woman, arctic Finland. Eskimo, Baffin Island. Polar Eskimo from Siorapaluk, the world's northernmost village. Polar Eskimo woman, northwestern Greenland.

Bottom: Eskimo with bone goggles. Eskimo fisherman, northern Labrador coast.

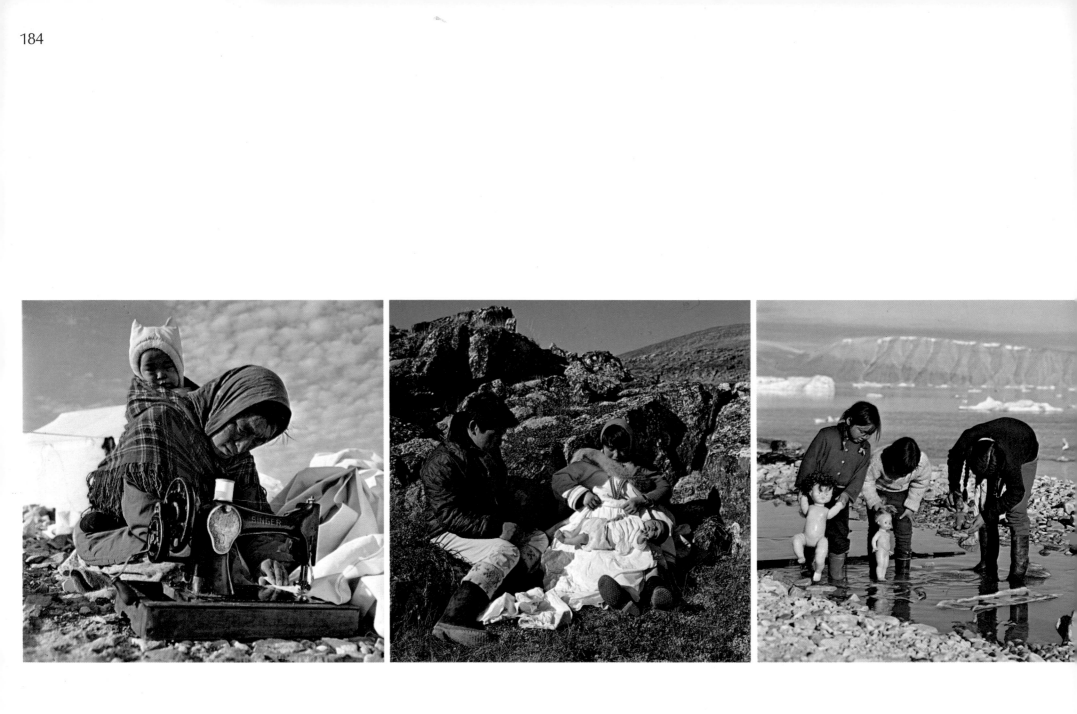

Children in the Arctic are well cared for. They receive love and attention, are rarely disciplined, and are nearly always happy.

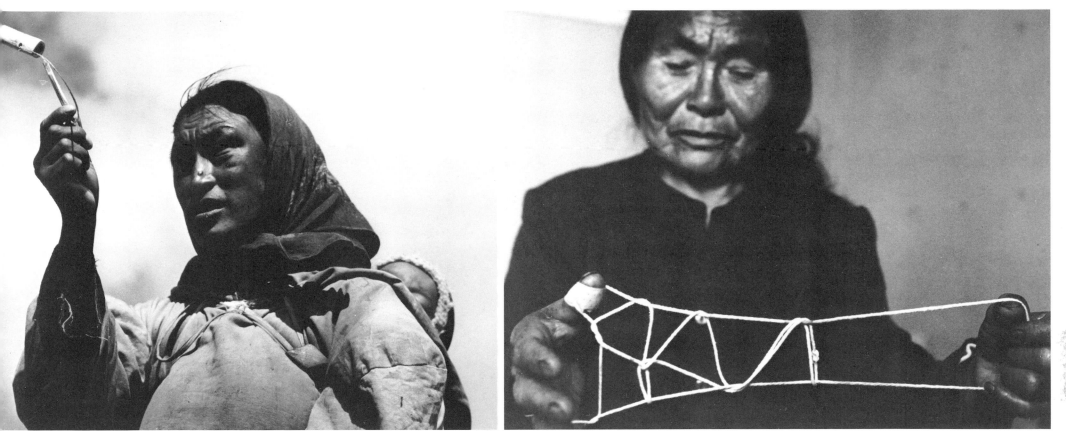

Eskimos play a wide variety of games.
complex jigsaw puzzle helps pass the time during a storm. A traditional game resembling dice, using
seal bones. An "ajaqaq" of hollow caribou bone and a wooden pin.
Most Eskimo women know dozens of cat's cradle figures; here a running caribou.

The arctic women's work is never done . . .

Scraping seal skins. Fishing for polar cod. Softening tough leather by chewing.
Sewing a new parka. Making snowshoes. Caring for the seal oil lamps. Making duffel socks.
Cleaning dovekies for supper.

Overleaf: His lasso at the ready, a Norwegian Lapp watches reindeer rushing past him.
Lapp reindeer herd on the spring migration northwest across the fells of arctic Norway to the coast.

Religion in the Arctic is a mixture of traditions.
Skoltt Lapps place small offerings of food into a hole of their raised wooden grave covers. These covers
symbolize the boats with which the graves were covered in ancient times.
Aleut service in their Russian Orthodox church on St. Paul Island.
At Davis Inlet, a Naskapi Indian altar boy lights candle. Skoltt Lapp funeral. Eskimo holding service in
northern Greenland. Graves at Baker Lake.

lruses killed by Polar Eskimos
northwestern Greenland
pulled onto the ice.

The Norwegian scientist and explorer Fridtjof Nansen extolled the life of the Siberian reindeer herder. He wrote in 1893: "And over these mighty tundra plains of Asia, stretching infinitely onward from one skyline to the other, the nomad wanders with his reindeer herds, a glorious free life. Where he wills, he pitches his tent, his reindeer around him; and at his will again he goes on his way . . . He has no goal to struggle towards, no anxieties to endure — he has merely to live!"

However, Nansen also pointed out the harsher realities of the herder's existence in 1893:

". . . Russian traders, who barter with the natives, giving them brandy in exchange of bearskins, sealskins, and other valuables, and who, when once they have a hold on a man, keep him in such a state of dependence that he can scarcely call his soul his own."

That soul, in a manner of speaking, had already been mortgaged to the missionaries. They came north brimful of kindness and zeal, eradicated the Lapps' nature-linked shamanistic religion, collected and burned thousands of their sacred drums (only 71 are left) and, while they were at it, burned a few Lapp shamans as well. The Lapps had believed in many gods, most of them benevolent and none truly evil. The concepts of "devil" and "damnation" were brought north by the missionaries.

"Saivo" was the Lapps' ancient name for the paradise, inhabited by infinite reindeer herds, they imagined good Lapps would go to in the hereafter. On earth, if perhaps not in heaven, the reindeer have certainly been a form of salvation for the nomads of the north. Possession of

reindeer set them apart, thus preserving, to some extent, their cultural identity; reindeer gave them a measure of security and independence; and far from withering away, reindeer have become of increasing importance to the Eurasian north, still looked after by peoples whose ancient culture makes them uniquely suited for this task.

Nomads now form an infinitesimal part of Siberia's population of more than twenty-five million. Yet it is primarily they who look after the reindeer which now number more than two-and-a-half million.

The Eurasian reindeer and the North American caribou are the same animal called by different names. But reindeer herding and the entire cultural complex based upon this specialized form of animal husbandry, though extending from northwest Norway to northeast Siberia, stops just short of Bering Strait. The Chukchi are both hunters and reindeer breeders, their neighbors to the east, the Yuit, Siberia's Eskimos, are exclusively hunters. And the art of reindeer domestication never crossed the Bering Strait into America.

Attempts to introduce a reindeer herding culture to the North American Arctic have ended in failure. Dr. Sheldon Jackson, Alaska's famous educator, imported several groups of reindeer from Siberia in the 1890s. Lapps, at first, then Eskimos looked after the reindeer. They prospered; at one time they numbered nearly a quarter million. But the essential trait of reindeer and reindeer herding, its vital nomadism, the alternate use of summer and winter pastures, was overlooked. The reindeer were kept in the same location all year, they overgrazed the slow-growing lichen, and in the 1930s and 1940s they died in thousands. Now only 30,000 reindeer are left in Alaska.

Canada, inspired by Alaska's early success, decided to establish reindeer ranches in the Mackenzie River delta. Three thousand reindeer were purchased in Alaska and driven from the Kotzebue region to the Mackenzie delta. It was an epic trek: with detours, rests, summer grazing and winter wandering it lasted four years and three months (1929 to 1935), "the slowest march since Moses led his people through Sinai," one writer put it. The arrival, unfortunately, was the end of the epic. A pilot project without a pilot, the enterprise has limped along for forty years. It might, in the opinion of Diamond Jenness, have endured the government's attempt to remote-control the herd from 3,000 miles away, the "excessive overhead" and the "meagre return," "but it could not survive the unwillingness of the Eskimos themselves to adopt the unfamiliar and arduous life of the reindeer herder as long as their traditional occupations, hunting and fishing, could supply most of their food . . .''

The life of the arctic hunter was different, but at least as arduous and a lot less secure than that of the herder. In the herder's existence, week-long periods of incredible strain and concentration are followed by months of relative ease. The hunter is under near-constant pressure to procure food: a lean spring caribou is but one meal for his family and his dogs; a seal is eaten in two or three days. To the herder, his reindeer give the security of an assured and always accessible food supply. The hunter, at the mercy of the whims and vagaries of weather and elusive game, is rarely certain of his next meal.

The herder's life had its ample measure of risk, hardship and effort, but its strong element of predictability and certainty emerges in a ''yoik,'' by the Lapp Nils Hotti:

''And the life of a Lapp is like this:
Skis on his feet
a lasso round his shoulder
and a dog behind.
The crust on the snow
took him far in a night,
and he stopped
where he found pasture.''

The Eskimo hunter's life fluctuated between the ecstasy of success:

''Here I stand
Surrounded with great joy.
For a caribou bull with high antlers
Recklessly exposed his flanks to me.''
and the fear of failure and foreboding of famine:
''I did so wish to see
Swimming caribou or fish in a lake.
That joy was my one wish.
My thought ended in nothing.
It was like a line
That all runs out.''

The herder's thoughts and dreams, his fears and hopes circle never-endingly around his reindeer, with whose existence his life is interlinked. Swedish Lapps have more than 60 specific words for every age phase of the reindeer. The hunter's language is full of words that describe his prey. Siberian Eskimos have 15 words for the walrus and the way it swims: ''putukak'' means ''walrus floating on the water with its head bent down''; ''ilgaxtyk'' — ''walrus sleeping in the water with only its nose visible''; and ''manilguk'' — ''walrus herd swimming towards the shore.'' The Lapps have more than a hundred words for the different parts of reindeer harness and sled; the Eskimos have about 40 terms for various straps: ''kaskak'' — ''strap made of the skin of a young walrus''; ''magnygrak'' — ''thick strap of walrus skin for whale harpoons''; or ''akmagin'' — ''strap for fastening loads on one's back.'' And the Eskimo language, so deficient in abstract terms and concepts that it lacks words for ''art'' and ''create,'' is extremely specific when it comes to spatial orientation. One word, ''pikna,'' means, in the Siberian dialect: ''that one, above the speaker, opposite to the sea, on the elevation.''

Eskimo, with its multitude of suffixes, is a complex, vivid, flexible, emotive language, full of imagery. ''Nunusagaq,'' meaning ''something that quickly comes

to an end,'' is also the word for ''candy''; and ''qahiaq'' — ''the ever-wandering one,'' is the poetic of the polar bear.

The Eskimos' forebears, believed to have belonge Mongoloid racial group, were the last of succe waves of immigrants from Asia, arriving about years ago, at a time when the rising sea had pro already drowned the land bridge. To the first discer proto-Eskimo culture, archaeologists have give somewhat cumbersome name of Cape Denbigh Complex of the Arctic Small Tool Tradition. Sha figures in the dim distance of time, we know of existence and their life only through the multitu stone tools they left behind: skin scrapers, spear h arrow points, microblades, and burin spalls (small c tools) delicately and expertly chipped from chert and obsidian. Denbigh people, originating in we Alaska about 4,500 years ago spread slowly east a the vast Arctic which they found uninhabited by but rich in game, and reached Greenland a 2,000 B.C.

Their material culture was meagre, but well adap life in the Arctic, and it changed little in 3,000 small pockets of people, eternally wandering, from mer to fall to winter hunting grounds; courageous face of real, physical dangers; oppressed by a mul of fears and fancies about the powers beyond the ke control of man; ingenious in the use of scant local rials, yet conservative to the point of stagnation, their lives with little change, without any real, u need for change and with no desire for change fo generations. In a harsh and often relentless land, be the uncertainties of hunt and weather, arctic man stubbornly to the familiar comforting continuum c changing life patterns. Temperamentally, said St son, ''the Eskimo expects to find everything next y he found it last year.''

Change did come, but with the imperceptible slov of an advancing glacier. Out of the Denbigh an subsequent Pre-Dorset, the Dorset culture evolved, ably in the region of northern Hudson Bay. Begir about 800 B.C., it spread gradually westward, nea far as the Mackenzie River and east to Greenland held sway over this immense region of the Arcti nearly 2,000 years, until about 1300 A.D.

People of the Dorset culture were distinctly Eskir probably in language and appearance, and certair

...ay of life. They used oil lamps, hunted sea and land ...nals, lived, in winter at least, in semi-subterranean ...s, they may have had kayaks and are thought to ...een the inventors of that symbol of Eskimo in... ...y, the igloo, but they probably did not possess dogs ...ulled their small, ivory-shod sleds themselves.

...sing his opinion upon an analysis of their art, Dr. ...e Swinton, the foremost expert of Eskimo art, pre... ...nd past, feels that the "Dorset people appear to ...een fearful, intense, severe, moody, mystical, and ...y credulous and superstituous." They were, ...ps, the greatest artists the Arctic has ever known. ...ir art is usually diminutive and delicate, tiny men ...nasks, bears and birds, some less than an inch in ...arved of bone, stone, ivory, or driftwood, and yet ...e their miniature size imbued with a tremendous ...g of power and force. In 1970 Father Guy Marie-...elière, O.M.I., and his Eskimo assistants discovered ...rge (seven inch high), Dorset culture masks made of ...ood on Bylot Island, both stained with ochre, the ...ragic and resigned, the other of nearly demonic ...ness. They were preserved in the desert-like earth of ...igh, north Baffin, latitude.

...e the art of the paleolithic people of Europe, the ...ificent paintings in caves at Lascaux or Altamira, the ...Dorset men, on a smaller, less flamboyant scale, but ...ss intense, probably had a religio-magic function. ...e Eskimos remember the Dorset people of long ago, ...ot as peaceful mystics. "Tunit" they call them in ...egends — a race of giants preternaturally powerful. ...y could haul a walrus across the ice as easily as we ...a seal," Igloolik Eskimos say. They were strong, ...ble but rather dumb; in their somewhat boastful ...he Eskimos recall with glee how they outwitted the

...e newcomers, direct forebears of today's Eskimos, ...the Thule culture people. Starting from northern ...a, around 900 A.D., they spread east, and in 200 ...they reached Greenland, replacing, eradicating or, ...ps, in some instances absorbing the introspective, ...ly, Dorset giants.

The Thule people were courageous, adaptable and innovative. While Dorset culture man laboriously hauled his sled, the Thule people travelled swiftly with dogs. They hunted all game of the land and, above all, of the sea, from the small ringed seal to the giant bowhead whales of the north. Dionyse Settle noted in 1577: "Those beastes, flesh, fishes and fowles, which they kil, they are both meate, drinke, apparel, houses, bedding, hose, shooes, thred, saile for their boates . . . and almost all their riches."

In the 18th century, Eskimo whale hunting declined and with it the Thule culture people's distinctive way of life. Perhaps increased ice cover during this cold period, the Little Ice Age, kept whales away from former hunting regions; possibly whales were already becoming rarer due to decimation by white whalers in the Davis Strait region. The large whale hunting villages were abandoned; the people scattered, and the modern phase of Eskimo life began, small groups of people spread over the infinite vastness of the Arctic, similar in language, custom and tradition from eastern Siberia to East Greenland.

Far to the west, the Eskimos' distant cousins, the Aleuts developed a more complex culture. They had powerful chiefs and shamans; they had an "upper class," but also slaves; they knew how to mummify their dead and preserved them in sacred caves; they were superb hunters. Procurement of food was relatively easy, the supply usually ample, leaving time for other pursuits, particularly man's favorite pastime — war. In a curiously contradictory sentence, Bancroft, the historian of Alaska, wrote of the Aleuts: "Notwithstanding their peaceful character, the occupants of the several islands were almost constantly at war."

"Shamans were
very clever in our days and
were even smarter than the doctors of today.
They used to know
if the patient would live or if
the patient would die."
Louis Tapatai, 1972,
in the Eskimo magazine
"Inuttituut".

Along Bering Strait and adjacent regions, where game was immensely plentiful and the living fairly easy, raids, warfare and enslavement occurred among Eskimo groups though less frequently than among the Aleuts. Farther east, where life was a lot harder, the Eskimos were, by necessity and perhaps inclination, peaceful. They feared and despised the Indians whom they called "Itqilit," the ones with the many louse-eggs. In their legends, both Indians and whites are considered the bastard descendants of an Eskimo woman who mated with a dog.

Indian and Eskimo fought each other, in stealthy, deadly ambush and raid, from Alaska to Labrador, and even in the Eskimos of East Greenland, removed in time and space by many centuries and thousands of miles from this ancestral foe, there lingered until recently an ancient, nearly atavistic terror of Indians, who stalked through their subconscious as bogeymen from a distant past. Generally, though, their choice of environment kept the antagonists apart. The Indians were a people of the forest; the Eskimos feared the forest, and felt safe and content only on the treeless tundra and the remote shores of the arctic islands.

Now Indians and Eskimos feel united by a common bond, a common fear and common fate, the crushing of their ancient, nature-linked cultures by southern values and technology, yet in a few isolated areas ancient dislike persists. Labrador Eskimos travelling from Hopedale to Nain, avoid stopping at the Naskapi Indian village of Davis Inlet, and if they have to, they usually ask the missionary to put them up. Among themselves they refer to the Naskapis as "allakuluk" — "wretched Indians." The Naskapi call the shrivelled, brownish dried apricots and peaches they buy at the store "Eskimo ears."

To the Eskimos white men appeared restless, time-obsessed, overweening, moody, totally lacking in manners and boorish. For the latter trait, some allowance was made because, after all, white men had a rather unfortunate ancestry, descended as they were from the union of a woman and a dog. When this offspring was born, their mother placed the young in a boat, but it leaked, they were busy bailing, and, says the genesis legend, "the circumstance that they had so much to do in their boat later on became a peculiarity of white men who are always in a hurry and have much to do . . ." And a Netsilik Eskimo confided to Rasmussen: "It is generally believed that white men have quite the same minds as small children. Therefore one should always give way to them. They are easily angered, and when they cannot get their will they are moody and, like children, have the strangest ideas and fancies."

Thus Eskimos and white men (with the notable exception of Rasmussen, who was born in Greenland, and his friend Peter Freuchen) viewed each other across a cultural chasm so vast as to render them mutually incomprehensible.

While I lived with the Polar Eskimos, a geologist from Europe arrived and chartered a schooner plus its owner for an extensive trip. On the way north, along the coast, they passed the Eskimo's home village and naturally stopped. The Eskimo went to visit all his friends, which meant just about everybody in the village. The stories were long, the meals copious and a day passed and a night. Then it was the Eskimo's turn to have all his friends over to his house. It was a long and convivial party, and another day passed and another night; everyone was in the mood for visiting, everyone was happy — except one man, the geologist. He was fuming up and down the beach, thinking of time and money.

In 1973, three Eskimos were working on an oil rig in the Mackenzie River delta. They were employed as "casual labor." They worked well and willingly, and the company, favorably impressed, decided to put them on "permanent staff," which meant a raise in status, security and pay. The Eskimos quit. The very casualness of "casual" had appealed to them. They felt free to go whenever the mood was upon them, to hunt caribou or white whales. But "permanent" frightened them, it meant fetters they were not yet willing to wear.

Jumping from floe to f
a Polar Esk
hunter harpoons a seal s
from the ice ec

Eskimo Art

Top: The only petroglyphs ever found in the vast region inhabited by Eskimos are on tiny, isolated Qikertaaluk Island, near the south shore of Hudson Strait. A Bathurst Inlet Eskimo works on a carving in his tent. Eskimo ceramist at work in Rankin Inlet.

Bottom: A petroglyph, the shallow incisions have been traced with black chalk. A woman in Povungnituk pulls a lithograph off the inked stone.

Top: ''Virgin Mary and Child,'' carved by Samisa Iviallaq at Povungnituk.
''The Giant Holding An Axe,'' part of an Eskimo legend, carved in soapstone by Sivuarapiq of Povungnituk. A soapstone sculpture made by Angutiqirk of Povungnituk. Eskimo man, carved by Angutiguluq of Povungnituk.
Bottom: ''Joseph,'' carved by Marcussi Aliqu, in the Eskimo church at Povungnituk.

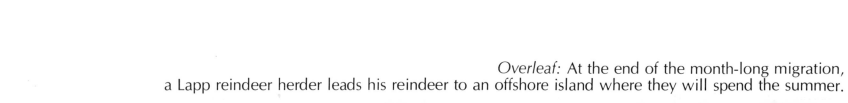

Overleaf: At the end of the month-long migration,
a Lapp reindeer herder leads his reindeer to an offshore island where they will spend the summer.

nding motionless
er an "agloo," a seal's
athing hole,
  Eskimo waits for the animal
surface.

Southern man's culture places great value on profit, property and progress. Northern man, in former days, knew nothing of profit, had little property, and abhorred progress. His culture valued survival, respect — self-respect and the respect of others — tradition and happiness. He was independent and self-reliant to a degree we, with our complex, interdependent society, can no longer comprehend. He accepted orders from no one and gave orders to no one (except, perhaps, his wife). An Eskimo does not say: "Shut the door!" He says: "One feels that there is a draught somewhere."

His possessions were few, but since they had enabled northern hunters to survive in the Arctic for millennia, they were obviously adequate. Even when he built a house, he was only its tenant not its exclusive owner. When he left, it became public property anyone could occupy. And few Eskimos occupied a house for a great length of time, because by need and inclination they were inveterate travellers. Until recently most Polar Eskimos travelled, by dog team, on foot, by kayak or schooner, thousands of miles each year.

In the past, when old beliefs were still alive, a shaman would speak magic words over a child travelling for the first time, such as these, recorded by Rasmussen:
  "I arise from rest with movements swift
  As a beat of a raven's wings
  I arise
  To meet the day.
  My face is turned from the dark of night
  To gaze at the dawn of day,
  Now whitening in the sky."
Although hunting was northern man's "work," he did not think of it in that term. It was the necessity of his life,

but also a passion, a constant challenge, a total involvement. And when he returned, successful, there was the double joy of food, not just for himself and his family, but food to share with others, the expansive pleasure of largesse, and the thrill of telling to others what happened on the hunt, to re-live it again in his own tale, and hold the others, all hunters like him, enthralled, absorbed, involved in everything that has happened.

As the hunter told his tale it became alive, the others would see and feel his tension, suffer the cold, crawl with him towards the caribou, and exult in his success.
  "I came creeping along over the marsh
  With bow and arrows in my mouth.
  The marsh was broad and the water icy cold,
  And there was no cover to be seen.
  Slowly I wriggled along,
  Soaking wet, but crawling unseen
  Up within range.
  The caribou were feeding, carelessly nibbling
  the juicy moss,
  Until my arrow stood quivering, deep
  In the chest of the bull.
  Then terror seized the heedless dwellers of the plain.
  The herd scattered apace,
  And trotting their fastest, were lost to sight
  Behind sheltering hills."
The hours ticked by, but he did not count them; partly because he had no watch, partly because he couldn't count, but mostly because time meant nothing to him. Few things annoy an Eskimo as much as the white man's obsession with time, measurement and exactitude, and nothing irritates white men as much as the Eskimos' total disregard for exactitude, measurement and time. When an Eskimo says he will leave tomorrow morning at 9 o'clock, one of the following things may happen: he will drop in at a neighbor's, talk all night, the morning will be superb, he will walk out at 6 a.m., harness his dogs and leave; he will wake up in a grumpy mood and not go at all; or, most likely, he will do this, that and the other, 9 a.m. will come and go, the day will pass and suddenly, about midnight, he will be up and away, because just then he felt like going. He does not live within a straight-jacket of measured time, he just lives; mood and impulse, need or joy determine his actions. On Victoria Island, Diamond Jenness observed that all Eskimos could count to three, most got stuck around five, and none got past seven. But Elisha Kent Kane noted that along the 600

miles of coast line forming the Polar Eskimos' land, the people knew every foot of ground, and "every rock had its name, every hill its significance."

We have fragmented our world, we live it in narrow specialized slots, cogwheels that intermesh to run the machine of a complex society. The northern hunter was a total being, and he was alone — or nearly. A woman needed a man to provide her with food, and a man needed a woman to cook for him, clothe him and care for his children (in Eskimo the word for "unmarried man" also means "lonely man"), and both needed the company, the esteem and, occasionally, the help of other people in their group.

"They exist both in love and community of resources as a single family," Kane said of the Polar Eskimos. But the arctic hunter could and often did exist alone. Freuchen tells of a Polar Eskimo family who left on a muskox hunting trip and "a whole year elapsed before they came back." Everything a man needed, he could make himself. He could build a kayak and construct a sled, carve a cooking pot out of stone or make needles from the hard wing bones of gulls and geese. He could harness and drive a dog team; he could find his way across a featureless waste in a white-out; he knew how to harpoon a whale and how to anticipate and avoid the lethal and lightning-fast charge of a polar bear. He could build a house out of stone and bone and hide, and with simple stone tools he could carve from ivory an exquisite figurine less than an inch in size. He knew the clouds that presaged bad weather and when bad weather came, he knew how to protect himself. His knowledge of animal behavior was uncanny, at times it seemed as if he knew, intuitively, just what an animal would do next. To this, he owed a good portion of his hunting success. He went where he liked and stayed as long as he liked. He was beholden to no one, dependent on no one. He was totally self-sufficient. Netsilik Eskimos, in search of wood and adventure, occasionally made trips that lasted several years.

To a man from the south, the Arctic was a forbidding region, harsh, barren, cold and hostile. To the Eskimo it was "Nunassiaq" — the beautiful land. He was a part of it; it brought him sorrow and it brought him joy, and he lived in harmony with it and its demands, accepting, fatalistically, its hardships, exulting in its bounty and beauty.

"O warmth of summer sweeping o'er the land!
Not a breath of wind,
Not a cloud,
And among the mountains
The grazing caribou,
The dear caribou
In the blue distance!
O, how entrancing,
O, how joyful!
I lay me on the ground, sobbing."
Men from the south saw the land very differently. Wrote George Best, a member of Frobisher's expedition in 1578: "I finde in all the Countrie nothing, that may be to delite in, either of pleasure or of accompte, only the shewe of Mine, both of golde, siluer, steele, yron and blacke lead . . ."

Addressing his land, a Greenland Eskimo said in 1756: "How well it is that you are covered with ice and snow. How well it is that, if in your rocks there are gold and silver, for which the Christians are so greedy, it is covered with so much snow that they cannot get at it! Your unfruitfulness makes us happy and saves us from molestation!"

The gold — and oil and gas and iron — won. The north, to quote a favorite government slogan, is "the treasure trove of today and tomorrow." The days of the hunter are nearly over, his ancient way of life has nearly ceased to exist. The new way of life that is offered him, is, as Dr. Swinton has so succinctly put it "technologically seductive, ecologically poisonous, and culturally ruinous." He hangs suspended between two worlds: one dear but dying, the other alien, empty perhaps, but enticing.

"Knowest thou thyself?
So little thou knowest of thyself!
While dawn gives place to dawn,
And spring is upon the village."

"I was surprised to se
how unspoiled and happy the
(the 'camp' Eskimos) wer
I didn't feel much of an Inuit besid
these happy peopl
and thought to mysel
'so these are the real Inuit
I felt I was an Inuit of toda
and not muc
in common with the old
My language is still ther
but what part of me is real Inuit?
**William Tagoona, 197
a young city Eskim
from the magazir
"Inuttituut**

Eskimo women at Baker Lake having a tug-of-wa

Children of the North.

Overleaf: Polar Eskimos travel across water-seamed ice in early summer.

A rare caribou skin tent and the now nearly vanished kayak of the inland Eskimos. Eskimos on a long hunting trip load their sled outside the igloo they built for the night.
Eskimo tents on the coast of Frobisher Bay in early summer.
A raised storage shed of logs with a sod roof holds supplies for an Indian family in Arctic Village, a small settlement in northeastern Alaska.

An Eskimo cuts snow blocks for his igloo with a hand saw.

The boats that made Aleut and Eskimo masters of the arctic seas were the oomiak and the kayak, and variants of either boat were used over a range of nearly 7,000 miles, from eastern Siberia to East Greenland. The Danish archaeologist Count Eigil Knuth found a remarkably well-preserved oomiak, dated from about 1500 A.D., on Peary Land, at the north tip of Greenland, less than 500 miles from the North Pole.

The large open oomiak (or umiak) of the Eskimos and the similar bidar (or baidar or baidara) of the Aleuts were, at least in this century, essentially transport boats. Long ago, Eskimos used the oomiak also to hunt the great whales of the north, the sixty-ton bowhead and the only slightly less bulky grey whale.

Dressed "in their best as for a wedding," as Hans Egede, the 18th century bishop of Greenland described it, the men paddled stealthily towards the mighty whale, then thrust their ivory harpoons into it and, usually after a long and often dangerous struggle, killed it with lances.

Oomiaks varied in length from 15 to more than 40 feet, were usually flat-bottomed and had great flare amidships which made them stable, roomy, and seaworthy. A large oomiak could carry 50 passengers or some five tons of cargo, yet was so light that, when empty, it lay only six inches deep in the water and four men could carry it

ashore. Its frame was made of drift-wood, mortised, tenoned and trenailed, and tightly lashed together, extremely strong yet flexible, and covered with the thick, durable skins of bearded seals, or with split walrus hide. On long sea voyages, such as the 57-mile trip from the east tip of Asia across Bering Strait with its fierce currents to the Diomede Islands and from there to America, the Eskimos lashed inflated sealskin bags to the side of the oomiak as sponsons to give the boat even more stability in this notoriously stormy sea.

E. W. Nelson, an American who travelled extensively in Alaska in the late 19th century during the summer of 1881, met "near Cape Lisburne . . . nine umiaks containing about one hundred people from Point Hope, who were on their way to the vicinity of Point Barrow to trade." At Hotham Inlet, Nelson saw 70 oomiaks drawn up on the beach and more than 200 kayaks neatly aligned on low scaffolds.

I once met an old Eskimo, Joe Talirunilik, in the village of Povungnituk on the east coast of Hudson Bay. He was a famous carver, and one of his best-known works is a soapstone oomiak crowded with people. Talirunilik is in that boat. "I am the child in the amautik of the woman, my mother, sitting near the mast," he said. The carving tells the story of his people's Odyssey a life-time ago. In the 1890s, the people of the Povungnituk region had fallen upon hard times. In spring, forty men, women and children piled into a great oomiak and set out for the un-

known. They travelled along the coast for two months, camping wherever game seemed plentiful. Then they hoisted their sail, made of sewn-together bearded seal intestines, and sailed west, out into Hudson Bay until, more than a hundred miles from shore, they came to the Ottawa Islands. There they lived for many years, but finally they returned to the mainland. North of Povungnituk, in the little village of Ivugivik, the last oomiak in Canada was built in 1960 — for the National Museum.

Oomiaks were traditionally paddled by women, and were therefore known throughout most of the Arctic as "women's boats." An early Eskimo convert to Christianity on the Labrador coast objected strenuously when the missionaries demanded that he shed all but one of his wives. "I need them to paddle my boat," he explained. While the men paddled their sleek kayaks to the summer hunting regions, the women followed in the oomiak piled high with tents, children, dogs, pots and bags with clothing and provisions.

In Canada, the oomiak had died out, replaced, like the kayak, first by the whaleboat and now by the ubiquitous motor-driven canoe. A few oomiaks are still used in Greenland, now invariably canvas-covered and usually much smaller than the oomiaks of the past. Only the Alaskan Eskimos still use the oomiak extensively (but not the kayak). With it, they still hunt bowhead whales off Point Hope, Wainwright and Point Barrow, pursue the walrus and cross at least the American half of Bering Strait to Little Diomede Island. Light, yet roomy, strong and flexible, the oomiak remains unsurpassed as the ideal boat for travel among shifting, current-and-wind-driven ice floes.

The bidar of the Aleuts was similar to the oomiak, though usually shallower and even broader. There was no lack of driftwood on the Aleutian Islands; cur-

rents from both north and south delivered it to the 1,000-mile-long island chain. Some logs had drifted far across the sea. An early visitor to the Aleutians saw a bidar, its frame constructed almost entirely of camphorwood from the tropics. The bidar was covered with sea lion skins and while it was mainly used, like the oomiak, as a cargo and family vessel, some of the more warlike Aleut groups employed it for raiding expeditions against their neighbors. Now the big bidar and the small bidarka have both disappeared. Only on St. Paul, one of the Pribilof Islands, are three enormous canvas-covered bidars still used to lighter cargo ashore in stormy weather. Each of these "primitive" boats, quickly and cheaply built, can carry a load of twelve to fourteen tons, and when the sea becomes too rough for the great metal barges, the bidars are pressed into service.

The oomiak was useful but dull. The kayak was exciting: sleek and swift, man and boat fused into a superbly harmonious unit. Just as the early Greeks were stupefied when they first saw men on horseback, riding west out of the Asian steppes, and elevated them in their legends to mythical man-beasts, the centaurs, so to early arctic travellers Eskimo and Aleut in his kayak appeared like a strange hybrid, part man, part marine animal. "These aquatic men are so closely confined by the narrow build of their boats, and keeping motion with them, too, that their appearance suggests the idea that some undescribed marine monster had just emerged from the depth below," Charles M. Scammon, a 19th century whaler, wrote of the Aleuts.

European sailors admired the speed

and dexterity with which Eskimos [pad]dled their kayaks, even in a storm. Wrote George Best, who accomp[anied] Frobisher to Baffin Island in 1578[:] ". . . they [the Eskimos] rowe the[m] with one ore, more swiftly a great [deal] than we in our boates can doe w[ith] twentie."

Kayaks, though not their origin[al,] been known in Europe for a long [time.] The odd one drifted across the no[rth At]lantic, usually from East Greenla[nd, to] be washed ashore, more or less b[roken,] on the west coast of Scotland, or [the] Orkneys and Shetlands. At least o[ne] kayak arrived complete with Eski[mo. In] his "General Description of the E[ast] Coast of Scotland," Francis Doug[las] wrote in 1792 about " . . . a can[oe] taken at sea, with an Indian man [in it.] He was brought alive to Aberdee[n but] died soon after his arrival and co[uld] give no account of himself. He is [sup]posed to have come from the Lab[rador] coast and to have lost his way at [sea."] This kayak is in the Aberdeen mu[seum.] It is of East Greenland origin.

Throughout their immense ran[ge,] from Siberia to East Greenland, k[ayaks] were all alike in basic design, bu[t varied] considerably in appearance from [one] region to another. Some of the lo[ng,] gracefully tapered Aleut bidarkas, [for] instance, had bifid bows that curv[ed] like oriental slippers. The Aleuts [also] constructed bidarkas with two ma[n]holes, and even with three, thoug[h the] latter type seems to have been bu[ilt] under Russian influence; the idea [was] that one Aleut paddled in front, th[e ...]

Boats

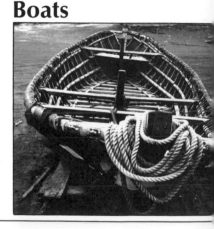

r in the rear, while their Russian
enger sat in comfort in the centre
. In the stormy, current-swept wa-
of the Aleutians, the two-man kayak
a definite advantage. While one
paddled and steadied the boat, his
panion sat poised with the harpoon
pture their prey.

e kayak of the King Islanders was
t but extremely strong. It had to be.
Island, in the northern Bering Sea,
steep cliffs and constant surf. There
o quiet coves where a kayak could
y be launched. Instead, the hunter
nto his boat while it was still on
. Then two other Eskimos picked up
k plus man and heaved both into
ea.

e relatively broad, flat-bottomed
k used by the Labrador Eskimos
those on Baffin Island was strong,
y (often more than 100 pounds)
fairly stable.

e kayak of the Caribou Eskimos
some groups of the central Cana-
arctic mainland coast, who often
ed their craft along on extensive
land migrations, was round-
omed, light (less than 30 pounds)
extremely cranky. A young Green-
Eskimo, member of Knud
hussen's Fifth Thule Expedition, who
dly considered himself an expert
kman, climbed confidently into a
bou Eskimo kayak and, to the joy of
romptly overturned it. His name
Qaivigarssuaq and I met him in
when, at the age of 70, he was
considered one of the best hunters
ng the Polar Eskimos. After half a
ury, he remembered vividly the in-
t that had happened on his four-

year journey with Rasmussen from Greenland to Siberia. "We saw many different kayaks," he recalled, "but those of the Umingmaktormiut were the most difficult to handle. They were so light, one could lift them easily with one hand, and as round-bottomed as a woman!"

Round-bottomed, flat-bottomed, or V-hulled like the Greenland kayak, all the boats, from the east tip of Asia to East Greenland were essentially the same: a wooden frame entirely covered with sealskin except for a hole in the top centre into which the man fits like a cork into a bottle. The frame was made of driftwood (or, by the Caribou Eskimos of thumb-thick dwarf willow "trunks"). In regions where wood was extremely scarce, small pieces were scarfed and pegged together with simple stone or copper tools and infinite patience, and joints in most kayaks were strengthened with bone or ivory gussets. The lashings, of sinew, rawhide or, mainly among the Aleuts, baleen, were applied wet and dried firm and taut. The boat was covered with the skins of four or five ringed seals, sewn moist onto the frame with the "blind stitch" technique which does not pierce the skin and assures waterproof seams.

In their kayaks, Eskimo and Aleuts became nearly as much part of the sea as the seals and whales they hunted. Georg Wilhelm Steller of Bering's expedition that discovered Alaska and the Aleutians described them in 1741:

"The boats of these Aleuts are about two fathoms long, two feet high and two feet wide from above . . . The frame is covered . . . with sealskins . . . About two arshins [8 feet 4 inches] from the stern there is a round opening with a skirt of whale's guts. By means of a cord, put through a hem, the lower border of the skirt may be tightly bound around the edge of the hatch and stretching out his legs the American draws the upper hem of the skirt around his body under the armpits and ties it with a noose; thus the water cannot penetrate into the boat."

Four years later (in 1745) and nearly half a world away, Hans Egede, the "Apostle of Greenland," gave an almost identical description of the boats used on the west coast of that island. Of the native boatmen he added:

"They do not fear to venture out in them in the greatest storms . . . though they may happen to be upset, yet they easily raise themselves again with their paddle . . ."

Not all Eskimos knew the technique of the "kayak roll" that Egede describes. The Aleuts could do it; when their bidarka overturned in a heavy sea they were capable of righting it again, either with their paddle or with the help of an inflated sealskin they carried along. (The Aleuts also used inflated sealskins inside their bidarkas, as "floatation chambers," to avoid disaster should their craft be punctured on one of the innumerable reefs surrounding their islands.) But the real experts at the kayak roll were the Eskimos of the West Greenland coast. These men seemed to the kayak born, as much home at sea as on land. In pursuit of harp, hooded and

ringed seals they ventured far out into the open sea, undaunted by storms and waves. If a wave overturned them, they used their paddle to push themselves upright again. If, by mischance, they were caught by a really heavy sea, they might have to employ the kayak roll to save their lives.

The immense weight of a great wave thundering over the boat could snap a man's back against the unyielding wooden coaming of his kayak. Thus, when a hunter saw a steep-crested wave approach, too high to ride, he would, in an instant, turn himself and his boat upside down and hang head down in the sea, while the wave rushed over the bottom of his boat and then right himself again to paddle fast towards the sheltering coast.

There was danger in a stormy sea, yet, strangely enough, there was danger, too, in a sea absolutely calm. The hunter, alone on the mirror-smooth sea might then succumb to that weird hallucination known as "kayak trance" or "kayak hypnosis." The sky is sunny, the sea smooth and infinite, the man sits still in his boat waiting for seals to surface. Bereft of any stimulation, visual or tactile, the hunter becomes drowsy, apathetic and slowly sinks into a dreadful trance. The sea, he feels, is rising, it will swallow him, yet he is helpless, paralyzed, he cannot move. The slightest rippling of the glassy surface by a breeze will break the spell.

The experience must hold a terror beyond comprehension, for the bravest hunters, men who laughed at the fier-

cest waves, if they were ever gripped by kayak trance would never go to sea again, doomed to a life of dependence and poverty on shore. More than 100 years ago the Danish government ordered a survey made of all Greenland Eskimos debilitated by kayak trance, and paid them a small pension in lieu of their lost livelihood in a sea which seemingly benign, had destroyed them.

The kayak, superb and efficient, essence and symbol of the sea culture of Aleut and Eskimo, is, like that culture, dying out. It has all but vanished from Alaska. Only three kayaks were left in the entire Canadian Arctic in 1970. All were on the Belcher Islands in Hudson Bay, and no longer used as true hunting boats, but only as easy-to-transport craft taken along in winter to retrieve seals shot from the floe edge. Only at old campsites, long abandoned, does one still find kayak skeletons, the wood clean and bleached, the lines still elegant, the joints still a marvel of craftsmanship.

In Greenland, though, the kayak still lives and with it a sea-oriented Eskimo culture. The Polar Eskimos, in fact, recognizing the superiority of the kayak have, in a law applicable to their region, banned the use of motor-driven boats for the hunting of all sea mammals except walrus.

Somewhere, in the remote past, man, the thinking mammal, arrived gropingly at the conclusion that, beyond the joys and dangers of the real, visible world, there lay another, filled by powers that could favor or threaten his life. Through religion, he tried to achieve balance and harmony with these powers; through myths he tried to explain them; through magic he tried to control them.

Perhaps the Arctic with its infinite space, its majestic grandeur, its solemnity and solitude, its dark and long, and dismal winters, its weird atmospheric mirages and distortions, its silent, dancing northern lights, gave northern man a special awe for the might and mystery of the world, impressed upon him his own insignificance, and made him both mystically-inclined and humble. An Eskimo expressed this in a poem about a successful caribou hunt:

"Here I stand,
Humble, with outstretched arms,
For the spirit of the air
Let glorious food sink down to me."

This feeling of awe and impotence before powers that could be sensed but not seen, was the basis for shamanism, the religio-magic belief complex of all arctic and sub-arctic peoples, and created the need for shamans to act as intermediaries between the world of man and the world of the spirits. A shaman, after all, was a very reassuring person to have around.

He knew how to mollify Sedna, the easily-disgruntled sea goddess and mother of seals, and whales and walruses; he could appease Sila, the nasty-tempered god of weather; he could explain disasters and pinpoint their cause to a broken taboo; he could cajole the spirits into being a bit more cooperative with man, and help him to achieve hunting success; and through his intercession he might dislodge the evil spirits causing sickness and stave off the threat of famine.

A shaman, nearly invariably, was called to his vocation. In rare cases he might be born to it, in even rarer instances he was created in a flash of blinding vision, in the case of one famous woman shaman, literally through a stroke of lightning. Usually, though, possession came gradually, through dreams, and visions, and voices, through fasting and fear, through weeks and even months spent in solitude and meditation. He might train under an old shaman, who imparted to him the rote and ritual of shamanistic seances, but its essence, the acquisition of familiar spirits, could be achieved only in the agony and ecstasy of total solitude. There a shaman became a man capable of seeing "things that to others are hidden."

Shamans did not form a priestly caste. Most of the time they lived and hunted like other men of their group; in time of need they were called upon (usually for a fee) to try and re-establish harmony between man and spirits. A few shamans were evil and feared; most were beneficient and respected. Some were thinly disguised phonies who pepped up their shows with ventriloquism and tricks of legerdemain; others were deeply committed mystics, who at times achieved what seemed like miraculous results.

Above all, with exceedingly rare exceptions, the shamans believed implicitly in their own powers, spirits, voices and visions, and were, equally implicitly, believed by the people whom they served. And finally, especially in winter when weather was bad and boredom lay heavily upon the people, a shaman seance, with its enormous tension and drama, was like an emotional steambath, a catharsis that left participants relieved and relaxed.

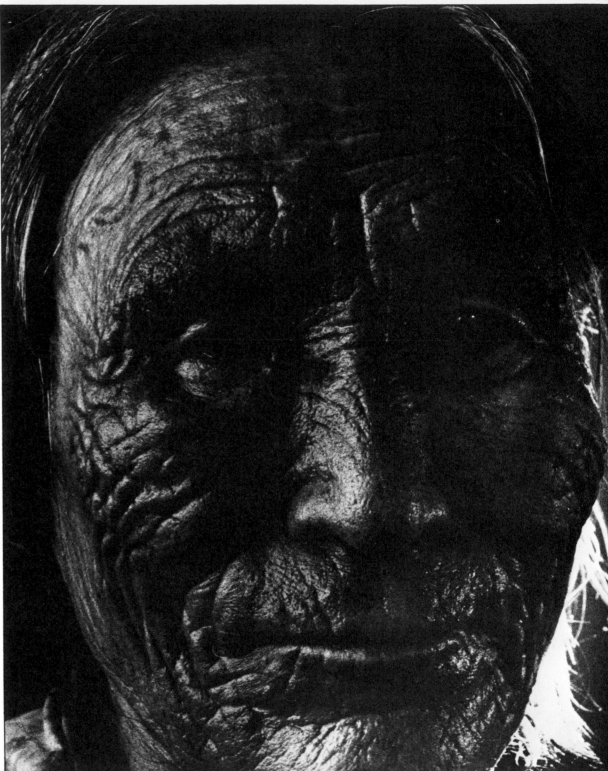

Shamanism

or the Eskimos, as indeed for all peoples of the circumpolar lands in her days, there was no sharp divi- between the possible and the im- sible, the natural and the super- ral, the world of man and the world nimals. One merged with the other, unreal simply became an extension he real. A Polar Eskimo shaman ex- ned the absence of bears in an area re they normally were numerous : "The bears are not here, because e is no ice here, and there is no ice because the wind is too strong, the wind is too strong because we e insulted the spirits."

he people were quite willing to ept the incomprehensible on faith e, and would no more think of stioning a shaman's assertion that he d turn himself into a gull, than y devout Christians would question doctrine of transubstantiation. "It is that it is so, and therefore it is so," as Rasmussen has pointed out, an matic Eskimo concept. Stefansson, superb and astute scientist, ran l of this mental world, when, meet- Eskimos who had never seen white and their technical marvels before, ould not resist the temptation to w off. e shot and hit a distant target. The mos were more impressed by the g than with the result. Can you hit a oou on the other side of the moun- they asked. No, Stefansson admit- Well, our shamans can, they in- ned him. Stefansson bragged a bit ut his immense travels. Have you n to the moon, the Eskimos wanted now. Again Stefansson had to say Several of our shamans have been he moon, he was told. It was a game ne-upmanship Stefansson could not because he was pitting his world of against their world of faith. he people of the north lived in an

intensely spiritual world. All things, they believed, and all beings had spirits or souls, except, perhaps, something as evanescent as snow or ice that melt. "The earth, and everything belonging to it . . . are sacred . . ." the Netsilingmiut told Rasmussen. Arctic man did not feel he had a God-given right to subdue the earth or have dominion over the ani- mals. In fact he felt that long ago, there was a "time when there was scarcely any difference between man and ani- mals." By imbuing all nature and all animals with feelings and souls akin to his own, northern man developed a re- verential attitude to nature.

"Life's greatest danger lies in the fact that man's food consists entirely of souls," an Igloolik Eskimo said to Rasmussen.

To lead a safe and successful life, the Netsilik Eskimo Qaqortingneq told Rasmussen:

"I must never offend Nuliajuk or Narssuk (the goddess of the sea and god of the air).

"I must never offend the souls of animals . . .

"I must . . . make offerings to animals that I hunt . . . (and) to lifeless things, especially stones or rocks . . .

"I must make my own soul as strong as I can . . .

"I must observe my forefathers' rules of life in hunting customs and taboo . . .

"I must gain special abilities or qualities through amulets.

"I must try to get hold of magic words or magic songs that either give hunting luck or are protective.

"If I cannot manage in spite of all these precautions, and suffer want or sickness, I must seek help from the shamans whose mission it is to be the protectors of mankind against all the hidden forces and dangers of life."

If the observation of a multitude of taboos, propitiatory rites and rules was often a nuisance and occasionally a hardship, it nevertheless provided for the people who implicitly believed in them, a shell of security and certainty in a harsh and uncertain world. The break- ing of a taboo, it is true, could have dire

consequences, not just for the guilty in- dividual but for the whole group, but usually a confession, freely and publicly given, and an assurance of remorse and regret would set the matter right again, because neither the Eskimos (though occasionally indulging in prolonged blood feuds) nor their gods were prot- ractedly vindictive, and both had a sav- ing sense of humor.

R. Kaare Rodahl, a Norwegian psychologist who has done extensive research into the emotional effects of "mørketiden," the long, dark arctic winter, reports: "The polar night has a tendency to bring out the least desirable elements in human behavior — envy, jealousy, suspicion, egotism, irritabil- ity." In the north of today, consumption of alcohol and incidence of crime rise sharply during the winter months. In the past, the polar peoples had no intoxi- cants, probably because cold discour- ages fermentation. Some Siberian tribes used a decoction of fly agaric, a pretty but poisonous mushroom, as a potent hallucinatory, but essentially all the peoples of the north employed but one thing, the drum, to achieve trance or transcendence, happiness or exultation, and for dance and divination.

To forestall the fear and tedium of the long dark winter, the Eskimos made it their most festive season. It was a time to tell again the old legends, faithfully preserved from generation to generation for hundreds, perhaps thousands, of years, with such exactitude some tales vary but little from eastern Siberia to eastern Greenland.

It was a time to dance by the flicker- ing light of oil lamps to the throb of the drums. It was a time to compose poems and sing them. In Eskimo, the words for "poem," "soul," and "breath" derive from the same root. "All my being is

song, and I sing as I draw breath," an Eskimo told Rasmussen. After a night spent with the Bathurst Inlet Eskimos Rasmussen wrote: "Towards morning I had to leave the dance-house. All those remarkable faces, bearing the impress of freedom and hardiness, women and men in beautifully harmonizing caribou skins, characters, personalities, simple natures who knew how to abandon themselves to the enjoyment of the moment, open, pleasure-ready minds, who had prepared me a welcome I shall never forget . . .

"A broad and swelling belt of the au- rora borealis had risen over the moun- tains round the village; frolicsome it came towards us, every shade gleaming in its celestial conflagration. Over- whelmed with the impressions of the day and the night I gazed into this flam- ing riddle, listening to the improvised festival hymns of the village beating out of uncorrupted minds with all the gorgeousness of the aurora borealis in their music.

"And it struck me that there, at that spot, in a bitterly cold night, I was ex- periencing the great fanfare of joy . . ."

"Glorious was life
Now I am filled with joy
For every time a dawn
Makes white the sky of night,
For every time the sun goes up
Over the heavens."

This was the spiritual world of the arctic hunter in the not so distant past. It was, perhaps, in some respects similar to that of Dorset culture people a thousand years ago.

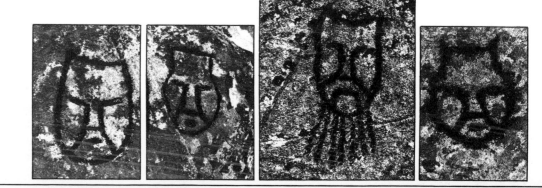

Bibliography

Arnberg, Matts, et al. *Yoik*. Sveriges radio förlag. Stockholm (1969).

Baird, Patrick D. *The Polar World*. Longmans, Green and Co. Ltd. London (1964).

Bancroft, Hubert H. *History of Alaska, 1730-1885*. Antiquarian Press Ltd. New York (1959).

Bandi, Hans-Georg and Maringer, Johannes. *Kunst der Eiszeit*. Hobein Verlag. Basel (1955).

Barnett, Lincoln and the editorial staff of LIFE. *The World We Live In*. Time Incorporated. New York (1955).

Birket-Smith, Kaj. *The Eskimos*. Methuen & Co. Ltd. London (1959).

Bodsworth, Fred. *Last Of The Curlews*. Dodd, Mead & Company. New York (1955).

Bosi, Roberto. *The Lapps*. Frederick A. Praeger, New York (1960).

Brower, Kenneth. *Earth and the Great Weather: The Brooks Range*. McCall Publishing Company. New York (1971).

Brown, Dale. *Wild Alaska*. Time-Life Books. New York (1972).

Carpenter, Edmund; Varley, Frederick and Flaherty, Robert. *Eskimo*, University of Toronto Press. Toronto (1959).

Carpenter, Edmund, and Heyman, Ken. *They Became What They Beheld*. Ballantine Books, Inc. New York (1970).

Carson, Rachel L. *The Sea Around Us*. Oxford University Press. New York (1951).

Conway, Sir W. Martin, editor. *Early Dutch and English Voyages to Spitsbergen*. Hakluyt Society. London (1904).

Conway, Sir W. Martin. *No Man's Land* (a history of S bergen). Cambridge University Press. Cambridge (1906).

Cornwall, Ian. *Ice Ages — Their Nature and Effects.* Baker Ltd. London (1970).

Crottet, Robert, and Méndez, Enrique. *Lapland.* Hugh Ev Limited. London (1968).

Daly, Reginald Aldworth. *The Changing World Of The Age*. Hafner Publishing Company. New York (1963).

de Camp, L. Sprague. *Elephant*. Pyramid Publications. York (1964).

Diószegi, Vilmos, editor. *Popular Beliefs and Folklore Tr tion in Siberia*. Indiana University Press. Bloomington (19

Durham, Bill. *Canoes and Kayaks of Western America.* per Canoe Press. Seattle (1960).

Dyson, James L. *The World Of Ice*. Alfred A. Knopf. York (1962).

Fejes, Claire. *People Of The Noatak*. Alfred A. Knopf. York (1966).

Freuchen, Peter, edited by Freuchen, Dagmar. *P Freuchen's Book Of The Eskimos*. Fawcett Publications, New York (1965).

Garfield, Brian. *The Thousand-Mile War*. Doubleday Company. New York (1969).

Gillsäter, Sven. *Wave After Wave*. George Allen & Unwin London (1964).

Hakluyt, Richard. *Voyages*. J. M. Dent & Sons Ltd. Lor (1962). Everyman's Library. Vol. I.

Hearne, Samuel. *A Journey From Prince Of Wales' Fo Hudson Bay To The Northern Ocean*. A. Strahan & T. Ca London (1795). [Macmillan Company of Canada Limited ronto (1958).]

Heizer, Robert F. *Aconite poison whaling in Asia America: An Aleutian transfer to the New World*. Smithso Institution, Bureau of American Ethnology-Bulletin 13 417-468. Washington (1943).

ess, Diamond. *The People Of The Twilight*. The Univer-
of Chicago Press. Chicago (1959).

ess, Diamond. *Eskimo Administration: II. Canada*. Arctic
tute of North America, Technical Paper no. 14, May.
treal (1964).

s, Gwyn. *The Norse Atlantic Saga*. Oxford University
. London (1964).

s, Gwyn. *A History Of The Vikings*. Oxford University
. London (1968).

ler, Lucy. *Freezing Point*. The John Day Company. New
(1970).

y, Howard. *The Vikings*. National Geographic. Vol. 137,
. (April 1970).

, W. Kaye, editor. *The Journals and Letters of Sir Alex-
r Mackenzie*. Macmillan Company of Canada Limited.
nto (1970).

Kay, Douglas. *The Honourable Company*. Tudor Publish-
Co. New York (1938).

ham, Clements R. *The Voyages of William Baffin*. Hak-
Society. London (1881).

den, Walter. *The Lemming Year*. Chatto & Windus. Lon-
(1964).

yer, Maurice, editor and translator. *I, Nuligak*. Peter Mar-
ssociates Limited. Toronto (1966).

son, Samuel Eliot. *The European Discovery of America*.
rd University Press. New York (1971).

at, Farley, editor. *Ordeal by Ice*. McClelland and Stewart
ed. Toronto (1960).

sen, Fridtjof. *Farthest North*. Harper & Brothers. New
(1897). Vol. I and Vol. II.

enskjöld, Nils A.E. *The Voyage Of The Vega Round Asia
Europe*. Macmillan and Co. London (1881).

y, Robert E. *Nearest The Pole*. Hutchinson. London
7).

rsen, Alwin. *Polar Animals*. George G. Harrap & Co. Ltd.
on (1962).

, Richard. *The World Of The Polar Bear*. University of
ington Press. London (1966).

Phillips, Paul C. *The Fur Trade*. University of Oklahoma
Press. Oklahoma (1961). Vol. I.

Poulson, Ivar; Hultkrantz, Ake, and Jettmar, Karl. *Die Re-
ligionen Nordeurasiens und der amerikanischen Arktis*. W.
Kohlhammer Verlag. Stuttgart (1962).

Powers, Alfred. *Animals Of The Arctic*. David McKay Company Inc. New York (1965).

Powys, Llewelyn. *Henry Hudson*. John Lane The Bodley
Head Ltd. London (1927).

Pruitt, William O., Jr. *Animals Of The North*. Harper & Row.
New York (1967).

Quimby, George I. *Aleutian Islanders*. Chicago Natural History Museum. Chicago (1944).

Rasmussen, Knud. *Intellectual Culture Of The Iglulik Eskimos*.
Gyldendalske Boghandel, Nordisk Forlag. Copenhagen
(1929).

Rasmussen, Knud. *The Netsilik Eskimos*. Gyldendalske
Boghandel, Nordisk Forlag. Copenhagen (1931).

Rasmussen, Knud. *Intellectual Culture Of The Copper Eskimos*. Gyldendalske Boghandel, Nordisk Forlag.
Copenhagen (1932).

Scheffer, Victor B. *The Year Of The Whale*. Charles Scribner's
Sons. New York (1969).

Scheffer, Victor B. *The Year Of The Seal*. Charles Scribner's
Sons. New York (1970).

Scholander, P. F. et al. *Studies On The Physiology Of Frozen
Plants And Animals In The Arctic*. Journal of Cellular And
Comparative Physiology, Vol. 43, Supplement 1. Philadelphia
(September 1953).

Scoresby, William, Jr. *An Account Of The Arctic Regions*. Archibald Constable and Co. Edinburgh (1820).

Scoresby, William, Jr. *Journal Of A Voyage To The Northern
Whale Fishery*. Archibald Constable and Co. Edinburgh
(1823).

Semyonov, Yuri. *Siberia: Its Conquest and Development*. Hol-
lis & Carter Ltd. Gt. Britain (1963).

Spears, Borden, editor. *Wilderness Canada*. Clarke, Irwin &
Company Limited. Toronto/Vancouver (1970).

Stefansson, Vilhjalmur. *The Three Voyages of Martin
Frobisher*. The Argonaut Press. London (1938). Vols. I and II.

Stefansson, Vilhjalmur. *My Life With The Eskimos*. Collier
Books. New York (1966).

Stonehouse, Bernard. *Animals Of The Arctic: the Ecology of
the Far North*. Ward Lock Limited. London (1971).

Swinton, George. *Sculpture Of The Eskimo*. McClelland and
Stewart Limited. Toronto (1972).

Taylor, Andrew. *Geographical Discovery And Exploration In
The Queen Elizabeth Islands*. Geographical Branch, Mines
and Technical Surveys. Ottawa (1964).

Taylor, William E., Jr.; and Swinton, George. *Prehistoric Dorset Art*. The Beaver. Winnipeg (Autumn 1967).

Tuck, Leslie M. *The Murres*. Canadian Wildlife Service. Ottawa (1960).

Tyrrell, James W. *Across The Sub-Arctics of Canada*. William
Briggs. Toronto (1908).

U.S. Department of Commerce, Coast and Geodetic Survey.
United States Coast Pilot; Alaska, Aleutian Islands. U.S.
Government Printing Office. Washington (1944).

Vibe, Christian. *Arctic Animals in Relation to Climatic
Fluctuation*. C. A. Reitzels Forlag. Copenhagen (1967).

Weyer, E M. *The Eskimos*. Yale University Press. New Haven
(1932).

Wiggins, Ira L., and Thomas, John Hunter. *A Flora Of The
Alaskan Arctic Slope*. University of Toronto Press. Toronto
(1962).

Wilkinson, Douglas. *The Arctic Coast*. Natural Science of
Canada Ltd. Toronto (1970).

Williams, Harold. *One Whaling Family*. Houghton Mifflin
Company. Boston (1964).

Woodford, James. *The Violated Vision*. McClelland and
Stewart Limited. Toronto (1972).

Place Locations

Place	Latitude	Longitude
Aberdeen Lake	64.30 N	99.00 W
Agparssuit	77.23 N	72.30 W
Alaska Peninsula	57.00 N	158.00 W
Alaskan North Slope	70.00 N	154.00 W
Aleutians	52.00 N	180.00 W
Altamira	43.23 N	4.08 W
Amur River	49.30 N	129.00 E
Anadyr	64.41 N	177.32 E
Astrakhan	46.22 N	48.04 E
Attu	52.55 N	173.11 E
Baffin Island	68.30 N	70.00 W
Baker Lake	64.20 N	96.10 W
Barden Bay	77.20 N	70.00 W
Barents Sea	75.00 N	40.00 E
Bathurst Inlet	66.49 N	108.00 W
Bear Island	74.23 N	19.26 E
Beaufort Sea	72.30 N	140.00 W
Beechey Island	74.32 N	91.52 W
Belcher Islands	56.00 N	79.00 W
Beverly Lake	64.40 N	100.30 W
Boothia Peninsula	70.30 N	94.30 W
Borden Island	78.30 N	111.00 W
Brock Island	78.00 N	114.30 W
Brooks Range	68.00 N	152.00 W
Bylot Island	73.30 N	79.00 W
Cape Deshnev	66.08 N	169.40 W
Cape Farewell	59.50 N	43.40 W
Cape Lisburne	68.54 N	166.18 W
Cape Sparbo	75.51 N	83.50 W
Chukchee Sea	67.00 N	168.00 W
Churchill	58.45 N	94.00 W
Coats Island	62.30 N	83.00 W
Cold Bay	55.10 N	162.33 W
Commander Islands	54.35 N	166.34 E
Coppermine River	67.00 N	115.00 W
Countess of Warwick I.	62.49 N	65.27 W
Crimson Cliffs	75.54 N	67.37 W
Cumberland Sound	65.00 N	65.00 W
Davis Inlet	55.50 N	60.45 W
Davis Strait	67.00 N	57.30 W
Devon Island	75.10 N	85.00 W
Diomede Islands	65.35 N	169.00 W
Disko Island	70.00 N	54.00 W
Dubawnt River	63.00 N	101.30 W
Dvina River	55.50 N	23.30 E
Ellesmere Island	80.00 N	80.00 W
Etah	78.20 N	73.00 W
Faeroes, The	62.00 N	7.00 W
Foxe Basin	67.30 N	79.00 W
Franz Josef Land	81.00 N	55.00 E
Frobisher Bay	63.45 N	68.30 W
Fury and Hecla Strait	69.50 N	84.00 W
Glacier Bay	58.50 N	136.30 W
Gulf of Alaska	58.00 N	144.00 W
Hakluyt Island	77.23 N	72.30 W
Hell Gate	76.40 N	89.45 W
Herbert Island	77.25 N	70.10 W
Hopedale	55.30 N	60.10 W
Hotham Inlet	66.45 N	162.00 W
Ilmen Lake	58.15 N	31.30 E
Inglefield Bay	77.30 N	67.00 W
Jan Mayen	70.10 N	9.00 W
Jens Munk Island	69.40 N	79.40 W
Kamchatka Peninsula	63.43 N	58.07 E
Kânâk	77.40 N	69.00 W
Kangerdlugssuag	77.16 N	66.30 W
Kautokeino	69.00 N	23.06 E
Kayak Island	59.55 N	144.30 W
Kazan River	63.20 N	69.10 W
King William Island	69.00 N	97.00 W
Kodiak Island	57.20 N	153.40 W
Kodlunarn Island	62.49 N	65.27 W
Kolyma River	67.00 N	160.00 E
Kong Karls Land	78.55 N	28.30 E
Kotzebue	66.51 N	162.40 W
Kuriles, The	45.00 N	150.00 E
Kvalöy — Tromsö	69.40 N	18.45 E
L'Anse-aux-Meadows	51.35 N	55.33 W
Labrador	55.00 N	60.00 W
Lancaster Sound	74.00 N	85.00 W
Lascaux	45.03 N	1.11 E
Lena River	66.48 N	123.27 E
Little Diomede Island	65.45 N	169.58 W
Mackenzie Delta	68.54 N	135.00 W
Marble Island	62.41 N	91.15 W
Meighen Island	80.00 N	99.00 W
Melville Bay	75.33 N	63.10 W
Moffen Island	80.09 N	14.36 E
Moosonee	51.18 N	80.40 W
Nain	56.30 N	61.45 W
Nantucket	41.17 N	70.05 W
Nelson River	56.25 N	94.45 W
New Bedford	41.38 N	70.55 W
New Siberian Islands	75.00 N	140.00 E
Newtontoppen	79.00 N	17.45 E
North Cape	71.07 N	25.00 E
North Kent Island	76.30 N	90.00 W
Novaya Zemlya	54.43 N	30.53 E
Novgorod	58.30 N	31.20 E
Okhotsk	59.20 N	143.15 E
Peary Land	82.49 N	35.00 W
Point Barrow	71.16 N	156.25 W
Point Hope	68.20 N	166.50 W
Pond Inlet	72.40 N	77.59 W
Povungnituk	59.45 N	77.20 W
Pribilof Islands	57.12 N	170.00 W
Prudhoe Bay	70.27 N	149.00 W
St. Elias Range	60.12 N	140.57 W
St. Paul Island	57.09 N	170.18 W
Schefferville	54.50 N	67.00 W
Schultz Lake	64.55 N	97.32 W
Severnaya Zemlya	80.00 N	100.00 E
Siorapaluk	77.48 N	70.58 W
Southampton Island	65.00 N	85.00 W
Spitsbergen	78.19 N	20.00 E
Thelon River	64.17 N	102.00 W
Thompson Pass	61.09 N	145.45 W
Thule	77.40 N	69.00 W
Ulugssat	77.25 N	70.10 W
Umnak Island	53.20 N	168.20 W
Upernavik	72.50 N	56.00 W
Ural Mountains	60.00 N	58.30 E
Ussuri River	46.49 N	134.30 E
Valdez	61.07 N	146.17 W
Verkhoyansk	67.35 N	133.25 E
Vest-Spitsbergen	78.22 N	15.00 E
Volga River	51.30 N	45.55 E
Wainwright	70.39 N	160.10 W
White Sea	66.21 N	37.30 E
Winter Harbour	74.14 N	110.00 W
Yakutsk	62.10 N	129.50 E

Printed in Canada: Montreal Lithographing Ltd. *Color and film preparation:* StanMont Inc. *Typesetting:* The Graphic Group